THE RAF IN COLD WAR GERMANY

IAN SMITH WATSON

FONTHILL

Dedicated to James 'Jim' Dyer Watson, son, brother, husband, father, and grandfather
RAF Brüggen (1974–1976)

In fulfilling our assigned role in NATO, we face impressive odds, further compounded by the troubled world in which we live. If you have ever doubted the worth of your contribution, you will have little cause to doubt it here. You are at the 'Sharp End' and it does not come much sharper.

RAF Brüggen Station Information Booklet (1977)

Fonthill Media Language Policy

Fonthill Media publishes in the international English language market. One language edition is published worldwide. As there are minor differences in spelling and presentation, especially with regard to American English and British English, a policy is necessary to define which form of English to use. The Fonthill Policy is to use the form of English native to the author. Ian Smith Watson was born in Irvine, Scotland, and educated mostly in West Yorkshire; therefore, British English has been adopted in this publication.

Fonthill Media Limited
Fonthill Media LLC
www.fonthillmedia.com
office@fonthillmedia.com

First published in the United Kingdom and the United States of America 2022

British Library Cataloguing in Publication Data:
A catalogue record for this book is available from the British Library

ISBN 978-1-78155-842-3

Typeset in 10pt on 13pt Sabon
Printed and bound in England

Preface

Now it has come to pass, and despite there being numerous books about the Cold War from various aspects and covering various facets, I thought I would try my hand at putting together both an historical analysis and a trip down memory lane for those that were there. The subject herein will strike the novice as an odd contrasting situation. For a start, whenever something is necessary, it usually is not fun. The permanent basing of what was in the 1960s the bulk of the RAF's tactical air assets based around a nuclear strike force at its centre was not for fun. Yet as you read through the following pages, you may pick up a sense that for all that was at stake, for all that sat on the razor's edge, those that served in Germany through the Cold War enjoyed a quality of life that was not matched back home.

Then there are the personal anecdotes and recollections at the end of the book. Service in Germany, for RAF personnel of all ranks, was a contrast of the peak of operational preparedness being maintained at the final step before what would be a very quick transition to a war footing, and life in the richest and one of the most liberal democracies in Europe.

When the news came through that the citizens of Berlin, both East and West, were swinging sledgehammers at sections of the Berlin Wall, that unmistakable symbol of the Cold War, the world rejoiced that it was about to move forward and upwards into the broad sunlit uplands promised forty-nine years earlier by Winston Churchill. That was not quite how matters developed in the intervening years through to the present.

Yet anyone back in November 1989 could be forgiven then for feeling a good degree of euphoria, that the stand-off between NATO and the Warsaw Pact was at an end. The threat of nuclear annihilation, which always sat at the back of so many people's minds, like death itself, had been removed.

As someone who played his part as a very tiny cog in this enormous wheel, researching the contents had a familiar and nostalgic feel, which naturally fired my enthusiasm all the more. This is not a work of fiction; it is factual. Many at the time were oblivious of the purpose of UK forces in Germany; certainly, the tension that existed day to day was not felt, even among some Germans. A few along with some in the UK felt the other side were the goodies really and that our crowd were the evil perpetrators; others plain just did not care at all, but perhaps I generalise too much.

If you have picked this book up off the shelf or ordered online because you have an impossible-to-restrain sense of curiosity, then I trust you will find your eyes open to a facet of military history that you might not have been fully aware of—or if you were, then that it fills in any blanks in your knowledge of the Cold War, and the role of the RAF in particular in maintaining the otherwise tranquil peace, which everyone believed was permanent and unassailable following the second world war. All the best—read on and enjoy.

Ian Smith Watson

Acknowledgements

As always, it has been necessary to pick the brains of some for first-hand accounts of the subject at hand—in this case, to broaden the understanding of what life was really like serving in the RAF in Germany during the frosty overcast era of the Cold War.

On this occasion, I have taken the personal perspective and placed it in a chapter at the end—Memories. If nothing else, this manages to keep the more sombre circumstances of the period separate from the droll circumstances people found themselves in at the coal face, so to speak. This book has been given a pleasantly light-hearted edge as a result of their input. Therefore, my deepest appreciation goes to John Houlston, Trevor Pearson, Paul Wheatley, Howard Lucas, Nick Wilcock, Paul Giverin, Tony Taylor, Tony Hawes, David Edward Langley, Patrick Rowney, Mike Turner, Peter Goude, Chris Liddle, Gareth Cunningham, Ian Gawn, Ian McFadyen, Roy Evans, and Peter Jefferies.

There are, of course the images provided, to which I am indebted to Hugh Alexander, Lee Harper, Peter March, Tony Paxton, and Adrian Balch. No book of this nature gets to mature without the input of many minds, and this one is no different. Finally, I would like to mention Jamie Hardwick and Jay Slater at Fonthill Media for their forbearance while I have tinkered around with this and another magnum opus heading their way at very much the same time. Finally, my sincere apologies to anyone whom I may have inadvertently left out.

Contents

Preface   3
Acknowledgements   5
Glossary   9
Introduction   13

  1   Prologue, Third Reich Collapse, and Red Star Ascent   19
  2   Germany Defeated   26
  3   The Post-War Settlement   51
  4   The Cold War Development   56
  5   The Nuclear Option   98
  6   The 1957–1963 Restructure   109
  7   The Canberra Question (TSR2 and F-111 Cancellations)   127
  8   The 1970s and Flexible Response   148
  9   The Tornado Arrives   177
 10   Down with the Wall   208
 11   Options for Change   215
 12   Memories   223

Appendix I: RAF Order of Battle in 2nd Tactical Air Force as
    of 1 April 1957   244
Appendix II: RAFG Order of Battle as of
    November 1989 When the Berlin Wall Collapsed   246
Appendix III: Rest of NATO Central Region Air Forces Order of Battle 248

Glossary

A&AEE	Aircraft and Armaments Experimental Establishment
AAIB	Air Accident Investigation Branch
AAFCE	Allied Air Forces Central Europe
ACAS	Assistant Chief of the Air Staff
AFCENT	Allied Forces Central Europe
AFN	American Forces Network
AFVG	Advanced Fighter Variable Geometry
AIRCENT	Air Forces Central Europe
ASM	Aircraft Survivability Measures (in respect of airfield hardened shelters)
ATAF	Allied Tactical Air Force
AWI	All-weather Interceptor
BAFO	British Air Forces of Occupation
BAI	Battlefield Air Interdiction
BAOR	British Army of the Rhine
B(I)	Bomber (Interdictor)
CAG	Canadian Air Group
CAP	Combat Air Patrol
CAS	Chief of the Air Staff
CAS	Close Air Support (in respect of operational role)
CDS	Chief of the Defence Staff
CGS	Chief of the General Staff
CIGS	Chief of the Imperial General Staff
CINCENT	Commander in Chief Central Region
CNS	Chief of the Naval Staff
FEAF	Far East Air Force
FRG	Federal Republic of Germany

GA	Ground Attack
GCI	Ground Controlled Intercept
GDR	German Democratic Republic
GTS/APU	Gas Turbine Starter/Auxiliary Power Unit
HAS	Hardened Aircraft Shelter
IDF	Interceptor Day Fighter
IDS	Interdictor Strike
IUR	In Use Reserves
JBG	*Jagdbomber Geschwader* (Fighter Bomber Wing)
JG	*Jagd Geschwader* (Fighter Wing)
JHQ	Joint Headquarters
KLU	*Koninklijke Luchtmacht* (Royal Netherlands Air Force)
LABS	Low Altitude Bombing System
MEAF	Middle East Air Force
MINEVAL	Minimum Evaluation
MAXEVAL	Maximum Evaluation
MRAF	Marshal of the Royal Air Force
MRPR	Medium Range Photographic Reconnaissance
NATO	North Atlantic Treaty Organisation
OCU	Operational Conversion Unit
OO	Orderly Officer
ORB	Operational Record Book
PHA	Polish Home Army
RAFG	Royal Air Force Germany
RCAF	Royal Canadian Air Force/Armed Forces
RNLAF	Royal Netherlands Air Force
SACEUR	Supreme Allied Commander Europe
SACLANT	Supreme Allied Commander Atlantic
SAM	Surface-to-Air Missile
SAM Sup	Surface-to-Air Missile Suppression
SHAEF	Supreme Headquarters Allied Expeditionary Force
SHAPE	Supreme Headquarters Allied Powers Europe
SRDF	Short Range Defence Fighter
SRPR	Short Range Photographic Reconnaissance
TACEVAL	Tactical Evaluation
TAF	Tactical Air Force
TF	Tactical Fighter
TFR	Terrain Following Radar
TFS	Tactical Fighter Squadron
TFW	Tactical Fighter Wing
TTTE	Tri-National Tornado Training Establishment
TWCU	Tornado Weapons Conversion Unit

UE	Unit Establishment
USAF	United States Air Force
USAFE	United States Air Force European Command
USSR	Union of Soviet Socialist Republics
VCAS	Vice Chief of the Air Staff
WDU	West European Defence Union
WGAF	West German Air Force
WILD WEASEL	SAM Suppression role

Introduction

So why was a sizeable chunk of the RAF, and the British Army, permanently garrisoned in the Federal Republic of Germany (and some of the rest of north-west Europe) through the latter half of the twentieth century?

To fully understand, you need to look at the events that brought it all about as part of a much wider and in-depth international proposition. In order to provide an overview in this introduction, let me wind the clock back a few stages. While the post-war honeymoon period between the Western Allies and the Soviet Union moved to establish the four respective zones of control through Berlin, there was no escaping the fact that 'the Russians were here'. So decisive was the defeat of Nazi Germany that nobody but those at the highest echelon of command could have imagined that the very nations that had fought side by side to bring about the cataclysmic end of such an incomparable regime could also foresee a future that would see the defeated Germany become an ally of the West, in a protracted stand-off against one of the principal former Allies. So unlikely must such a development have seemed in 1945, every aspect of the vanquished enemy's character placed it in terms of reason, sense of pity, and morality, somewhere between Imperial Rome and the Middle Ages.

Yet with such a tyranny truly destroyed, the world would soon find itself descending toward another equally divisive ideological disagreement that most thought they had managed to put firmly behind them.

The need to destroy the Axis nations' (essentially Germany and Japan) military hegemony had pushed the Allied powers, including the Soviet Union, an equally totalitarian state itself, to a military standing never previously witnessed. During the First World War, the United Kingdom had reached a supreme level of arms expenditure and fielded the largest army in British history by the war's height. However, the overall effort required to meet the demands of defeating Hitler surpassed even that by a considerable margin. The First World War brought many new facets of war to the fore—the submarine, the armoured fighting vehicle (tank), and the aeroplane.

Before August 1914, the Royal Engineers had introduced hot air balloons for the purpose of spotting. Aeroplanes were already being developed, and the early demands of the war inevitably found a purpose for such machines and the introduction of a military air arm. By the end of the 'war to end all wars', the light air arm, not at all unique in its existence, had expanded and been granted complete autonomy and independence from the army. The new independent air force was formed from the Royal Flying Corps and elements of the naval counterpart, the Royal Naval Air Service. The Royal Air Force was born and formally recognised on 1 April 1918.

Essentially, it was the former that became an independent force, re-identified with the greater title—the Royal Air Force. The years following the end of the First World War pushed the newly independent service into the spotlight, largely due to army and navy attempts to have things back as they were pre-1918, with air power back in its place as respective arms of each. This was because of the perception that peacetime resources would be placed at an even tighter premium, which in turn would subsequently risk their respective requirements not being met.

The new RAF was casually viewed as a rich playboy's new pursuit in the form of a 'flying club'. The expectation was clearly that the air force was a one-off, simply to cope with the circumstances of a global conflict, but now it was over, it was time for this new facet of military activity to be relegated back where it rightly belonged—as respective elements of the navy and the army.

The RAF spent the next two decades battling its Cinderella-like unhelpful image both in public, largely through the Hendon Air Pageant and the Empire Air Days, and through the significant contribution made in overseas campaigns, significantly in Iraq and a series of counter-insurgent operations across the Middle East (notably Iraq), Egypt, and Palestine.

The RAF had gained traction through this mix of self-promotion and active service, despite naval and army attempts to have the service returned to respective branches of the two far more venerable services. One could argue this would have been exceptional folly given what was to come, regardless of the continued existence of a military air service to whatever degree. Had the RAF been disbanded, it would have been concentrated in two specialised forms—as a support function essentially for fleet defence and battlefield support.

This would inevitably have resulted in nothing like the kind of fighter force that would need to be in place by the start of the Second World War. It was not foreseen, but while the First World War introduced military aviation, the Second World War would firmly establish its prominence and proliferation within the armed forces of most nations. The impact and utility of air power matured quickly through the Second World War.

Until 1935, when concerns that conflict in Europe could happen again, the British people were far more preoccupied with the Depression. The expansion of Germany's very new and radical military complex was approached internationally with a mix of concern, diplomacy, wishful thinking, and even praise from those who were impressed with Germany's economic turnaround.

The British government reluctantly took steps to prepare for any eventuality; this was against a not insubstantial degree of opposition. The National Labour party under the leadership of George Lansbury did not oppose the government's rearmament schemes as excessive but advocated the complete and comprehensive disbandment of the armed forces—despite the clear direction of Germany's dismissal of the Treaty of Versailles' limits, including expanding army and a second smaller one that developed from Hitler's personal para-military bodyguard, the Waffen SS. Also forbidden was the creation of an unprecedented and uniquely modern air force.

Another global conflict was predicted by many, and it came sooner than imagined, following a series of annexations and territorial claims that went unopposed. The line was crossed with the invasion of Poland. Beforehand, the German Army were ordered into the Rhineland, in breach of Versailles. Next came the annexation of Austria and the Sudetenland along with the further invasion of most of the rest of Czechoslovakia. Germany had been accommodated over one breach after another.

Opposition to any resistance to German hegemony largely disappeared by this time within the British political establishment. The British prime minister, Neville Chamberlain, often described as an appeaser, was busy doing what we demand of leaders today—to exhaust every diplomatic avenue to avoid military conflict. However, the German invasion of Poland could not be ignored. The inertia of the Phoney War, which followed, led to the famous last words of 1914 being uttered once again—'it will all be over by Christmas'. From spring to summer 1940, German military successes abounded. Nowhere was Britain and its Allies, chiefly France, even holding ground, everywhere German forces prevailed. An accommodation with Hitler was not sought by the British government, despite approaches made by Berlin.

That Britain, under the stewardship of its new prime minister, Winston Churchill, chose to hold out whatever the seeming futility determined the future shape of the world. Air power would play a much greater role this time; in the future, it became an indispensable weapon, one which demanded heavy resources and investment both in terms of manpower and technology. The balance in British arms toward the RAF was the inverse of the previous conflict and so was the effect. Air power consumed considerably but transformed the ability of the country to both bring destructive power to bear, supply, and re-supply allied forces, provide close support, and defend against the impact of hostile aircraft. Ultimately, the final point reached by military conflict is still the soldier on the ground, to hold and oversee, until the conflict which put him there is settled.

Through the spring of 1945, the war in Europe reached its climax and consequently, Nazi Germany's downfall. Not just Germany's cities, but many across the battleground of Europe were transformed into endless plains of jagged ruins, piles of bricks and rubble under which countless bodies rotted.

The Western Allies under the operational leadership of the supreme allied commander, US General Dwight Eisenhower, had reached as far as the river Elbe; here they met the Russians, which was the position they found themselves in by 7 May. Their respective forces occupied not just German soil, but all the land they had crossed to get there.

Now the dust was settling on the aftermath, the consequence of running the German war machine to earth was to unfold.

This was the stage for an unprecedented period in history that polarised the industrialised nations into two opposed ideological camps, a seemingly indefinite period through which those allied forces in the West would need to remain on German soil, while Soviet forces remained in that part of Germany (and the European nations ceded to them and their administration and oversight). This included the likes of Poland and Czechoslovakia, two countries whose gallant sons had contributed so much to the victory over Nazi Germany. They had suffered dreadfully under occupation and were now to be rewarded with continued occupation under another outside authoritarian power.

Initially, no actual hard border (to use a modern choice of expression) existed between the Soviet zone and those of the West. As far as the victorious powers were concerned, they would remain as forces of occupation until the long-term future of Germany was settled. In due course, the political development resulted in worsening relations and the western occupation forces changing their posture to become a component element of a wider line of defence looking east. The British Army occupation force would transition to become the British Army of the Rhine (BAOR).

As was now the case, a part and parcel element of any comprehensive military proposition is the air component. The element of British airpower that supported the British 2nd Army from Normandy through to the German surrender was the 2nd Tactical Air Force. In 1945, 2 TAF became the British Air Force of Occupation (BAFO). By 1949, the BAFO once again took the title 2nd Tactical Air Force; it was to become the basis for not just the RAF presence in north-west Germany but the cadre of what was to become a larger NATO air component as 2 ATAF (2nd Allied Tactical Air Force), of which the RAF element became a component part re-badged as Royal Air Force Germany (RAFG) in later years.

This posture was maintained through four decades during which the Sword of Damocles hung over the future of the very existence of civilisation itself. For make no mistake, the standoff between East and West (or more specifically, the Warsaw Pact and NATO) placed the world on a permanent knife-edge.

People went about their business, seemingly unconcerned on both sides of the fence, but the tension that developed ensured the routine at each of the RAF's stations in West Germany was such that through the decades, a level of readiness just short of a war footing could never be relaxed.

More specifically, for the better part of this chapter in history, aircraft armed with live nuclear weapons, as it was deemed necessary, sat fuelled and ready to launch, at times with crews at cockpit readiness. Elsewhere, other aircraft (such as defence fighters) also waited, armed and ready to confront any challenge to West German airspace. This meant anything from a simple border violation by a light aircraft to the feared opening attacks in support of an invasion across the inner German border; all would meet a physical and visible response.

Many a British citizen back home was quite aware of the nuclear balancing act between East and West, but not too many knew or comprehended the size of the presence of British forces in West Germany (far too many were blissfully unaware) and the high level of readiness maintained. Together with the air arms of other NATO countries—Belgium, Netherlands, USA, Canada and indeed, in time, the reformed Luftwaffe of the Federal Republic of Germany—a large enough tactical air force was formed with its own doctrines, aims, and purpose. The spear point of NATO's air arms was sharpened through a growing list of highly testing no notice exercises, devised and implemented to ensure the quickest and most effective response, these were the Tacevals, Maxevals, and Minevals, which became the bugbear of every airman and airwoman's life in the RAF in Germany in the 1960s, '70s, and '80s.

For all those who served in Germany and lived through these moments of pandemonium, the interruptions to sleep not knowing if 'this was it!' whenever the station Tannoy system crackled abruptly and noisily into life, usually about 3 or 4 a.m. As often as not, the tannoy presaged nothing more to worry about than another station manning response exercise, to be followed by a normal day's work, if it all sounds familiar, then this book is for you. There was the other side to the airman's life in Germany during the Cold War—the unique holiday abroad experience. This involved mixing in the local communities, meaning young airmen became a feature of many northern German and Dutch towns where the nightlife threw into sharp relief what they were used to back home. Instead, the continental atmosphere of bars seemingly open around the clock (certainly well beyond midnight), combined with clean streets and a relative crime-free atmosphere, provided a paradise-like existence for the more conservative social life that British squaddies and airmen were used to back home.

This book is a comprehensive account of the course taken by political and military leaders through the twentieth century to maintain the best diplomatic relations while making clear their resolve not to accept any unacceptable degree of compromise, resulting in NATO's Cold War stand-off with the Warsaw Pact. In turn, this all boiled down to circumstances requiring a young British airman or soldier being based in Germany either wearing a gas mask on exercise, or in the local *Gast Haus* drinking his weight in *Bier*.

This is the history of the Royal Air Force in Germany, from occupation force through the change in international relations which switched to a forward based, permanently primed component of NATO's first line of defence.

A tactical nuclear strike force supported by air superiority quick response interceptors and offensive support aircraft stood ready to respond in conjunction with the army in the event of hostilities that would be brought about by the Kremlin reaching the conclusion that they had no choice but to send their vast numbers of tracked armoured vehicles rolling over the inner German border, to preserve peace, as the Kremlin viewed it. The political game of chess to avoid such a travesty in the first place, a delicate balance to avoid appearing too aggressive while also managing not to leave the impression that resistance from NATO would merely be token at best, was the essential objective. It may have been the West's politicians' responsibility to move the chess pieces, but the military personnel on the game board had to ensure their conduct at no time signalled the wrong impression, which could so easily be taken to heart by the Kremlin. Finally, and perhaps most nostalgically, the anecdotal memories of those who were afforded the opportunity to find their way around; *ein Bier und ein Schnellimbiss* (a beer and a snack) while praying never to see the 'bucket of instant sunshine' (a long-established euphemism for nuclear weapons) tipped over anyone's head, so to speak, memories of those who successfully held the balance between Armageddon and diplomacy and so lived to tell the tale.

1

Prologue, Third Reich Collapse, and Red Star Ascent

The Soviet drive westward during the Second World War did not always follow a clear line of attack against the Germans in order push further west. The Red Army had advanced along a broad front, and in the summer of 1944, it had entered Eastern Poland; by the end of July, they had stopped on the eastern outskirts of the capital, Warsaw. Some 10 miles east, on the banks of the Vistula, the Soviet steamroller halted at the end of Operation Bagration. Prior to their getting this far, Moscow had encouraged the commander of the Polish Home Army by radio, repeatedly, to revolt against the occupiers. On 1 August 1944, the PHA began their uprising in the city; eighteen days later, a similar uprising in Paris began. One succeeded, following belated military support from the 2nd Free French Armoured and US 4th Infantry Divisions; the other enjoyed scarcely any support and consequently failed.

There remains to this day speculation about Stalin's motives for halting that element of his army which faced Warsaw. They were arguably justified, certainly initially, to avoid overstretch and to allow re-supply and other logistical considerations. However, as their numbers and re-supply increased, the Warsaw Home Army uprising was starting to gain momentum. The Soviet force, it has been said, initially faced a sizeable German force of four Panzer divisions. It could also be argued that the Russians regarded Warsaw as not a legitimate objective; this certainly was the case with Paris where the Western Allies were concerned. Yet when news of the Paris uprising reached SHAEF, Eisenhower changed his mind and the resistance in Paris received the military support denied the Poles.

Back in Warsaw, the Germans were preparing to leave. As soon as Hitler realised the Russians were not going to move in, he ordered an end to the withdrawal and began reinforcing the Warsaw garrison. His troops went on the offensive when it became clear the Poles were on their own. By 4 August, the Germans had halted their retreat west and began receiving reinforcements of their own. The German reprisals, largely conducted by units of the SS, were brutal—clearing each house in turn, shooting Poles even if unopposed, then burning the bodies.

Meanwhile, Stalin's armies moved to secure bridge crossings over the Vistula further south. Large chunks of the Red Army continued to move south, driving down toward the Crimea to envelope Hungary and Romania; the Russians were casting the net far and wide to envelope as much of Europe as possible before entering Germany. Stalin had claimed he would not support the uprising until a recognised legitimate government was established; he now regarded the home army, fighting in their capital against the Germans, as no more than terrorists. A legitimate government would not happen unless the home army prevailed. It seems beyond question that Stalin encouraged the uprising to expose the Poles to a still large German presence, then left them to their fate, knowing this would destroy any chance of Poland falling inside the west's proposed sphere of influence. It may have worried Stalin that the proposed line of separation would be drawn along the Vistula instead of the Elbe.

Whether the Russians could assist the home army initially or not can be argued over; what is more damning of Stalin was his refusal to allow Allied aircraft to land on airfields in the Soviet-occupied parts of Poland. Had they done so, the Western Allies alone could have supported the home uprising directly; they at least could operate from bases in the Soviet so recently re-occupied east of Poland. To re-supply the Poles early on was crucial when, single-handed, they managed to reach a stage where they controlled more than half of the city. The RAF officer in charge of the proposed air bridge, Air Chief Marshal Sir John Slessor, afterward said of Stalin: 'How after the fall of Warsaw, any responsible statesman could trust the Russian Communist further than he could kick him, passes the comprehension of ordinary men.'

Some RAF aircraft, crewed as well by Poles, Canadians, South Africans, Australians, and New Zealanders flew sorties direct from bases in Italy to drop supplies as they could not land to refuel; they were flying a considerable distance, so their impact was limited. They were forbidden to fly over Soviet-held territory, and there are claims they were shot at by Red Forces if they attempted to do this.

Through August into September, Churchill continued his attempts to fly in supplies from bases in Italy, insufficient though it was without access to airfields in Eastern Poland. He even proposed what amounted to hostile action against Stalin by suspending arms supplies by sea to Murmansk and Archangel. He urged Roosevelt to join him in this response, which would clearly hammer away at the alliance between West and East with who knew what consequences. Churchill was emotional and a hostage to the debt Britain owed to Poland; Roosevelt was pragmatic as he could afford to be.

The die was cast; the Soviet drive into the Balkans brought Stalin Romania, Hungary, Czechoslovakia, and then Poland. The home army had fought on for more than two months, street after street, building after building, sewer after sewer.

The problem for the West now was how far the Soviet steamroller was going to go. This matter was partly addressed at the Yalta Conference the following February and this is where the foundations of the Cold War were laid, which saw a substantial Anglo-American force permanently based in north-west Europe (essentially West Germany) up toward the end of the twentieth century. This is where the big three compromised with one another over the map of Europe, after the German surrender. Stalin and Churchill in particular were going to be left unsatisfied; Roosevelt for his part was prepared to be more trusting of Stalin. He accepted him at his word, perhaps reluctantly; so did Churchill as they had little choice. Stalin had promised free unhindered elections in the Europe that he controlled.

Consequently, the Western powers ceded Poland and Czechoslovakia; this is where Churchill had to keep his fingers crossed and accept that the Soviet promise that the Lublin government (made up of Soviet-approved 'Poles') was a temporary interim Soviet administration of those European nations occupied by the Red Army and not permanent.

Churchill was especially concerned about Poland. He had hoped to redress the failure of Britain and France to come to Poland's aid back in 1939. Then there was the Atlantic Charter, which he and Roosevelt signed in 1941, prior to America's full entry into the war. The charter pledged to protect territorial rights. No changes would be made against the wishes of the people and this would go for all; this was a stated aim following victory.

By March, Warsaw was under Soviet administration. Churchill told Roosevelt that it was as 'plain as a pike staff' that Stalin would drag out his promise of free elections long enough to establish a communist administration to follow on from the Lublin committee. The US ambassador to Moscow, Averell Harriman, on 21 March, reported to Roosevelt 'that the Soviet program is the establishment of totalitarianism, ending personal liberty and democracy as we know it'.

The die was cast—the Soviet drive into the Balkans had also cut off Romania, Hungary, and Czechoslovakia from the liberal democracy and prosperity of the western sphere. There was a fleeting chance for Czechoslovakia to be liberated by Patton's Third Army; the opportunity was missed or was it simply too late to change the pre-set map of post-war Europe?

The Czech president in exile in London, Edvard Benes, had agreed that Czech territory liberated by Soviet forces would fall to Czechoslovakian civil administration; however, this would be in accordance with Soviet foreign policy, meaning adherence to the Soviet sphere of influence. No doubt salvation from Nazi occupation, from any quarter, was the most desirable and imperative outcome in the mind of Benes. Czechoslovakia was one-third communist anyway, which explains perhaps why Stalin was happy to allow local civilian administration, albeit under Red Army supervision.

The Americans had signalled the Soviet forces in the area but not to tell them they were going to liberate Prague, more to assist the Czechs. The Russian response was to misleadingly tell the Americans that they were already fighting the Germans in the streets of the capital; this was not true and Czech resistance fighters remained fighting the Germans, alone, after 7 May 1945.

Churchill had urged Eisenhower to take advantage of the situation and get to Prague first. Stalin would be furious, but Czechoslovakia (or some of it) would be snatched away from the pending communist yoke. Eisenhower contacted Soviet General Aleksei Antonov, Eisenhower's Soviet counterpart. The following is an excerpt from a report by the Czech journalist and officer Zdeněk Vršovský, sent to the Czech department of the BBC:

> Unfortunately, he decided to ASK about the possibility of Americans pushing forward to the logical line given by the rivers the Vltava and the Elbe, instead of simply ANNOUNCING that that was going to happen.
>
> General Antonov replied the next day, May 5, by protesting that the Prague Operation of the Red Army has already started, the US and Soviet armies could accidentally clash with resulting friendly fire, etc.
>
> However, we now know that he was misleading Eisenhower. Soviet troops were at that time only beginning to take up positions on the move towards Prague around Dresden. In fact, the operation did not start until May 7.

Czechoslovakia consequently fell to Soviet occupation. Another near flashpoint, as the war in Europe reached its climax, was Denmark, despite pleas from the German commander on the island of Bornholm for a British contingent of troops to surrender to. The British acted in time to liberate the rest of Denmark, but Bornholm was the most easterly of Danish territories, sitting north of Poland and south-east of Malmö in the Baltic Sea. The Soviet Army sent a delegation to occupy the island and remained until the following year when diplomatic negotiations resulted in a quiet withdrawal from this single Soviet foothold in Western Europe.

Once the Allies reached the river Elbe, that was as far as they were to go; to proceed further would have been operationally legitimate only if the Russians were not already on the east bank. This might explain Eisenhower's refusal to regard Berlin as a legitimate target for the forces under his command.

The fate of Poland was a clever checkmate by Stalin before the Yalta Conference. This was the last time that the Western Allies felt they could trust Stalin at his word. By assisting the uprising in crushing the Germans, he risked losing the capital to the PHA. If he had helped to liberate the city, he subsequently risked a confrontation with the Poles on their own soil, in their own capital.

There was still some benefit of the doubt toward Stalin from the Americans—Stalin did not want to squander that just yet. Even worse would be for the Allies to follow up the crushing of the Germans in Warsaw by flying in troops to take control of the resistance and seize the moment by securing the city for the exiled Polish government. Poland then would fall into the West's sphere, possibly all of Germany as well. The fear of the latter in particular frightened Stalin most of all. Even worse, any attempt by the Russians to meddle unsuccessfully at this time could destabilise everything and possibly bring about Stalin's nightmare situation and the German High Command's (if not Hitler's) dream—an Allied/German unholy pact, to counter the Soviet advance west.

Both sides were keen not to upset the other for fear of losing their allegiance against the common foe. I doubt that either had much to worry about, truth be known.

Poland would have to wait until January to be liberated, when the Red Army was already fighting on German soil. The Germans left in Warsaw found themselves in the Russian pocket, cut off from Berlin. They had destroyed about 85 per cent of the city—an apocalyptic landscape of rubble and ruin. There was another point over which Churchill and some American commanders were to find disagreement, this time with Eisenhower. On 14 April 1945, two days following the death of President Roosevelt, US General Bill Simpson, commander of the 9th Army, requested permission from General Omar Bradley for his units to continue to Berlin. They had reached Magdeburg, on the banks of the Elbe three days earlier, but permission was denied to go further. There was some concern initially that the president's passing may have had the effect on US policy that some had irrationally feared, and Goebbels had forlornly hoped for—a radical shift in US policy toward a focus on the defeat of the USSR instead of Germany. This was unlikely in the extreme and something which would not have troubled Churchill, who had a far better insight into the US wartime administration than to be beguiled by such flights of fancy.

The supreme commander had declared Berlin no longer a strategic objective back at the end of March, and therefore permission was denied. Furthermore, Ike cabled Stalin with his intention before even contacting General of the Army George Marshall in Washington, DC. Churchill thought Eisenhower exceeded his authority, especially as he communicated his intent to Stalin before anyone else. This might have been seen by some as the last chance to bring Berlin fully within the West and give away to Stalin only the parts of Germany up to the Oder River line.

However, Eisenhower had his reasons—the estimated Allied casualties in heading to and invading Berlin would cost about 100,000 deaths. What was also not taken into consideration was that the agreed division of Germany was currently, for operational reasons, in default. The Americans were already occupying nearly half of Stalin's Germany—why expend Allied lives for territory that they would have to yield again to uphold the agreement? Further, the German tenacity to fight on was still stubborn in some elements; three German divisions had held off an initial attempt by Simpson's army to establish the first of two eventual bridgeheads across the Elbe.

Ike did permit Montgomery's 21st Army Group to advance eastwards as far as Rostock to seal the access to Denmark's Jutland Peninsula over fears that the Danish mainland was being eyed up by Stalin despite what was agreed at Yalta. This was quite a distance and put the 21st Army Group almost parallel along a line north to south with Berlin.

The handing over of much of Europe as far west as Poland and Czechoslovakia as well as German territory up to the agreed inner German border was the price of victory and the geographical setting for what was to become the Cold War.

On 3 May, the Air Ministry advised all RAF commands that in the event of a cessation of hostilities between Allied and German forces, a simple message—'CEASE FIRE'—accompanied by a time at which this would take effect would be transmitted. Norway and Denmark were classed separately to Allied-occupied Europe as they were still under German occupation. On 4 May, Fighter Command issued an instruction that none of its aircraft were to attack ground targets anywhere on the European continent, except for Norway; German forces here were still expected to offer resistance.

This same day, the first articles of surrender were signed by General Admiral von Freideburg, at Luneburg Heath, of German forces in the north-west of Germany, the Netherlands, and in Denmark. Accepting the surrender was 21st Army group commander, General Sir Bernard Law Montgomery. As Allied forces advanced through from the Low Countries and France into Germany in the early months of 1945, the scale of devastation through Allied bombing became increasingly evident. More shocking for the advancing troops, however, was the finding of examples of the apparatus that characterised the horror of the dying regime—concentration camps, extermination camps, the inflexibility of the Gauleiters, the Gestapo, the SS execution squads, and the mixed reaction from the German citizens. There was a mix of relief, superior indignation, and righteousness as well as bewilderment and surprise. There was also the fearful anticipation and panic of the small-town officials who sought to ingratiate themselves with their new masters to those who denied outright that they had any knowledge of the camps. Many mayors and Gauleiters preferred the easy way out.

There were those who could not deny their role as an accomplice who tried in vain to claim they were merely following orders. There were those who simply resented the imposition of the Allied troops' presence on German soil. So thick-skinned were some among the vanquished that one could only imagine these were the Germans who honestly had no knowledge of the savage and macabre activities committed in their name; to suggest otherwise indicates that they were indeed utterly pitiless.

There were those who were utterly helpless to do anything; these are the men and women who would find the greatest difficulty in convincing the occupiers of the honesty of their benign position, particularly so with the level of compromising evidence everywhere. What even the most hardened and indifferent mindset among the liberators had become attuned to, paled to nothing compared to what they happened upon. What they uncovered was never imagined possible despite the growing reports through the preceding years that such ghoulish goings on were real.

In what became the British zone of occupation, the most significant find was the Bergen-Belsen extermination camp. The commandant had earned the most appropriate nickname—the 'Beast of Belsen'. This was SS *Hauptsturmführer* (army rank of captain equivalent) Joseph Kramer, who was thirty-nine years of age. Following his arrest, he was detained at Celle, also the location of a Luftwaffe airfield that soon became RAF Celle. Kramer did not reach Nuremberg; he and his staff were dealt with in short order being tried by the British Army and sentenced to hang, a duty for which the celebrated British executioner, Albert Pierrepoint, was commissioned. Kramer was hanged on 13 December 1945.

This was the Germany that the initial British Forces were confronted with, doubtless far from their minds was the slightest notion that they would, in a short few years be the guardians of these people and its land side by side with German forces, among other NATO Allies against the threat of a possible military intervention from the Soviet Union—one of the victorious nations of the war would pose a threat against the defeated enemy and the rest of north-west Europe. With the absolute and unconditional surrender of German forces having taken effect, the Allies were faced with a monolithic task to administer Germany, a task made that much easier certainly in so far as the country was divided into four principal zones of occupation. The British occupied the north-west, meeting the borders with Belgium, the Netherlands, and Denmark.

2

Germany Defeated

In the early hours of the morning of 7 May 1945, the supreme commander of the Allied Expeditionary Force, General Dwight David Eisenhower, received notice of the unconditional surrender of all German land, sea, and air forces in Europe. The articles of unconditional surrender had been signed and witnessed that morning. The German delegation that delivered the official German offer of surrender included Hans Georg von Freideburg, who carried the unusual rank title of general admiral; he had already signed unconditional articles of surrender of German forces in the north-west of the country, Norway, and Denmark—the two Scandinavian countries remained under German occupation. The signing was witnessed by Field Marshal Montgomery. Von Freideburg had been instructed by the man who was now *Führer* of the Greater German Reich, Grand Admiral Karl Dönitz, to seek a conditional surrender.

Dönitz had sent *Generaloberst* (colonel general) Alfred Jodl, chief of operations at OKW (*Oberkommando der Wehrmacht*, Armed Forces High Command), and his chief staff officer, Colonel Wilhelm Oxinius, to negotiate not a surrender as much as a pact. Jodl's mission had been to try and persuade General Eisenhower of the need to extend the alliance in the West to include all German forces in a surprise counteroffensive against the Red Army. Jodl among the German delegation held a rather high degree of hope that he would be accorded the respect and recognition due to any senior officer.

Even representing a defeated army under terms of surrender, he had a right to expect this. If only he knew, he had a most unlikely ally regarding Dönitz's proposition. So aggrieved was the British prime minister and mistrusting of Stalin, he commissioned a draft for a plan for the continuation of war against the Soviet Union (Operation Unthinkable). He would find no takers in Washington, DC.

However, the depth of Jodl's predicament could not have evaded his thoughts entirely. He was not dealing with Churchill, nor for that matter the new US President Harry Truman. His next point of call was a man who was uncompromisingly pitiless toward the Nazis.

The logic of Dönitz's proposition was to slow down and halt, as far east as possible, the communist drive westward, which may very well have continued into Europe west of Germany. The German officers were sure that the Anglo-American commanders and political leaders were acutely aware and quite sensitive toward this possibility. Jodl, Dönitz, Von Friedeburg, and many others of doubtless greater notoriety—such as Göring and Himmler—were hopeful that at least Eisenhower would prove reasonable enough and manage to persuade his political masters of the serious threat the Soviet forces presented to all Western interests.

Their hopes of a new western union of nations, including the remnants of the Third Reich, forming a bulwark against the 'Red Menace' were desperate in the extreme as they knew they had presided over the most inflexible, pitiless, totalitarian, and bloody occupation across Europe in Christendom. From Moscow to Cherbourg, from Narvik to the Mediterranean, they knew the reason for Allied—and especially Soviet—enmity toward them. They would have known they were hated, but whatever their own individual knowledge of the depth and range of the systematic brutality they had been at the helm of, they still hoped for—even expected—some form of shared interest wrapped up in a gentlemanly agreement with the Americans, British, and French.

So, it was with a sense of hope, Jodl arrived at Eisenhower's HQ in Reims on 6 May 1945. He along with his delegation, Admiral Von Friedeburg and Colonel Oxinius. Jodl's instructions from Dönitz were to try and secure a forty-eight-hour period of grace before any surrender terms would come into effect; this was to give time for the surrender to be communicated to all German units still fighting. They were afforded twenty-four hours.

Eisenhower would not speak to the Germans himself and appointed his chief of staff, Lt Gen. Walter Beddell-Smith, to communicate directly. Given Stalin's paranoia about German relations with the US and Britain, Eisenhower kept the Russian western representative, General Susloparov, fully informed and involved in what was transpiring.

Susloparov was reassured by Eisenhower that the German surrender would be comprehensive, not a partial surrender to Western forces only, as Jodl was ordered to secure by Dönitz. Susloparov still had to speak to Stalin before he could agree to sign the documents of surrender. As often happens in such circumstances, Stalin could not be contacted, but Eisenhower managed to convince the Russian general just the same, knowing the risk he personally was taking should Stalin even come to learn he had acted without his consultation. That risk was realised as General Susloparov was summoned back home and arrested by the Soviet secret police.

Just after midnight on 7 May 1945, the German delegation had made no inroads to persuade the Allies; they were now resigned to their fate and that of Germany. Meanwhile, the one man who was conspicuous by his absence was the very man Jodl especially felt he needed to talk to.

Eisenhower insisted on unconditional surrender on all fronts; further, if the Germans refused to accept this, he would cut off the access to the West through which German refugees and service personnel were desperately making their way into Allied territory—such was the desperation to avoid falling into the hands of the Red Army, from whom they expected stark retribution. Eisenhower had made it clear that he would also order a heavy bombardment of that part of Germany, which lay to the east of the Western-occupied regions. This left no room for Jodl to manoeuvre, and this bleak situation was what he had to communicate back to Dönitz in Berlin. So it was that the articles of unconditional surrender were signed by Jodl on behalf of all German armed forces at 2.41 a.m. on 7 May 1945.

The surrender came into effect at 11.01 p.m. local time in Reims on 8 May. After the signing, Eisenhower received the German delegation in his office on the second floor of the school, utilised as SHAEF Headquarters. He reportedly spoke briefly but directly to Jodl, only to ask if he understood the terms of the surrender articles and to warn that he would be held responsible for any failure of German forces to honour the surrender. They were then ushered back out. Any expectation Jodl and Dönitz still retained of some degree of accord had now disappeared.

Von Friedeburg, before the surrender took effect, was back in Berlin to be present to sign the Soviet articles of surrender.

A separate signing had been insisted on by Stalin as he feared that what the Germans had hoped for was going to meet with sympathy from the Western Allies, although his suspicions were misplaced. He gave as his reasons that Susloparov was not authorised to sign the articles. Truth be known, the Soviet concerns about the surrender in Reims were not entirely unjustified. Although the surrender terms affected all German forces, German resistance continued in the east, and quite effectively. The Prague uprising was being put down by German units with the same robust response as that in Warsaw previously.

Prague was after all, situated just a sliver west of the Elbe. Patton, like Simpson before him, requested permission to push onto Prague; Eisenhower again refused, concerned about upsetting the apple cart by risking a shootout between Americans and Russians. The Americans having been misled by the signal on 5 May that Soviet forces were already in the area and that they were already fighting the Germans in the streets of the capital; this was Stalin's *fait accompli*, keeping Americans out beyond 7 May 1945.

It was on this date that Soviet forces launched their offensive against Prague. Prague was subsequently liberated officially, at 12.01 a.m. on 9 May.

The Americans did maintain an offensive drive into western Czechoslovakia; elements of US V and XII Corps confronted the German 7th Army and made gains. Eisenhower intervened and ordered Patton not to enter Prague. The larger-than-life Patton was indeed keen to press on as he was ready to liberate all of Czechoslovakia, but Patton was neither the diplomat nor the politician that Eisenhower was; he was a soldier, a general, no more.

There is a small Czech town, Konstantinovy Lazne, which was liberated by the Americans and was as far as they were allowed to go. The town has a memorial in tribute to the Americans and they routinely celebrate that particular liberation.

Stalin had agreed to hold only that part of the country which Soviet forces had liberated. However, all parts of the country taken by US forces were afterwards abandoned as all moved to their side of the dividing line (Iron Curtain). Czechoslovakia fell to Soviet occupation.

The river Elbe was, to all intents and purposes, the declared border between east and west, and meeting point between Soviet and Western Allies. Ultimately, the Elbe could not be relied on to mark the line that should never be crossed. Also, parts from either side fell west or east of Elbe out of alignment with where everyone should be. It followed what would become the final confirmation of the inner German border and along some other national boundaries. Hamburg and Schleswig-Holstein, by this strict rule, should have been Soviet territory; instead, thanks to Montgomery's move, it remained along with Denmark in the west. Yet the Russians got the lion's share of land west of the Elbe further south, including the Thüringen region, Lower Saxony, and the north-west region of Czechoslovakia.

Russian fears were still unassuaged by the end of 7 May, when Dönitz had ordered German forces confronting Soviet forces to continue to do so. Meanwhile, on 8 May, a German field marshal, Ferdinand Schorner, broadcast to units continuing to fight that OKW had not surrendered to the Soviets; only the struggle with the West was over, but the 'Bolsheviks' must be resisted at all costs. For this reason, German heads of the armed forces currently located at Flensburg were flown by the Western Allies to Berlin that day where they were kept waiting until 10 p.m. before the Soviet delegation, led by Marshal Georgi Zhukov, arrived with amended copies of the Reims articles of surrender. The amendment had been applied to clarify that any Germans continuing to resist Soviet forces would not be classed as combatants, and should they attempt to flee to the sanctity of Western-occupied zones, they would immediately be handed over to the Soviet authorities for trial as war criminals.

German Admiral Von Freideburg, present at both Luneburg and Reims, was also present for the Soviet surrender ceremony in Berlin. Von Freideburg signed on behalf of the *Kriegsmarine* (naval forces) and the commander in chief of the OKW. Field Marshal Wilhelm Kietel, Jodl's immediate superior, signed on behalf of the *Heer* (army) and General Hans Jürgen Stumpff for the Luftwaffe (air force). Although Marshal Zhukov outranked Eisenhower, the latter held a higher appointment as supreme commander and therefore had a representative in Berlin to sign the revised articles on his behalf; this was RAF Air Chief Marshal Sir Arthur Tedder, who would become the RAF's chief of air staff from January 1946.

To ensure that no one's nose was left out of joint, President de Gaule insisted that he had a representative in place in Berlin to receive the German surrender on behalf of France even though all French forces, as with all British, Canadian, and other Free Forces were operating under direct command from SHAEF (Supreme Headquarters Allied Expeditionary Force). To remedy this, General Jean de Tassigny, commander of all French forces in Germany, also signed in Berlin.

That was it as far as Europe, the Middle East, and North Africa were concerned—the war was over. The clear-up, the demands for justice, the rebuilding, and the reshaping of Europe and the world order were now to begin.

The first appointed peacetime commander of the British air element of the Allied forces of occupation was Air Chief Marshal Sir Sholto Douglas, KGB MC DFC, while the overall governing post of commander in chief of the British forces of occupation was given, not at all surprisingly, to Field Marshal Sir Bernard Law Montgomery. Montgomery was assigned a political adviser—Sir William Strang KCMG CB MBE. The chief of the air staff, Sir Charles Portal, had struggled to assign Strang his very own air transport— an indispensable requisite evidently but a scarce commodity—which was not available until 28 October 1945. This was a period where despite the number of aircraft of various types providing the RAF with a very long inventory, everything was needed. Hence Strang had to wait until the end of October before Portal was able to make available an Avro Anson 19 for the adviser's personal use.

Strang was so humbled that he felt the need to write back to Sir Charles to thank him personally for what seemed, even for a man of his standing, a rather ostentatious accommodation. Writing to the CAS, he said, 'you may be assured that I should not wish to keep any machine standing idle if it were wanted for someone else. I really have a tender conscience in these matters'.

For all the abundance of aircraft, the demand on them remained high while the government moved as quickly as possible to return the country's armed forces to a more realistic peacetime footing; this not at all surprisingly meant many unit disbandments. For the forces of occupation (namely, 2nd Tactical Air Force and 2nd Army), a redesignation more reflective of the new role was in order. Like their American, French and Soviet counterparts, they were busy hunting down not just the architects of the Reich, but the heavy lifters—those who got their hands dirty.

The occupiers were exposed to the depth of the horror of Nazi excesses that had already been uncovered and the lines of investigation, the gathering of evidence, and the roundup of suspected German military personnel and officials, whatever their rank, progressed. There were the administrators, who for all the world had the appearance of harmless desk clerks, to the brutish thugs in grey uniforms, to the severe looking officious commanders and district Gauleiters.

The war in Europe was over; now the mess had to be cleaned up before anyone could look forward to a future that left the aftermath of the war behind. The time for celebrating victory was brief.

One would have imagined the British position to be one of elation and joy—we had won and found ourselves sharing this victory with many other nations with similar aspirations. Yet as the late American historian Stephen Ambrose said, the British faced as many problems in victory as the Germans did in defeat. He was not wrong; the economic circumstances of Britain compared with those of the U.S, with whom we shared the crown of victory, were the polar opposite of each other—woeful in the extreme. Britain's cities, while not flattened to the same degree as Germany's, had sustained high levels of bombing. Cynics or rather pragmatists with a hint of dry humour have pointed to the advantages brought about by the bombing of London's East End.

The levelling of many of the slum houses helped to force the post-war governments to instigate a housing construction programme on such a scale that the resources were simply not at their disposal. The early post-war administrations achieved miracles, and given the circumstances, it is difficult to comprehend the great strides taken to create a National Health Service while faced with an acute housing shortage. The latter was ably dealt with thanks to the prefab homes; some, originally built between 1945 and 1948, are still lived in happily to this day. Yet Britain was to be transformed. Social security and public spending would, in 1950s and 1960s Britain, see industrial cities benefit from new developments. Rows of brick-built modern houses added to a new skyline of high-rise blocks of flats, which gradually appeared through the early post-war years. The country that would in time, emerge from an era of austerity, which was defined through the continuation of rationing up to 1956, would be different.

Life for the returning British servicemen struck a sharp contrast with that of their American counterparts, or so it seemed. Some GIs returned not to comfy apartments and leafy neighbourhoods, but instead to trailer parks—the equivalent of the British prefab. They rapidly went up from seemingly nothing in the weeks and months that demobbed servicemen and women returned home to spouses, parents, and other loved ones. Stephen Ambrose did acknowledge something else—the United Kingdom had emerged from the war as the moral victor. For all Britain had lost, we could sleep easily at night. The Soviet Union had been wilfully duplicitous; they had entered the war as Hitler's unwitting partner in crime and had invaded Poland simultaneously with Germany. Hitler's invasion of the Soviet Union, from which flowed such an enormous loss of human life, placed the USSR in an unenvious position; the fight for survival was their only course of action, which reinforced an inbuilt mistrust of other countries. The appalling level of inhumanity on the Russian plains alone dwarfed everything else. Yet it was an invasion that the *Führer* had made no secret of so far as his intentions went.

The United States had kept a safe distance initially. There was support for the British position, namely President Roosevelt himself, but the wider US population had no appetite for any further overseas interventions. Meddling, as had come to pass, during the previous global war was to be avoided, permanently. To jump in again was widely regarded as ill-advised and would cost the US treasury and the lives of America's young men. There should be no more unnecessary interference and folly on a continent—Europe—which simply never seemed to learn.

In the early stages of the Second World War, a very tiny fraction of the US population, as in every country, were indeed more sympathetic toward Germany, even though the official position of Washington, DC was to support British interests. There were certain notable individuals who, in at least one case, actively worked against the British position and championed Germany as the side to back—none other than the American ambassador to the court of St James, Joe Kennedy Sr, the father of JFK. Kennedy Snr passed subjectively written cables back to the US president. These reports carried the impression that Britain was on the point of capitulation, that it was merely a matter of time before surrender and the inevitable arrival of German forces on UK soil.

This position was not wholeheartedly accepted by Roosevelt who established a separate line of communication with a senior US Army officer, Colonel William 'Wild Bill' Donovan. Donovan later became head of the OSS (office of secret services), but at the height of the Battle of Britain, Col. Donovan provided the president with a balanced assessment about Britain's prospects. This inevitably improved the US administration's assessments and prompted better faith in Britain's chances of survival.

It would take a miracle to change the minds of Americans, to convince them to feel any different about seeing American boys sent into another world war. This war would see GIs deployed, across the globe, exceeding 12 million by the peak of the Second World War.

With the German war over, allied forces were sprawled across Europe, garrisoned in towns and cities, with airfields accommodating allied air force squadrons while farm fields had to be utilised for the same purpose. As a result, many locations that the Allies were relying on to serve as airfields were served by personnel living in tents as they had in 1939 to 1940 during the Phoney War, while based in France when there were so few substantial aerodromes. Instead, lengthy grass strips belonging to chateaus and stately mansions served as RAF air bases. At the other end of the spectrum in 1945, established air bases now relinquished by the Luftwaffe housed allied air arms. Yet so myriad were the makeshift stations and so fluid was their establishment and disbandment that from the point when the first allied aircraft touched down on the continent following D-Day, these instant makeshift air bases were assigned a letter and numerical reference code such as B1.114 to B1.124 and so on.

Now in the summer of 1945, much of the military sprawl was surplus. The allied forces and their vast numbers struggled, at least initially, to coordinate and manage liaisons between the different armies still established on a war footing but tasked now to govern Germany between them. During a tour of the occupied zone in July 1945, the chief of the air staff, MRAF Sir Charles Portal, had one of his Avro Ansons made available for his personal use so he could fly into Field Marshal Montgomery's personal airfield at B.115. His aircraft was grounded due to bad weather after reaching the continent, so from here he attempted to contact the airfield at B.115, no quicker way to expedite the matter was available so he took a staff car to 30 Corps headquarters, which sat 15 miles from the airfield in question.

The army officer he was to rendezvous with, General Weeks, had since moved on to Berlin where Portal was ultimately headed. Another Anson was made available at another airfield, designated B.116, Sir Charles was unable to make the meeting in Berlin due to his flight being delayed another hour; the cause of the delay was the Russian control of Berlin airspace. They were already exercising jurisdiction here to the inconvenience of the Western Allies.

July 1945 was a pivotal point in how the future would unfold for the Western Allies. On the 15th of that month, the RAF's continental expeditionary command—2nd Tactical Air Force—received formal notice that henceforth, it would be recognised as the British Air Forces of Occupation (BAFO). Regarding the wider picture, 17 July 1945 brought the final strategic meeting of the 'Big Three'—Truman, Churchill, and Stalin, the three leaders of the principal victors over Germany. The final conference was held in the Cecilienhof, the former residence of Crown Prince Wilhelm, in Potsdam Square. The square stood at the central point of the zones of occupation; when erected, the Berlin Wall cut the square in half, so blunt was the Soviet insistence on literally drawing demarcation borders exactly in accordance with zone limits.

To point out that Truman was in the strongest position of the three was way beyond doubt. There was no relative comparison as the American economy was in good stead, having survived the war with Germany, indeed expanding as a result.

The Americans had many debts to call in, but that could wait. The States had also avoided the kind of devastation inflicted on all the other key protagonists, leaving America at the dawn of its own form of imperial standing. The UK was at the end of its day in the sun.

British Prime Minister Winston Churchill was in the weakest position; he was prime minister of a hitherto waning and fading empire, and from here, the erosion would be hastened by economic hardship and the global shift away from the old imperial order maintained by Britain and other European states. The changes were already started much closer to home. Churchill's fellow countrymen and women had twelve days earlier gone to the polls to vote in the first general election since 1935 when Stanley Baldwin was returned with a majority of 242. A lot of water had flowed under the bridge since then and promises had been made for the post-war era. The National Health Service was on the starting blocks, but while this project got underway under the Conservative-led wartime coalition, the blueprint for the NHS had been drafted and pursued by Liberal MP William Beveridge, who was serving on the National Government's committee to survey social and allied services. He subsequently produced the now historic 'Beveridge Report', which made several recommendations as solutions to one of the five pillars of evil: disease, want, ignorance, squalor, and idleness. This included National Insurance contributions and the setting up of the National Health Service.

While Churchill had become the nation's saviour as the wartime prime minister, the beckoning peace (the war still persisted in the Far East) called for a party and leader perhaps judged to be more sympathetic to the implementation of the Beveridge Report, especially given, or even despite, the economic circumstances the country was now mired in. The party waiting in the wings most likely to build the new Jerusalem was not the Liberal party, but the Labour party. Equally identified with noticeably higher concern for social and economic equality, they naturally appealed to a war-weary electorate as the antidote to the past. Churchill, whatever his public mood, was aware of the likelihood of his being rewarded by the nation he had led and guided to ultimate victory over the threat of Nazi hegemony, with defeat at the ballot box. The country to whom he was a most unique saviour was now about to forsake him for a prime minister and party that would secure the peace.

Churchill probably was not too enraged by the result; his wife, Clementine, commented at the time about the ingratitude of the electorate. 'Not at all,' he said, 'they've had a hard time.' Above all, Britain was bankrupt as its vast empire could not be maintained following the demands of six years of total war, the material production, and the human and material sacrifice, much of which had to be offset and repayment terms agreed. This then was the price of bearing the accolade of the moral victory as well as a prominent position in contributing to the absolute military defeat of the greatest physical threat to humanity on record, certainly since the dawn of the age of enlightenment. While that military threat had been vanquished, another loomed on the horizon.

The results of the election held on 5 July were not yet known, hence Churchill attended Potsdam first. Due to the means of conveying counted ballots, the final result was not known until 26 July. On this day, Attlee replaced Churchill as prime minister and thus Britain, midway through the conference, changed from a Conservative to a Labour government. Attlee was immediately flown out to Berlin to attend the remainder of the conference. Labour had polled 393 seats in parliament; the Conservatives had lost nearly as many seats as the 204 they were left with. As one might assume, being from the left of the centre, Attlee had a more everyman view of the post-war world and was more interested in seeking international cooperation. The chiefs of staff shared the outgoing Churchill's concerns—not that Attlee was to prove weak on international diplomacy and national security, but he did wish to seek an accord where his predecessor was less trusting.

If there is one thing Attlee's premiership promised, at least as far as Britain's place in the world and how we related to other countries was concerned, it would not be a radical shift away from the pacifism of the Labour party he took over from George Landsbury. However, there were certainly going to be changes. So, while the outgoing Conservative cabinet, alongside the military establishment, were already worried about the future implications of Soviet hegemony (in particular they were exorcised about Stalin's interest in Turkey), the new government of Attlee was eager to avoid any further clashes abroad and risking fresh conflicts. The new American president was looking to avoid an isolationist position once again, but also hoping to reduce the level of US forces in occupied Europe.

The new British government endeavoured to at least avoid looking imperious. Stalin's outlook was, as he had said himself, to take what he could at the least cost. Comrade Stalin, the president of the Union of Soviet Socialist Republics (USSR), was in a position of advantage, in certain strategic respects. An ally of Britain and the USA during the war, from the point of the German invasion of the USSR's incomparably vast geographical mass on 22 June 1941, he had before this collaborated with Hitler in a strategic pact, which resulted in splitting Poland in two.

Now Stalin wanted to return to the borders of 1940, he had no intention of moving any part of the Red Army from Central Europe; it and his people had paid too high a price. Stalin believed in the goal of global communism. He was opportunistic and prepared to take advantage whenever it presented. He was not, however, prepared to engage his country in any costly endeavour to achieve any of this. Yet what he had so far, he was not about to let go of.

This is where the arrival on the scene of a Labour government in Britain could have much greater impact on the future development of the redrawing of Europe and the US presence in it. The Labour party in truth was instrumental in government in the instigation and development of NATO, of recognising the threat from the Soviet Union and ensuring the United States fulfilled Roosevelt's claim to be the arsenal of democracy.

However, unlike the Conservative party, Labour was founded on ethical principles that were retained in pure form by a substantive element of its members, which would rise to the surface on more than one occasion in the years ahead. These principals were the pursuit of international interests at the expense of national interests. The true socialists within the party believed their party should be reaching out to oppressed people in other lands and seeking solidarity between workers across the global community. They eschewed the idea of maintaining a military posture and armed intervention, particularly where Britain and other Western countries were concerned. They perceived the communist revolution as a milestone toward a worldwide socialist community, and they hated the political direction that Attlee took Britain's foreign policy in. Attlee was not always a believer in the efficacy of maintaining a substantial military posture; he was once an adherent of the party's more left-leaning wing.

A statement made in parliament by Clement Attlee in 1936 began:

> I beg to move, in line 1, to leave out from 'That' to the end of the Question, and to add instead thereof: as the safety of this country and the peace of the world cannot be secured by reliance on armaments but only by the resolute pursuit of international understanding, adherence to the Covenant of the League of Nations, general disarmament, the progressive pursuit of international labour standards and economic cooperation so as to remove the causes of war, this House cannot agree to a policy which in fact seeks security in national armaments alone and intensifies the ruinous arms race between the nations, inevitably leading to war.

Attlee was placing his own corrections in response to the following statement to the house by the prime minister, Stanley Baldwin:

> I beg to move, that this House approves the Defence proposals of His Majesty's Government which are outlined in Command Paper No. 5107 (Statement relating to Defence). In moving the Motion which stands in my name and the name of some of my right hon. Friends, I want to remind the House that defence requirements and foreign policy are so closely and so firmly interrelated that one cannot be considered apart from the other. I propose, therefore, to say something about the objective of our foreign

policy, something about the means of attaining that objective, and then, and as a consequence, something about our essential defence requirements. The objective of the foreign policy of the United Kingdom and the end to which every endeavour is being steadfastly and continuously directed may be summed up in one sentence: to secure peace for the peoples of the British Empire and for the nations of the world, and the means of obtaining that objective are collective security and friendship. With a view to obtaining collective security we are members of the League of Nations, which seeks to substitute a reign of law in international affairs for a reign of force. Friendship we seek with all the peoples of this world. But the disappointing results of our efforts to secure international disarmament, the growth of armaments in other countries, combined with the development of a number of very disquieting features in the international situation, have left us no alternative, pending disarmament, for which we shall continue to work, but to review the state of our Defence Forces to see what is needed, first, to fulfil our obligations under the Covenant of the League of Nations, and, secondly, to enable us to safeguard ourselves.

By early 1938, the Labour party still opposed the Chamberlain government's re-armament plans because of the amount of money that would need to be borrowed and also because they felt the need for re-armament was a result of the government's failed foreign policy. The suggestion was that, despite what was evident to all, negotiations with Hitler were straightforward enough as to negate any preparation for a different outcome. It could easily be argued that the party's natural pacifist disposition affected their judgement, but in due course, the British left found themselves supporting guerrilla warfare in Spain and the volunteering of British citizens from all walks of life, to fight with the anti-government forces, in war which Britain had no interest in. When German forces were deployed to support General Franco's government forces in Spain, in 1936, many from across Europe and elsewhere flocked to join the fighting. Yet still the government's own clear attempts, however hapless at times, to respond to the growing likelihood of expanding German hegemony through military means were met from the opposition by criticisms over failed foreign policy and wasteful arms expenditure.

All the more curious given the Attlee led Labour party's 1940 view of Chamberlain as an appeaser for the lack of progress in checking German expansion and, presumably, the failure of the government re-armament programmes which seemed to follow one after the other. Now in 1945 and following such a catastrophic conflict in which the USSR had become the UK's most unexpected ally, many on the left found it difficult to accept that the USSR would not continue as an ally, instead of becoming an increasingly isolated state and hostile to the West. The communists had ruthlessly overthrown the tsar in 1917, the authoritarian state which had prevailed since and kept its brutal iron grip on its people in very much the same way the Nazis did in Germany. To the British left, the violent despatch of Tsar Nicholas II and his young family was a necessary step toward the greater good of all, bringing down imperialist privilege and the inequity of capitalism.

This mindset was an ingrained characteristic of an element of the party sitting on the government benches in Westminster and about to negotiate the future map of Europe, the long-term future of the defeated Germany, and what relationship would exist between each of the leaders now at Potsdam. For his part, Attlee was like many on the right of the Labour party, often described as centrists or Atlanticists, the latter due to the lean toward the United States as an ally on security grounds and for economic cooperation. This did not mean he failed to share the same economic and cultural principals of socialism as the left of his party, but it did mean that he had his eyes open over Stalin and the Soviet Union.

In the new world order about to be forged, he was far more drawn to the liberal democracy, enterprise, and 'get up and go' progressive nature of the United States, especially the enlightened approach to equality and egalitarianism of the US Democrats, also the party of Roosevelt and Truman. There was also ruthless capitalism and, for better or worse, engineered mass consumerism for profit—more characteristic of the years ahead. The left of the Labour party was, logically, more anxious to develop links with the Soviet Union, or at least develop an agreeable relationship. Despite the history of brutal suppression of even fellow socialists, they reluctantly over the years ahead came to accept the undeniable evidence that Soviet Communism held Eastern Europe in a state of curfews, political arrests, imprisonment without trial, and executions.

On the other hand, they were unhappy about the capitalist hegemony of the USA and, more importantly, could scarcely accept the argument that a reinforced defence posture in the West, when it came, was the way to confront the growing Soviet military force. With western civilization essentially sitting on the edge of the inner border that split Germany into the Western zones one side and the Russian zone on the other, it was, nevertheless, shear anathema for true socialist DNA to welcome, even accept, any move toward a military posture from your own side. Instead, it was far more practical to seek support on economic strength and workers' and peoples' rights internationally, and to reach accord on these concerns.

To those rightly repelled by the mass casualties and destruction that were certainties in war, reaching out was seen as a much more likely and promising way to achieve the ultimate goal and was certainly seen as achievable. The Potsdam conference was supposed to produce the blueprint for a lasting peace throughout the European continent, if not the world. It was instead the starting pistol for the Cold War. The Second World War was not yet over, and cooperation was vital between the three powers. Interestingly, Truman chose to mention to Stalin that the day before they sat for the first day of the conference, a couple of thousand miles or more away, the Americans were testing a new bomb that possessed enormous destructive power for the first time. Stalin responded with seeming indifference; inside, however, he was deeply concerned that the atomic bomb, now in the hands of the Americans, would render his army, no matter how vast or how well-equipped, superfluous. He was well aware of 'the bomb' as Klaus Fuchs had kept him abreast of what was going on through 'Sonya', a Russian intelligence officer whose real name was Ursula Kuczynski; with aliases including Ruther Werner, Ursula Beurton, and Ursula Hamburger, she was a German left-wing activist and Soviet spy who operated during the 1930s and 1940s. Fuchs was a German physicist who fled his homeland, after the Reichstag fire, and sought refuge in the UK. Here he received his PhD from the University of Bristol and a DSc from the University of Edinburgh.

After being interned on the Isle of Man following the declaration of war in September 1939, he was released in 1941 and proceeded to work on 'Tube Alloys', researching a British atom bomb with Rudolph Peierls. There was no likely threat of Fuchs pursuing any hidden loyalty to the *Führer*; he had joined the German communist party in 1932, hence his flight from Germany. Both he and Peierls were sent to New York University, to work on the Manhattan Project. From here he went to the Los Alamos laboratory, from where he supplied details to Ursula Kuczynski. He was arrested in 1950 after confessing to this significant breach of security and served nine years in prison. His British citizenship was removed, and when released from prison, he settled in the German Democratic Republic (East Germany), where he remained until his death in 1988.

However, Stalin's seeming lack of interest may have influenced Truman's thinking. The American president was not given to the idea of spreading American hegemony and influence across the world and was looking forward to bringing America's boys back home at the earliest convenience. This alarmed Churchill, who was seriously concerned about what would happen in Europe should Truman commence a comprehensive withdrawal. Atom bombs or no atom bombs, Stalin's army would certainly dominate and would become a tool with which to intimidate and influence. Germany was no longer a sovereign state; its vanquished population had accepted the imposition of the victorious powers.

Senior officers and soon judges from the victorious, now governing, nations were afforded significant arbitrary powers to take control of the country and oversee the start of clearing away rubble and reconstruction work. There was also the matter of the application of the rule of law, the restoration of democracy, and the establishment of an international war crimes tribunal to try an as yet undeterminable but quite sizeable list of Nazi war criminals.

In Berlin, entire streets were cleared of inhabitants to make room for the entourage of visiting, high-ranking officials, with many attending the Potsdam conference. Fraternisation between servicemen of the occupying powers and the Germans was strictly forbidden. The Germans for now were treated as outcasts in their own homeland. Overall, the immediate matter to be confronted was the collation of evidence against those German leaders arraigned to stand trial. It has been said that the trials, not necessarily limited to but characterised by the Nuremberg Trials, amounted to nothing short of victors' justice. Indeed, there have been conflicts before and since which have seen the most diabolical depths reached by otherwise seemingly well-adjusted and rational human beings, but authoritarianism and ignorance have never been far away; in such circumstances, understanding brutality seems clearer but not excused, not always anyway.

One only needs to observe some of the pejorative vehement comments which pass for political debate in some democracies, including Westminster, at times. One can easily gain some impression of how easy it is for people, brought up in relative domestic and civilised communities, to quickly change and become agitated and ever more hateful. But the men (predominantly so, many women stood trial as well) in prison awaiting trial—not just at Nuremberg, but across Germany—were not all that faced post-war retribution, they were perhaps lucky to face the legal process.

Elsewhere, lynch mob justice was prevalent—this was a very ugly period. Even the Luftwaffe, like the *Heer* and *Kriegsmarine*, the legitimate military arms of the nation, did not escape allied justice, even among more junior ranks. A significant number of Luftwaffe personnel were to face trial for war crimes, not simply the crews of bomber aircraft, but also those who treated prisoners inhumanely. These poor souls were taken to camps selected for various so-called experiments into finding ways of combating extreme conditions faced by aircrew, such as rapid decompression at altitude and extreme temperatures.

The Germans had built pressure chambers which could lower pressure to that experienced at altitudes as high as 66,000 feet. They did not even operate manned aircraft with that kind of performance, nor was it realistically within reach at the time. The RAF also had an interest in pursuing war crimes, the charges against certain members of the SS who had been involved in the execution of fifty airmen who were rounded up and shot following their escape from *Stalag Luft* III. Generations have come to understand the incident—the Great Escape. This state of affairs continued for many more months—indeed a few years after the German surrender, an era of war crimes trials and non-fraternisation rules, which the ruling military authorities eventually had to concede were impossible to enforce.

Before the trials at Nuremburg could get underway, Truman's atomic bomb was introduced to the world when it was dropped on Hiroshima on 6 August. The seeming slow and unclear response from the Japanese resulted in a second bomb, with a greater yield, being dropped on Nagasaki three days later. On 15 August, the Japanese unconditional surrender was announced to the world, and on 2 September 1945, the formal articles of surrender were signed. The dropping of the devastating new weapon had forced the emperor to accept the unacceptable—a weapon that would come to cast a long dark shadow over Europe, and many of them, in the years ahead. The two bombs used were Little Boy (12.75-kiloton yield) and Fat Man (22.5-kiloton yield); they were dropped, respectively, on the Japanese cities of Hiroshima and Nagasaki. The war was at an end and the polarisation of the world into East and West was about to become apparent.

This polarisation centred on continental Europe, those of the western democracies, and those of the Soviet-overseen eastern block. It was never expected that the USSR would be able to counter America's nuclear advantage with nuclear weapons of its own but that they would was predictable; they did and the threat of Armageddon was now just around the corner.

For now, peace reigned as the people of the United States, the United Kingdom, France, and other nations were getting on with putting civilisation back together.

Most people were unaware that from north to south, a line ran in rough fashion from just east of Jutland down through Germany, dividing the occupied country into west and east. Southwards, it went west of Czechoslovakia, then on around the Austrian border, continuing to segregate Czechoslovakia, then Hungary; on it went, dividing Italy from Hungary until it reached the Adriatic Sea. This new border then followed between the Soviet-occupied nations north of Greece until reaching the Black Sea.

To the north of Germany, the Baltic states of Lithuania, Latvia, and Estonia were firmly inside the Soviet Union. Where Russia met Finland, the Iron Curtain continued between the two, eventually dividing the last strip, separating Norway's north-eastern tip from Russian soil. All to the east was theirs, as far as Mother Russia extended away from the European theatre. All to the west of the line was ours.

Unfortunately for ease of settlement, Berlin sat, most awkwardly, inside the Soviet zone of occupation. This became a little complicated as well as unprecedented as the three Western powers were responsible for corresponding zones of occupation in Berlin. As Germany was split into left and right, so was Berlin. The divided city would remain, until the day the wall was brought down, a city under military occupation and by opposing armies.

On 25 August 1945, the British Army of Occupation, while retaining that role, changed its name to the British Army of the Rhine.

This was soon to be the settled situation. On 20 November 1945, as the Nuremberg Trials got underway, the wider processing of German military personnel was making progress as well. In January 1946, HQ BAOR were seeking approval to cancel the discharge papers of all German service personnel who had volunteered to serve in the *Einsatzgruppen* (deployable special service groups). On the other hand, permission had already been given for German officers, irrespective of rank, to be discharged if they were invalided, mentally unstable, or aged seventy and over. Some 34,000 German servicemen had, by 31 January 1946, been transferred from the British to the Soviet zone of occupation. Some 4,351 had been handed over to the Americans, 7,977 to the French, 2,291 to the British zone in Austria, and 3,632 to the French zone in Austria; 24,736 had been discharged. Non-German members of the armed forces of the Reich processed so far amounted to 15,000. Altogether, 274,166 former *Wehrmacht* personnel had been processed by the BAOR disbandment unit.

Some 70,000 Germans were still detained, classed as dangerous and subject to further screening, in addition to a further 30,000 non-Germans. There was an attempt to be quite fair with everyone, and German officers eligible for discharge whose addresses sat in other zones of occupation—i.e. the Soviet zone—could change to the British zone. The process of discharging and investigating *Wehrmacht* personnel went under the title Operation Clobber.

Specifically, German Air Force personnel were dealt with initially by the RAF (BAFO). There were some Luftwaffe personnel whose discharge the RAF wanted to defer. Of these personnel, the army were expected to take custody of them, but if the RAF had not already made such arrangements, they were advised to conduct summary trials of those Luftwaffe personnel in question. Even then, if the offences warranted a sentence of more than one year in prison, the RAF were to refer them to the military government for trial.

Apart from the disbandment of German personnel, the RAF and other allied arms were engaged in dismantling and disposing of enemy equipment and military apparatus in Germany and all the former German-occupied countries. Itemising of German equipment found inside the zones of occupation included recording everything, even down to kitchen pots and pans. A laborious, tedious, and unglamorous pastime, in Holland, they had managed to salvage some 60 per cent of enemy materials, which had been requested by the University of Delft and the National Aeronautical Research Institute. As such, the Dutch authorities were notified by the RAF that this requirement would be satisfied. BAFO still existed and operated at its wartime size and was now being addressed; units of BAFO were, as of January 1946, apart from those involved in Operation Clobber, warehoused in the Low

Countries. Detailed proposals for how these units would be moved from their current location had to be notified by 6 January.

As the BAFO started to work toward some form of establishment, various standards and procedures were to be approved and enforced. The desire to return to a peacetime environment at the earliest had a sense of formal informality. Headquarters BAFO had issued an order that as a concession to democracy, certain relaxations of discipline were to be made. However, such relaxations were described thus:

> The continuation of corporate pride and unwavering obedience under difficult conditions which made the RAF the striking force during the war is to be made possible, these relaxations must not be taken to imply anything more than a cutting out of unnecessary parades and formalities.

One such routine order requested by the BAFO was the provision of motor transport (MT) for recreational purposes.

This was no low-level attempt to override priority for more pressing operational or administrative purposes. An official letter was sent from the office of AOA (air officer administration), which had been written to BAOR OC 'Q' movements. The Air Ministry was fully supportive, and for some curious reason, the Admiralty were as well. However, the Treasury wanted to know why the RAF needed extra vehicles purely for recreational use when the BAOR had made no such request for the army in Germany. The RAF's case was the special circumstances of serving in Germany and the need for additional transport, as described, for recreational purposes. The treasury wanted the BAOR to support the application before authorisation; this may have meant the same accommodation being extended for the army, but not necessarily.

Set tours of duty were now being set for personnel and criteria for service families to accompany personnel stationed in Germany. In February 1946, eligibility for an accompanied tour by family required a tour of duty ahead of more than one year. Tours of duty for airmen were being set at eighteen months (two years for commissioned officers). Although no one could promise anything, matters were moving fast and BAFO were forecasting a date of 1 May 1946 for the arrival of the first families to join their husbands. By September, permission had been granted for recreational transport; this was to be extended for the benefit of RAF families now living in the British zone of occupation.

In January 1947, air headquarters, BAFO, recorded an assessment of the general wellbeing of personnel and dependents in occupied Germany:

> The background to BAFO activities is an unhappy one due mainly to the lack of food and fuel amongst the German population but more important issues

seem to be lurking behind these immediate problems which must necessarily occupy first place during the bitter weather the country is experiencing.

The Germans had an expectation that the Anglo-American occupation would see the economic input and fusion of both bring about (the Germans seemed evidently unaware of the British economic difficulties) a general improvement in their wellbeing. They were therefore sadly disillusioned.

The Americans, the BAFO noted, were further along the road to German rehabilitation and autonomy by March 1947. Their military posture was reduced to review, observation, and advice only. The recent severe winter had resulted in a lack of food, fuel, and clothing and a dislocation of public services. This caused a deterioration in public morale, and, as one RAF officer noted, 'with typical Teuton inconsistency the occupying power is blamed'.

The British military administration were the focus of this unhappiness and anger that had resulted in strikes, but these had been resolved. Within BAFO, there was a rising number of incidences of theft due to a shortage of RAF police staff. Two incidents of note were the theft of a large safe from one RAF station and £350 worth of goods from one of the Malcolm clubs. The Malcolm clubs were started by the wife of 1st Baron Tedder, CAS, back in 1943, in Algiers. By the end of the war, they had become widespread across overseas RAF stations, and later became particularly synonymous with the RAF in Germany. They were generally regarded as a better-quality amenity than the more widespread NAAFI service. The clubs took the name Malcolm after a young Scottish wing commander, Hugh Malcolm, who had posthumously been awarded the Victoria Cross during operations over Tunis.

In January, civilian airline services began from airfields in the British zone. Again, this brought its own problems, particularly pertaining to security, customs, transit hotels, and booking centres. This was being addressed in conjunction with the opening of civil aviation in the American zone. Operationally, the RAF practiced deploying 135 Wing from Faßberg to Alhorn, to test the potential of combined operations; this included participation by units of Transport Command and an exchange was arranged between British pilots of the BAFO and American fighter pilots from their 12th TAC (Tactical Air Command).

The rate of aircraft accidents in this era was nothing less than severe by modern standards—in the month of February 1947, the rate was 49.4 per 10,000 sorties. The worst accident that month was the collision of two Spitfires. Both pilots were killed and the initial entry in the ORB (operational record book) alleged a breach of flying discipline as the cause. It was noteworthy that only two squadrons—3 and 69—had not seen any accidents at all for four straight months.

This, however, was the least of command concerns, as by March, word had come from on high that 1 Corps (BAOR) were earmarked for disbandment.

Together with further manpower reductions, this did not bode well for two of the three air groups—2 and 84—whose continued existence was now in the balance. No. 84 Group was seen as the most likely operational element of the RAF to remain in Germany being a close air support and tactical bomber formation, but with the disappearance of 1 British Corps, the continued existence of 84 Group, formerly the Desert Air Force, was now in question. The decision was to disband 84 Group and retain 2 Group as the principal element of BAFO for now. British 1st Corps also disbanded in March; this left a small British military contingent in Germany, reduced to three divisions—2nd and 5th Infantry and 7th Armoured—together with two districts—Hamburg and Hanover—with an occupation force assigned to the British zone in Berlin.

The 5th Infantry and 7th Armoured Divisions were both to be disbanded later in the year, indicating a desire to reduce the British presence significantly in Germany—at the end of the war, all that remained were eleven British divisions together with the 1st Free Polish Division and the 3rd Canadian Division (with British troops within). Now the two divisions, together with British forces in Berlin, made up the force left in the British Army of the Rhine. Even though the military presence was winding down, there had been an identified need for night photographic and night visual reconnaissance, but the day fighter reconnaissance aircraft available from the RAF were unsuited.

The two aircraft in mind were the de Havilland Mosquito for the photographic role and the B-25 Mitchell for the visual task. Preferably, a single type to cover both tasks would have been ideal. Meanwhile, apart from the BAFO HQ at Bad Eilsen, the RAF had only three operational airfields—Faßberg, Alhorn, and Gütersloh in the British zone, supporting ten operational squadrons. There were other commandeered airfields; these were utilised for other roles, including that of advanced landing ground and were still assigned a reference number such as B.116, which happened to be assigned to what would shortly become RAF Wunstorf.

There was also, following the post war rationalisation of the armed forces, a significant lack of personnel in certain key trades that were found, in some cases, to be deficient of personnel by almost half. As a result, those airmen in the affected trades were, due to their short supply, not to be assigned secondary duties. This prompted one RAF officer to describe the situation as follows:

So serious that personnel in these trades are entering an airman's golden age, in which they are to be excused all station duties. Naturally, this is left to the discretion of the Station Commanders, but with these trades showing an average deficiency of 46% there seems no alternative.

It is generally accepted that the Cold War began its gestation period with the Potsdam conference, which left division between Stalin and the other leaders, even though the wartime alliance persisted long enough to see the comprehensive defeat of Japan. There was certainly a resumed fear of Soviet hegemony after the war. Yet as of spring 1947, air headquarters were expecting the disbandment of 1st Corps to result in an inevitable further corresponding reduction in the size of BAFO.

The size of land force left available to BAOR dictated that BAFO would need to be tailored to provide the kind of cohesion needed between the army and air force, such as was the relationship during the war. Back when they were 2nd Tactical Air Force and 2nd Army, the principal British air and land forces, they were also the two principal component parts of Montgomery's 21st Army Group. The latter also included the 1st Canadian Army and associated elements.

This further restructuring of the army was expected to see a corresponding reorganisation of the air force to meet the right balance. On March 11, the Air Ministry edict was for a reduction in BAFO of 2,400 personnel, but no cuts to the operational unit configuration. Germany was moving toward a greater degree of autonomy within the British and French as well as American zones, where elections were now being held. Despite this, denazification still proceeded with several arrests of former senior Nazi officials and SS men during the preceding February.

A year later, in March 1948, peacetime manpower levels for the armed forces were being assessed. The proposal for the strength of the RAF had developed into a rough figure arrived at by the DGO (director general of organisation), which was somewhat significantly higher than that arrived at by the joint planning staff. The figure of 244,600 was deemed appropriate; however, it was also seen as prudent to round the figure up to 245,000 when placed before the Ministry of Defence.

Of the 245,000, only 69,800 were classed as operational personnel. Everyone else fell under the various descriptive headings—Air Ministry Command and group HQs; RAF Regiment; research, experimental and development; training organisation, maintenance organisation; general supporting services; and miscellaneous unallocated (the latter included the 'special duty list'). The total number of operational flying squadrons was 144, with four flights. What also had to be accounted for was the ratio of peacetime national service personnel. The army strength proposal for the long term was mooted to be 346,000, of which 121,000 were national servicemen—the largest ratio of the three services. The RAF had originally proposed a peacetime strength of 225,000, once what was termed as stability having been reached. A force of 1,858 aircraft also formed a part of the long-term standing.

The target number of aircraft would need to be larger now that a figure of 245,000 personnel had been arrived at. This was described though as a broad overview. It has to be considered that at the end of the war, in early 1945, the

RAF personnel strength stood at about 1.1 million, although it was already being reduced where possible.

Prime Minister Clement Attlee had told the defence chiefs that the armed forces would have to meet certain priorities and that over the next few years would not be able to provide the kind of services that were required. Therefore, the chiefs of staff committee would need to agree upon the specifics of their roles. He had noticed some disagreement over the functions of the Royal Navy and Royal Air Force in a future war. There was difficulty in determining the future role of the army, partly due to the task it had of conducting occupational duties both in Germany and elsewhere, during what was still very much the climate of the aftermath.

The prime minister wanted the army to determine what its role in a future war would be and as a consequence, what it would need to be trained to do, and what its manpower requirements would be as a result. In order to crystallise these issues, Attlee said that in reply to the question, the current extraordinary post-war army commitments should, for the moment, be disregarded. The chief of the imperial general staff, Field Marshal Montgomery, replied that the army's role would be to hold the position in whatever area of the globe the government's foreign policy required us to maintain—in other words, to defend the UK's current consolidated interests abroad. This would vary depending on the international situation.

This function would be discharged in the first instance by the regular army, but behind it should be a territorial army of 600,000, which, with the help of national service, would already be trained to go to war. There would not be a need for lengthy training, which had been the case in the past. The Territorial Army should include a field army of nine divisions. Beyond this was the direct defence of the UK itself. Here Montgomery determined that the army would need to counter invasion, including from airborne forces, and provide for the anti-aircraft defence as well as aid to the civil power (police).

The extent to which the army should be deployed overseas was a matter for the government of the day to decide, after weighing up the needs of home defence. The then minister of defence, Albert Alexander, felt some sympathy with Montgomery's concerns about being able to defeat an invasion but believed that the Royal Navy and the RAF would not be easily neutralised by an invading enemy. What he was saying was it would be unwise to 'invest too heavily' in air and sea defences as they were less likely to be challenged by any recognisable threat. To defend the Middle East successfully, Montgomery said a force of about nine or ten divisions would be required, but the build-up would take some time. The new Labour administration certainly differed from the outgoing Conservatives, but at the time, there was a broad consensus on defence, and an incumbent Conservative government would be looking to reduce the scale of the armed forces as well in the immediate post-war world.

The discernible differences between the Conservatives and the Labour party in respect of national security concerns lay with the priorities and understanding of the efficacy of military strength in terms of overseas responsibilities. The Labour party had international cohesion at heart and were currently in government—albeit a government administered by men who placed greater store by the nation's position internationally and understood that liberal democracy would be better served through continued good relations with North America.

Opposed to this were those members, including many MPs, who were more mistrusting of the USA and had difficulty seeing their own country's position and benefits in supporting the national interests overseas. This element within Labour preferred to take a more internationalist outlook based around a common bond with the disenfranchised across the globe. The Soviet Union and its client states across Eastern Europe began to emerge as a more discernible military threat, noticeably toward Western Europe and more directly to the Western zones of Germany. Labour's more orthodox left-wing contingent naturally felt deeply uncomfortable with any moves to exploit this by polarising Western interests, including those of Britain, on the one side while socialism was left represented by the interests of the Soviet Union and satellites. Yet this is where their instinctive sympathies lay, which certainly represented something of a party dilemma.

Despite these differences, both Conservative and Labour governments over the next thirty-four years maintained a *status quo* on European security and defence against the likelihood of Soviet hegemony. The radical element within Labour would always fail to see the military threat from the Soviet Union and Warsaw Pact or any kind of threat that might be confronted with a standing navy, army, and air force. They did eventually manage to seize control of the parliamentary party and the executive in 1980.

For all that, Clement Attlee, whose socialist principals were beyond reproach and who may have taken a different view in the 1930s, was committed to the defence of Europe and understood the need for America to remain engaged. His cabinet included fellow centrists/Atlanticists Ernest Bevin and Hugh Gaitskell; these are the men at the heart of the creation of NATO and the development of the 'British Bomb'.

It is important to provide the political backdrop to the tension in Central Europe about to develop; to understand why, as early as 1945, the British government was in concert with the other leading West Europeans, increasingly uncomfortable with their forecast relations with Stalin, a principal leader of the war coalition against the Axis; and why this led to the creation of NATO resulting in a British commitment to the maintenance of a substantial Armoured Corps, with a second in reserve, and a large Tactical Air Force in north-west Germany long past the need to base (alongside the

Americans, French, and other Allies) forces of occupation there. Even after the establishment of West Germany as a sovereign nation and the construction of the *Bundeswehr* (German Federal Armed Forces), the military posture, which in time was equipped with tactical nuclear weapons, was determined to be utterly indispensable.

Throughout the coming decades, the West would see democracy served by various anti-establishment elements who could not help but see the West as the provocateur and enemy of the piece—or more specifically, US capitalism alongside Britain's imperialist past and the emergence of West Germany as an economic success and NATO member, requiring the resumption of its own standing armed forces; all were challenged from within. The rise of the anti-nuclear movement in Western countries was no doubt prompted by the news that the USSR also had the bomb. Yet their concern was not with Russian missiles, but those in the hands of NATO.

Radical left-wing groups on the continent years later developed a particular enmity toward the Americans. In West Germany, radical and progressive thinking among essentially university students developed into the creation of a terrorist movement that was paranoid about the acceptance into the country's post war political life of former officers, soldiers, and officials of the Nazi state. This was undoubtedly the case, but such men were also among those who led West Germany from ash and rubble through an era of reconstruction back to economic strength and respectability.

The other side of the divide had no such challenge to its security. Even so, in wider circles within the British establishment, the notion that Britain was on the wrong side of the fence was well supported. Many intellectuals who had served the country well against Germany and Japan were now making the case for a more sympathetic relationship with the Kremlin and were increasingly critical of Washington. The continuing argument that Western defence policy was particularly aggressive and was dangerously over-extensive to the point of making the chance of war and Armageddon more likely persisted.

Sympathisers of the USSR's position within Western establishments earned themselves the tag 'useful idiots'—an expression supposedly originally used by Lenin but unsubstantiated. Back in 1947, the threat posed by Moscow was not absent but prompted no undue concern. After the Second World War, Europe was understandably preoccupied with reconstruction and returning to peacetime levels of provision—things getting better and moving forward into broad sunlit uplands. Any suggestion of another return to arms after the last de-mob suit been mothballed was not going to be welcome. The British government were already in the process of continuing the wartime draft under the new peacetime legislation called 'National Service'. This was more to meet the still widespread demands of policing and garrisoning the empire. It was also the first time that young British men faced obligatory military service with no immediate threat to national survival.

During the war, Stalin had managed to get his army as far into the West as possible. Now they were in the eastern quarter of Germany and all countries on the other side of this demarcation and they certainly were not about to withdraw.

3

The Post-War Settlement

Relations between the victorious powers began to sour when the European recovery programme—more widely known as the 'Marshall Plan'—was first presented on 10 October 1946 at the Paris Peace Conference. It was rejected by Moscow, even though Stalin was interested initially and sent a Soviet delegation to Paris.

His own rejection was decided by the American insistence on full economic cooperation and that a good deal of aid would go to Germany. This was unacceptable as it would squeeze Soviet influence and control out of all participating countries, meaning the satellite states of Eastern Europe. The Kremlin both resented and feared American imposition on countries now just over a year following the war. At the Paris conference, the Soviet Union's negotiating team made their position clear; they walked out of the conference, to which sixteen European countries had sent delegations. The Russians also keenly objected to the Anglo–American intention to rebuild Germany with minimal delay.

The Kremlin opposed cooperating in the rapid regeneration of the former foe's means of sustenance and rebuilding of infrastructure, demanding instead that the Germans first set the bill straight for war reparations. Clearly, this would not do. Also, any involvement in the economic rebuilding of Europe would require economic cooperation from the beneficiaries, though this was again out of the question. The American position was strengthened by the British foreign minister, Ernst Bevin, and his French counterpart, Georges Bidault's demands that any aid should go hand in hand with the creation of a European united economic block. This was quite unacceptable to Stalin and his own ambition for a Soviet-controlled command economy imposed upon the East European states.

Apart from having the irritating presence of an ideologically opposed island of capitalist bourgeois decadence in the middle of the Russian-administered part of Germany, the impositions of the Marshall Plan were regarded, not surprisingly, as a hostile act by the West. The Americans regarded the Soviet response and their subsequent influence over the East Europeans, who for the most part were quite happy to comply, with little surprise. The Russians only had to allude to the consequences of failure to reject the Marshall Plan and subscribe instead to the 'Molotov Plan' in order to ensure compliance.

The imposition of the Western economic revival demands would ensure the loss of Russian influence and grip on the hard-won East and, as the Kremlin saw it, give the American commercial sector a free hand in hoovering up industry across 'their Europe'. This could lead to the Americans consolidating a vast expansion eastward toward Russian borders; this was absolutely anathema to Stalin and the *Politburo*. It would be humiliating and plain unacceptable.

The situation worsened into 1947 when in elections in some West European countries, the communists fared poorly; this was also blamed on the Marshall Plan. Stalin had hoped to influence events at Paris through the USSR's initial involvement, but the Americans insisted strict rules of economic management must apply. Another provocation to generate Soviet objections, again surprising no one, was the introduction of the new *Deutsche Mark*, which was not recognised in the Soviet German sector.

Stalin branded those countries in receipt of aid from the plan as enemies and the USA of fomenting anti-Soviet activity across Europe. This was the next step in hardening attitudes and the future position between East and West. The result was that the city of Berlin became a volatile flashpoint and a constant headache for diplomacy.

Concern about long-term Soviet intentions brought about a defence alliance between the United Kingdom, France, Belgium, Netherlands, and Luxembourg. A new treaty on mutual defence and security, the Treaty of Brussels, was signed by the contributory powers on 17 March 1948, with the notable exception of the United States; the WEU (Western Defence Union) was born.

Despite America's absence from the embryo framework of the defence union, the British prime minister, Clement Attlee, was working to convince President Truman to come on board, believing the only way to realistically hold Stalin's possible expansionist intentions in check was for the US forces to remain in Europe. Washington alone had the means and the numbers to even the balance, if they agreed. The basic framework of cooperation between the member states, agreed by the respective military chiefs of staff, were to provide all logistical aid to each other's armed forces.

For example, should the armed forces of one country find themselves on the soil of another member, the host would provide every support possible. This would take place without transferring rights or control of whatever resources were made available. Agreement was also required between all regarding the transit ports to be used. For British forces and forces under British control, Antwerp and the Hook of Holland were to be used to maintain and reinforce troops on the Rhine concurrently with the build-up of a base further west. Medical facilities were prepared to move west in the event of hostilities or any other crisis situation; this meant medical staff and whatever equipment that could be moved would transfer. As far as the BAFO was concerned, this would be RAF Gütersloh to Volkel; RAF Wahn to Gilze-Rijen; and RAF Wunstorf to Eindhoven. The RAF general hospital would move to Maeseyck, near Eindhoven. Stores of medical equipment, to equip and maintain 200 beds, would be in place by April 1949.

By 1 April 1948, much of the aftermath of the Second World War had been settled, that is to say judicial process had run its course for the greater part with the more prominent Nazi officials and senior political and military figures. Having had their day in court at Nuremberg, where they had been confronted with the bleak depths of the genocide programme that they had not only defended and been party to but had sought to impose across the continent of Europe from the Bay of Biscay to the eastern reaches of the USSR, many were sentenced to hang; a significant number had avoided this fate and were now serving prison sentences ranging from a handful of years to life. Some indeed were acquitted, although those who were, in some instances, then faced arrest and charges brought by the federal German authorities now operating under the watchful eye of the occupying powers. The status of Anglo-American- and French-occupied parts of Germany were already moving toward a different posture. The Soviet Union had not changed their position amounting to a complete lack of trust in the Western powers and especially the new Federal Republic.

What allied forces of occupation remained on German soil had continued to reduce their presence—the French had based troops in their allocated zone and the Americans were rapidly reducing their strength through Operation Magic Carpet from a strength of more than 12 million personnel at the time of the German surrender, including more than 7.6 million overseas. The US force total by 30 June 1947 had been reduced to 1,566,000. This figure includes all service branches and is significantly smaller than the US military strength at the end of the Cold War. Surprisingly, HM forces were not much smaller, having reduced from a peak of 4.8 million. The general rundown of allied forces continued. The common ground the Western Allies and the USSR had forged, through their being united against a common foe, was coming to an end.

The Russians now resented what they perceived as the sanctimonious American/Western political imposition as exercised through the demanded prerequisites to access the Marshall Plan. For their part, Western European countries could not be reassured over the prospect of possible Soviet hegemony. At a time when leaders on the continent presided over people trying to get over the nightmare of the recent ordeal of German occupation and pursue the interests of a more secure future, there was naturally a strong desire to find common ground and unity among nations, as far and wide as possible. No one could say for sure just how long there would be an allied military presence on German soil, but as time went on, the loss of a noticeable military force from the continent was more a prospect to worry about than one to hasten.

The war in Europe had left few with any idea of seeing the Germans as an allied independent nation ever again, yet the Soviet Union, whatever the relationship in May 1945, now bore closer scrutiny; no one was prepared to see the equally authoritarian USSR through the rose-tinted spectacles that were needed to defeat the Axis.

The past was exiting, the future beckoned, and the victors' view of it was polarised, not that there was any realistic expectation of anything different.

General Patton had caused discomfort and public embarrassment for his superiors following the German surrender by calling for the war to be continued against the Russians, much as the German leadership had very much hoped would find favour with the other allied victors. It would not be the case at all, that Western politicians or military leaders would regret not having followed Patton's advice, but relations with Stalin were not developing as had been hoped, rather as has been feared.

The Soviet reaction to the Marshall Plan was not surprising, but Washington, London, and Paris could not back away from their united position on democratic determination for the people of all participating nations. Relations were about to reach a post-war low in 1948, making it the defining year where the first rock was thrown. By March, the British chiefs of staff—Lord Frazer of North Cape (first sea lord), Viscount Montgomery (chief of the imperial general staff), and Lord Tedder (CAS)—had to hand all the studies needed to form an idea of how the future defence needs for the British people were going to develop. A report of the effects of weapons of mass destruction was being compiled by Sir Henry Tizard, the Ministry of Defence's chief technical advisor.

Even though Soviet Russia did not have nuclear or chemical weapons at the time, the Tizard report was of particular concern and interest as further into the future, everyone expected that Russia may be in a position where they may be more likely to go to war. This and other air ministry reports were urgently awaited. Allied resources with regard to the UK and the continental Allies were described as so meagre that 'they would be hopelessly discouraged if we had to plan to go to war without American support'. This directed the British military chiefs to seek assurances that America would intervene from the outset prior to any further talks with the rest of the Western Union countries, especially prompt participation by the US Air Force.

To the British chiefs, it was evident that the main strength of any allied military response centred on the USAF Bomber Force and its supply of atomic bombs. Initial contact with the continental Allies would be to address three points for future defence planning: stocktaking of available resources; review of measures for the immediate improvement of our military strengths; and the assurance of the United States that they would participate at the outset of war with Russia. Providing they could rely on this, then matters could with confidence be taken forward. Russia was described as embarking on an expansionist policy.

4

The Cold War Development

On 18 June 1948, the Western powers took another step forward that angered Stalin. After having had his nose put out of joint at Paris in 1946, the Western powers now announced the introduction of the *Deutsche Mark*. The new currency was intended to consolidate the occupied zones of both West Germany and West Berlin and was implemented on 21 June. The same day, Soviet military police halted a US Army goods train heading toward Berlin, turning it back. On 22 June, Moscow announced that a new German currency—the *Ostmark*—was to be introduced in their zone.

The post-war honeymoon was now over. Stalin was more inclined to regard West Europe as a capitalist or even a fascist empire, not that he was planning an all-out war to liberate the proletariat of the continent when the opportunity presented itself. However, the claims that he wanted any future conflict to be contained as far as possible from Russian soil would certainly have made sense. Everywhere that trouble could arise, a deep line of allied satellites buffered the USSR from any likely aggressor; this was how the Soviet Union planned to secure its long-term future and made sense of Stalin casting the net wide and far regarding wartime aims.

With the greater part of Germany now outside his overall control, he had his paranoia added to with the apparent collaboration between the West Europeans and North America. This made him wary of the chunk of Germany governed within the allied zones. The first question was the German capital— should Berlin be whole again? The Russians thought it should and they had the strength of argument on their side, certainly in terms of practicalities and logistics. Berlin was firmly inside East Germany, so from a simple and rational viewpoint, the whole city should become East German and communist. On the other hand, to concede this would set a most dangerous, not to mention, treacherous precedent as far as the Western Allies were concerned.

The part of the city occupied by the Americans, British, and French formed a solid area, just like the corresponding zones of the West, so it was easy to protect, rather than if the three western sections were in any way separated. The hard bit was that Berlin sat 98 miles east of the Iron Curtain or IGB (inner German border); the British zone, west of the IGB, directly faced the western sectors of Berlin. Bearing in mind that Stalin did not wish to risk an all-out confrontation with the West, certainly not while America retained substantial forces in Europe, he was certainly prepared—in fact, eager—to exploit any opportunity to expand and consolidate the communist hold.

1948 was to be a year of 'change and strain' for the BAFO, with the latter six months being especially trying. Thus, the first trial of relations between east and west began to unfold. On 5 April, a Russian Yak fighter crashed in Berlin while supposedly attempting to intercept a BEA Viking heading toward RAF Gatow. An order to BAFO was issued instructing that 'armed' fighter escorts were to accompany all transport flights in and out of West Berlin with immediate effect. The next day, the chief of the imperial general staff, Field Marshal Montgomery, was due to fly into Berlin; BAFO were to provide an armed fighter escort with orders to 'attack if fired upon'.

The RAF presence in Germany as of this point was described as a mere shadow of the initial occupying force in 1945. The Air Ministry had, at the beginning of the year, ordered BAFO to contract yet again through reorganisation. The plan was about to be wrong-footed—a trend that appears to scupper any attempt by government to adjust to a seemingly more settled vision of the future. BAFO had been set as an overseas command in January, with a fixed tour of duty for personnel of two and a half years.

The first major development that would confirm the need for a firmer defence alliance in the West came quickly. The strained relations, according to RAF Wunstorf, between the USSR and the West had finally reached a snapping point 'ostensibly' with the introduction of the new currency.

Stalin now decided to move. On 24 June, Moscow ordered the closing of all road and rail links into West Berlin. This placed the governing western powers in a most desperate position. Stalin aimed to not just hinder but to shut off movement of supplies, food, oil, coal, and other raw materials. The clear intention was to starve the inhabitants of the Western militarily governed sectors into submission and force the Western powers out.

The events that followed involved not the RAF units based in Germany were not to the fore but the bulk of RAF Transport Command, which flew many sorties direct from stations in the UK to RAF Gatow in West Berlin while other flights staged through RAF stations in the British sector of the country. RAF Wunstorf recorded in the ORB that one city and one operation dominated June—this referred to Berlin and Operation Carter Paterson, later renamed Plainfare. The preamble to this early East/West international crisis was, many on the left would effectively argue, the fault of the Western powers who had accepted the terms of the Marshall Plan.

RAF Wunstorf's ORB further recorded:

As all surface methods of reaching BERLIN were closed by the Soviets, and as we were determined to stay there, the immense airlift, about which so much has been written and spoken, was organised. This operation was built-up with the full and unstinted co-operation of the BAOR and the USAFE, together with a substantial German Labour Force. Transport Command collected York and Dakota aircraft from the air-routes of the world and sent them to BAFO airfields, firstly, Wunstorf. Aircraft landed at this airfield, ready for the Berlin run, having a few days before been flying the England-Singapore and other routes. Into the American Zone bases of Wiesbaden and Rhein-Main poured Skymasters and Dakotas from the States, Central and South America, Japan and the Pacific Islands.

The UK's counterpart in the USA—the Military Air Transport Service—was also stretched to the limits of capacity. This presaged the one means of access that remained open: the air links; in this case, imposing such restrictions would be far more difficult for Stalin if he wanted to avoid going down in history as the man who started a third world war. Closing ground routes very easily places the responsibility for resorting to armed intervention on the Western side, should they try to drive through road and rail blocks.

In the air trying to enforce a blockade is different. To prevent an unarmed transport aircraft from flying about its business would leave the blockader two options—try and force the aircraft to land, or open fire and shoot it down. Bearing in mind it would be unarmed and carrying food and fuel supplies, this would clearly place responsibility with the Kremlin for an act of unprovoked military aggression—namely, an act of war. Two days after the Russian block began, on 26 June, the United States Air Force made the first flights taking cargo into Tempelhof Airport under the codename 'Vittles'. By choosing the name Plainfare, it was the Brits for once who opted for a more obvious and revealing code. The BAFO had reduced its presence in Germany to fourteen stations (not all of which were airfields and only two that could be classed as fully operational: Gütersloh and Wahn). This was because the ten BAFO squadrons were concentrated here during Operation Plainfare essentially to free up the rest, especially Faßberg and Wunstorf, to act as hubs for the air bridge into Berlin.

There were other airfields. Celle was effectively redundant during this time but available. Oldenburg was in the hands of the army as a maintenance depot for vehicles repaired by the REME. Gatow was at the other end of the air bridge, while Jever was being used as a camp for refugees or displaced people. Schleswig saw all flying units leave at the end of 1945 and housed a parachute-servicing unit and a transport support practice unit, but these were here only briefly in the summer of 1948.

There were two more stations in Austria—Schwechat and Zeltweg—but these were residual bases for occupation and sat on the periphery of BAFO operations. Alhorn was a fuel and ammunition store only temporarily before becoming surplus while Wahn briefly provided lodging for various squadrons, typically operating PR Spitfires and Mosquito fighter bombers, but the ebb and flow was continuous and unsettled. Finally, there was RAF Uetersen, which became home to field and LAA squadrons of the RAF regiment.

Many of these stations would not be in RAF hands beyond the end of the 1950s.

The first British Dakota, laden with flour, took off from Wunstorf at 6 a.m. on 30 June 1948. Operation Plainfare—a scheme to feed and supply by air 2.25 million people, in defiance of Soviet pressure—was underway. The operation increased in scope and improved in efficiency.

No one wanted to countenance the loss of West Berlin and its inhabitants, who were very much now the dependents of the occupying powers. As 1948 wore on, the operation to counter the Berlin Blockade picked up pace and in July was retitled 'Combined Airlift Taskforce' as the all-encompassing title for all involved. The captain of a USAF C-54 Skymaster went to the trouble of adding bags of sweets, chocolates, and chewing gum to be distributed among Berlin's younger residents; his efforts were the spur for the title 'Candy Bomber'.

Against the backdrop of the airlift, the chiefs of staff (including the military governor of Germany, General Sir Brian Robertson) gathered to review the state of Berlin and the ability of its people to withstand the ongoing blockade of which there was no end in sight. Chairing the conference was the RAF's chief of air staff, MRAF Lord Tedder. The committee had two telegrams before them, one each from the military governor and the commander in chief Germany.

The committee met on 12 July 1948. First on the agenda was consumption. General Robertson said that by imposing a 75 per cent cut to industrial activity and on transport in Berlin, they had cut down the city's usage to 3,200 tons per day. At that time, the air bridge was providing 1,800 tons of supplies per day, but this was under normal flying conditions. What was described as normal rations were being maintained, but Sir Brian forecast that a fortnight on, if matters had not improved, it would be necessary to 'cut Berlin down to a minimum scale of life'. This meant further reduced rations and electricity supply limited to the absolute bare essentials, such as the sewers and water supply. British families living in Berlin had not yet been moved out as the general thought was that to do so would have an unfortunate effect on morale.

He would only consider evacuating families if rioting broke out on the streets. At the time, he felt this was not likely simply because the Russians were not sufficiently sure of themselves to instigate rioting. More on the upside, Sir Brian reported that morale in the western sectors was high and the Russians had 'lost a lot of ground'. Sir Brian also said that he thought six weeks on, the minimum scale of life was about as much as the Berlin population could stand.

Predicting the next Russian move could only be a guess, but the general believed that they might resume allowing a few trains through. They would not allow any military traffic movement but would allow sufficient goods through in order to meet the necessities of life for the German population so that circumstances could be maintained as critical during the council of ministers. This would mean the Russians were able to use the situation as leverage during the meeting of the foreign ministers. It was, in his opinion, important that should the Russians allow any goods trains through that the press and the public should not see it as a sign of Russian withdrawal. Field Marshal Montgomery met with the other British chiefs of staff on 28 October 1948 to put together a strategy for the defence of Western Europe, which was to form the basis for planning until further orders.

This kind of initiative was crucial to involving US support both economically and perhaps more importantly at the time, militarily. The Americans would need to see some cohesive, realistic initiative within Europe to become convinced of the worth of committing any substantial effort of their own. The policy was quite simple—if the present situation between the West and Russia should lead to a clash between the two, 'then the forces of the Western Union will defend their homelands'. Further, 'a great struggle would develop'.

In November, the first of the new Handley Page Hastings Transport aircraft joined operations, flying its first sortie from Schleswigland. Proposals to build the Tegel airfield were also confirmed. It was built in the French sector of Berlin, specifically to handle the intensifying airlift. The decision to do so was taken on 24 June. The land was intended for vegetable growing. Ironically, the blockade changed minds; it was to become an airstrip instead. Work began on the ground on 5 August. The field was ready in time to receive its first flight— an American C-54 on 5 November. Tegel became the principal West Berlin airport. It remained in use after reunification, but was eventually superseded by the old East Berlin airport, Schoenfeld. Impacted largely by COVID-19, Tegel eventually closed in November 2020.

USAF C-54 Skymasters of the 317th Troop Carrier Wing began operating from the RAF station at Celle, in addition to Wunstorf and Faßberg. This necessitated the move of RAF units from these bases elsewhere to make room for the Plainfare aircraft—C-54s, DC-4s, Hastings, Yorks, and Sunderlands.

The operation was quite considerable. Wunstorf saw no fewer than fourteen RAF transport squadrons operate detachments here during the airlift. Tragedy also struck when an RAF Dakota crashed in the Russian sector; none of the crew survived. The Russians were described as 'remarkably co-operative over this accident'.

Meanwhile, the operation to counter the Berlin Blockade picked up pace with civilian airlines joining the fray of the all-encompassing humanitarian mission. How long the Allies were prepared to continue with the air bridge and how much time Stalin thought would pass before something would give is perhaps a matter for conjecture, but the operation reached its maximum effort on 16 April 1949. The tempo had continued to build through summer 1948 into winter then spring. People in the UK and USA offered clothes and blankets to be flown over. RAF Transport Command were now equipped with some quite impressive purpose-built transport aircraft; alongside the Avro Yorks and Handley Page Hastings was the venerable wartime workhorse of air transport, the C-47 Skytrain, known in commercial use as the Douglas DC-3 Dakota.

The Short Sunderland (a wartime maritime reconnaissance and anti-submarine warfare aircraft), still in use with Coastal Command, was called upon to assist. Groaning with supplies, they took to landing on the surface of the river Havel near the RAF Base at Gatow. Stalin relented just shy of a year of this continued stand-off. Arguably, the expected loosening of the Western powers' grip on Berlin and eventual relinquishing of the city had not come to pass, nor was there any indication this would happen. The blockade came to an end in May 1949, but due to the lack of supplies, the air bridge continued.

Looking to the future, it was expected that for the next few years, however long it may stretch, that the Soviet Union would hold numerical military superiority.

Montgomery told the chiefs of staff that it was vital that the line on the Rhine was held to prevent the homelands of the west being overrun and that the Russians were kept out of Africa. He went on to speak in both bleak and positive terms simultaneously about fighting back to regain, with American aid, territory temporarily lost to the Russians during initial battles. The doctrine must form the background to planning in Western Europe. He stated the role of the forces of the British empire, again aided by America, was to hold the bridge between Africa and Asia and thus deny the Russians this route into Africa. It was therefore required of every officer and man in the Western Defence Union to be imbued with a single ruling mindset—'that he is trained to fight and to kill, and that he himself will not be killed without taking at least two Russians with him to the next world.'

This was uncompromising stuff from the head of the British Army, during a period with tension reaching the pinnacle point, with the recent Russian attempt to choke off access to West Berlin.

Europe was now recognisably divided into east and west; what Churchill described as the 'Iron Curtain' had descended across Europe—an impassable dividing line running through the approximate middle of Germany then separating Czechoslovakia from Austria. To the west were the nations of the Western Union—the United Kingdom, France, Belgium, the Netherlands and Italy—and across the Atlantic were the nations of North America—Canada and the USA. Further north, in the western hemisphere, Denmark, Norway, and Iceland sat firmly inside the West's protective umbrella—not Sweden and Finland, which maintained their neutrality.

While characteristically neutral, Sweden clearly identified with the Western alliance and took its contribution to its own defence arrangements quite seriously. There was one anomaly here—Finland. The most north-easterly Scandinavian nation fell between the East and the West. A grey area, Finland was engaged with the Soviet Union through the Finno-Soviet Pact of Friendship, Cooperation and Mutual Assistance. This would place pressure on Finland's relations with the USSR to avoid any defence alliance with any other Western states.

Secretly, economic support was provided from the USA. They also developed trade links with the UK, allowing them to make war reparations to Moscow, which had been demanded following the sterling resistance of Finland to the USSR following the latter's invasion on 30 November 1939. The war resulted in Finland being overwhelmed and the Moscow Peace Treaty signed on 13 March 1940. The relationship of the two countries was given the name of 'Finlandisation' by the West German press.

What is little understood from a wider modern perspective is that Berlin was not the only divided city, garrisoned by forces from the allied powers; Vienna was in the very same boat in 1948. Yet a further British/American garrison sat on the border with Italy and Yugoslavia disputably inside Soviet territory. The Free Territory of Trieste—this Western stronghold on the edge of the east—was threatened by a territorial dispute between Italy and Yugoslavia. In each case, these cities under occupation, but bordered by Soviet forces, were considered weak and capable of internal security duties only. They could not under any circumstances be expected to confront a military assault; this was the understanding of Field Marshal Montgomery.

Montgomery referred, for now, to a master plan or grand design—a strategy to avoid treating any one section of the line from the Baltics to the Mediterranean as a whole constituent. The defences of the line had to be able to respond by mobilising into action without delay. For the present, any military response had to be planned defensively. Montgomery also recommended the withdrawal of all allied forces to positions west of the Rhine line. The Rhine was the border west of which no Russian soldier would cross.

There was another neutral country—Switzerland. Montgomery offered Switzerland a form of ultimatum—she could remain neutral, but she should be ready to fight for her integrity against any forces from the east and deny access. If at any stage a prelude to conflict arose, should any belligerent intentions on the part of Yugoslavia become clear toward the Free Territory of Trieste, then the allied forces here would be evacuated to either Malta or the Middle East.

As for Italy, it was not a part of the Western Defence Union at the time and so WDU forces would not fight there should the need arise. The gap between the mountains and the sea at the south end of the French–Italian border would be defended. Should Russian-led forces cross the Rhine, allied forces would withdraw toward the south-west.

No amendments were received from the Air Ministry, but some were from the Admiralty. At the time in question, West Germany could not be expected to render any kind of military assistance, and so the reason for immediately withdrawing west of the Rhine was to establish a definitive defensive stance. Garrison troops in West Berlin would be left to their own devices. Any attempt to break through to them to affect an evacuation of any Western military personnel and or dependents still present at the outbreak of war was out of the question. What placed the Berlin garrisons in a particularly nasty position was the view that it would be politically unacceptable to withdraw them prior to hostilities.

The defence of Austria was deemed impracticable. Furthermore, the defence of Austria was not in accord with the concentration of allied forces to hold the Western Front as had been established. Italy was viewed strategically important, concerning access to the Mediterranean. As no forces could be spared to defend Italy, much was placed in the hope that the Italians could be encouraged to defend their homeland, but their resistance was not expected to be effective or prolonged. Spain and Portugal were equally important to the defence of the sea lanes through the Strait of Gibraltar. Spain remained neutral in 1948 but the Spanish were expected to put up fierce resistance against a Soviet attack. With strong forces, Spain could deter a Soviet assault.

As for Portugal, all the WDU required of them was continued access to naval and air bases. As far as the United Kingdom was concerned, the greatest concern came from those countries that were near Russia, if further north. For example, the territorial integrity of the Scandinavian block was of great importance to Britain's air defence and the defence of allied shipping in the North Atlantic. All the same, the defence planners did not consider the Scandinavian block as vital as the maintenance of the defence of France and the Benelux Countries.

Given the scale of the defence posture involved and the need for greater integration of all involved, it was clear that a 'supreme commander' would be required. It would be his responsibility to coordinate the military withdrawal to the Rhine, but the defence of Scandinavia, Italy, and Trieste fell outside the proposed remit. So it was, as the tensions brought about by the Berlin Blockade and the continuing airlift, the three British service chiefs came to an agreement:

a. The shortage of allied forces to meet all commitments in the event of war within the next few years precludes the successful defence of any line further east than the Rhine.

b. The main allied strategic aim should therefore be the defence of the line Yssel (Gelderse Ijssel)—Rhine—Switzerland—Franco/Italian frontier on the Mediterranean.

c. The relief of the Garrisons in Berlin and Vienna will be out of the question.

d. The successful defence of Trieste is not possible.

e. Allied forces of occupation in Western Germany and Austria should, if possible, assist in the defence of the line Yssel—Rhine—Switzerland—Franco/Italian Frontier. It may, however, not be possible to withdraw British forces in Austria which would then have to fall back on Italy.

f. If Swiss neutrality is not respected, it will be necessary to integrate the defence of Switzerland with that of the Western Allies.

g. The Allies will be unable to assist in the defence of Italy, whose resistance, if she fights, is unlikely to be either prolonged or effective.

h. The best that we can hope for is that the Scandinavian countries should remain neutral and be prepared to defend themselves as far as possible if attacked.

i. Spain is likely to remain neutral at first but would fight if attacked. It is in our interest that Spanish forces should be strong enough to deter Russian aggression.

j. All that we require from Portugal is her agreement to the continued use of air and naval bases in the Azores.

k. A Supreme Commander is required to command the continuous front from the Zuider Zee to the Mediterranean.

The British government reached out to the USA in January and received proposals from the US embassy. These were received in the first instance by the chancellor of the exchequer, regarding the methods by which the United States might provide financial assistance to the WDU. The chancellor, Sir Stafford Cripps, thought the proposals to be vague and may not necessarily have come from Washington, but he had come to the interim conclusion that the United States government were offering to pay half of any additional money allocated, individually, by the WDU countries to defence.

The Americans wanted to know how this would impact on each country's economic recovery programme. As evidence was due to be given to Congress on the progress of European recovery later that month, they would want to know how the WDU rearmament programme was likely to affect the overall economic recovery. The US embassy needed answers to this and other questions concerning specific concerns and objections quickly. Just to hurry the Europeans along, the embassy advised that they needed a clear commitment in the time left available, otherwise it might prove difficult to secure additional 'financial appropriations' in the year 1949–1950.

The chancellor thought the Americans to be well intentioned but wrong-footed and thought the idea of Washington was to double what further expenditure on defence the WDU countries were prepared make. They were not taking into account the already 'enormous' level of defence spending committed to by the WDU. Also, the expectation that every country would be treated the same took no account of what each country could afford. The chancellor therefore cautioned that all countries involved should decide among themselves just what level of contribution they each could make to their collective defence according to each country's financial and economic limitations.

Once this had been done, it should be possible to see where the gaps lay, then go to the Americans and ask them what form their assistance they might take. He certainly believed the whole exercise required far greater study, and it would certainly be a mistake to go to the Americans with rough figures and approximations as this may well be later quoted as authoritative.

The chief concern the chancellor had was that any answers they gave to the questions put by the US embassy may give the impression that we were in favour of their concept of what we had asked originally. This may not be the same understanding of the White House, but the British response to the embassy may gain acceptance in Washington and become the default in place of something better, from which there would be no reverse.

There was general agreement that we should not give the impression of being ungrateful toward the Americans for any assistance offered. At the same time, the Americans should be left under no misunderstanding that the British government saw serious flaws in their approach to a problem which they thought required the most careful and detailed consideration. The British believed the first essential step was for the WDU countries to determine just what they could do, and that it should be pointed out to the Americans that machinery would need to be put in place for the setting up of a financial and economic committee. The Americans would be associated with this body and would have full opportunity to watch it come to its conclusions. On this basis alone, the Americans should have a sound base to decide just what assistance they could provide and how it should be divided between the WDU countries. As for the UK, the need was more for manufactured goods rather than financial support for greater armaments expansion, although Britain would be glad of some raw materials—steel in particular.

It was suggested that the Americans should be given an idea of the UK's principal equipment shortages, but only as an indication of what sort of specific requests may eventually emerge. There was some evidence that the proposals for financial assistance were perhaps only part of a wider arrangement designed to strengthen the Western Defence Union. Equipment requirements for training purposes in 1949 could probably be met by satisfactory financial arrangements between the Western Union countries. The equipment requirements for war were of an entirely different order and called for outside assistance on a large scale. The British also wanted to avoid confusing defence assistance with the economic recovery and wanted to keep the two issues separate.

The differing degrees of strain on the individual European countries' economies and the on the UK economy was very heavy. The British also suggested that the WDU countries should provide a percentage of their respective national income to a pool. That pool would then be divided out over the WDU countries on a basis of relative need. The US Congress was expecting to authorise 'military assistance' on an understanding of mutuality based on self-help by the European powers.

Paris, Brussels, and the Hague were working out their own requirements and priorities. Any figure presented to Congress would need to be a sum total, as a whole single sum is what Congress would authorise.

It would be for the five governments to divide up the total. If ultimately equipment then had to be transferred from one country to another, the US would expect this to be done 'without compensation'. US military observers had worked out a plan just for the UK; they had drawn up three alternative programmes amounting to £50, 75, and 100 million respectively, which the US government could provide half of 'no strings attached'.

The British need for military equipment was largely due to a lack of spare productive capacity, circumstances arising out of the lack of raw materials. Some of the other countries were devoting considerably less as a percentage of their GDP on defence expenditure than the UK but also had a considerable idle capacity for defence production. If the UK were to increase defence expenditure, it would involve a corresponding increase in inflationary pressure unless it were balanced by increased taxation or compensated by reductions in spending on social services or other areas of state expenditure.

Britain's economic resources were under considerable strain, partly due to the measures taken for economic recovery and partly through the already increased expenditure for rearmament. The needs of the other WDU countries were not known in detail, but it was known that they were devoting widely differing shares of their own resources to defence. For the UK, any additional assistance with rearmament would preferably be in the form of increased military equipment rather than personnel.

The service chiefs had not yet given fully considered observations. It was agreed that priority should be given to aircraft and radar, but the needs in these fields could not necessarily be met by UK production. There was also a need to develop airfields to take larger and higher-performance aircraft. The army would like to make good deficiencies and replace equipment that might then be made available to the other Western Union countries for training purposes.

The British, French, Belgian, Dutch, and Luxembourg governments sent representation to Washington, DC, early in 1949 with a view to seeking the USA to join the defence union. As well as the Western Defence Union countries and the United States of America, other nations in the western hemisphere were signatories to the new treaty—Canada, Portugal, Italy, Norway, Denmark, and Iceland. The new alliance was ratified on 4 April 1949.

The place of Italy in the defence of Western Europe was of particular interest, or indeed concern, to the US and UK defence planners. Being a former Axis power, Italy was (despite the country's changed political position by the latter stages of the war) subject to post-war limitations on the size of forces it was allowed. The forces Italy was allowed were, as of 1949, deemed insufficient to defend the country against the perceived threat from the Soviet Union by 1957.

It was also initially accepted by Western planners that the other allied forces were not strong enough, nor were they expected to be so by 1957 either— certainly not if they were to put some kind of reinforcement contingent together to send to Italy. There was no feasible way to address this, and so the path of least resistance was adopted, meaning Italy was to be excluded from allied defence planning.

There was to be an exception—Sicily, which was seen as vital to Mediterranean communications. The interest in Sicily brought a change of heart, and the country was later recognised as a part of the Mediterranean theatre, as far as peacetime defence planning was concerned, and associated with the Mediterranean chiefs of staff under the new Atlantic Treaty, there being no officially settled title for it yet.

Therefore, Italy would become a full member. Still, she remained a source of concern for the Americans. They considered that Italy should be supported as far as practicable and that the Italian government should be persuaded to take on the defence of Sicily. However, they recognised that it would be almost impossible to both repel an attack by Soviet forces and maintain order in mainland Italy in the face of heavy disruption through fifth column activities, involving disorder inspired by the Italian communist party.

The British chiefs of staff now prepared an emergency plan for a response to an invasion of the Western allied controlled zones of Germany, or the Federal Republic of Germany as it became on 23 May. The main ports along the channel coast were not considered vital enough to have anti-aircraft defences allocated, but they fell within the confines of radar coverage. The other WDU nations were not to be handed the current emergency plan; instead, the British chiefs of staff would co-ordinate a revised plan for submission to the military chiefs. The revised plan would show the base requirements for all. Under existing arrangements, the BAOR had been ordered to develop a British maintenance area in Germany, west of the Rhine, and to place all manner of theatre reserves and supplies there.

The army had selected Mönchengladbach as the principal location, and preparations were already taking place. Should a war footing prevail, or a rise in tension yielding sufficient warning, then it would take about thirty days to change the route through which equipment and stores moved from the current one through Hamburg to a new route through a port west of the Rhine. It was not economical to change to the wartime port in peacetime because it would be located outside Germany and currently the cost of providing labour, accommodation and transport was found from German occupation funding. The RAF (BAFO) had already pre-stocked airfields in Holland at Eindhoven, Gilze Rijen, and Volkel, all of which were to become prominent KLU air bases.

Here was stored thirty days' worth of explosives, aircraft, and MT lubricants, fourteen days' worth of servicing spare parts, seven days' worth of packed aviation and MT fuel, fourteen days' worth of rations, and sufficient basic airfield and squadron equipment for the force on deployment. An additional twenty-three days' supply of aviation and MT fuel was held in bulk by the Dutch petroleum company Shell on behalf of the RAF. All quantities of fuel, explosives, and spares had been calculated based on the maximum rate of effort and were measured in terms of how long they were expected to last—a most unreliable method.

The most suitable ports considered as base ports were naturally deepwater. The list included Antwerp, the Seine ports Le Havre and Rouen, a number of satellite ports like Cherbourg, the Brittany ports Brest and Lorient, the Loire ports St Nazire and Nantes, and Bordeaux. Antwerp being only 90 miles west of the Rhine would be within easy reach of all Soviet aircraft. The railway station at Eindhoven was to be used as the principal point of evacuation to Ostend and any other ports while the airfield would be used to provide air evacuation of casualties. In the backdrop to all this, the British government was in contact with other west European nations as confirmed moves toward a better-coordinated defence arrangement were firming up.

The Western occupied zones of post-war Germany were now clearly facing uncertainty; there was no knowing what would come around the corner next as trying to second-guess Stalin and the Kremlin was a pointless endeavour. In April, the prime minister had approved an official interdepartmental committee 'to form a focal point for discussions of financial, military and supply questions in regard to the Western Defence Union'. This committee was not to be limited to matters concerning the WDU but all countries that were represented by the new Atlantic Pact. The UK Foreign Office remained responsible for dealing with the US embassy.

By November 1949, the air bridge had ended, the first facing down of Soviet attempts to railroad and force the Allies into a corner had failed, and West Berlin remained free of the communist block. Plans were now afoot to brace for yet further developments that could arise. The chance of a widening escalation toward an ever more likely full-scale conflict appeared not so much to be likely as inevitable.

At the time, this would not have resulted in the Armageddon theory through the balance of nuclear strike capability, which became very much the worry less than ten years on, but at that time, the likelihood was an overwhelming attack by Soviet land forces supported by the Soviet Air Force. As such, the commander of BAFO received notice of an update to operational instruction 1/49 originally posted in February during the blockade; the message, effective upon receipt revealed codewords for the gradation of transition to a full-scale war footing:

Whole Operation	Abigail
Single Alert	Barker
Reinforced Alert	Pastime
General Alert	Battledore

Whole operation was later replaced by the term 'Military Vigilance', while single alert became 'Simple Alert'. These terms marked the level of military posture on the way to general alert, which in layman's terms means a comprehensive war footing. The signal marked 'Top Secret' carried the instruction that under no circumstances were the codewords to appear on any document that included references to preceding codewords.

Further to this, the British chiefs of staff considered what action would be taken in response to a Soviet-led invasion into the West-controlled regions of Germany. This was not exactly a new development; as far back as August 1948, the subject of the Kiel Canal and denying its use to the Soviet armed forces in an emergency was approached. The method of how to go about this was in the hands of 'Flag Officer Germany' and the Admiralty.

In September 1949, an *aide memoire* was presented by the British foreign secretary, Sir Gladwyn Jebb, to the US secretary of state. The *aide memoire* contained proposals from a British working party instigated to review and report on the current situation on the European continent, with specific regard to the inner German border. It proposed setting up five regional groups under the partner nations of the hitherto Western Defence Union, the United States and Canada.

Two of these groups—the North Atlantic Ocean Group and the United States/Canadian Group—would probably have their headquarters in Washington, DC, also the United States had announced its intention to play a full part in all the groups' activities. In the other three groups, the Northern European, the Western European, and the Western Mediterranean would probably have their headquarters in Europe. The United States would provide for their participation under their terms, but having been requested, agreed to participate actively in the defence planning as appropriate.

The British chiefs of staff had not yet been able to find out from their US counterparts precisely what form participation by the Americans would embrace, and consequently, they were still very much in the dark. To further add to the British sense of uncertainty over the future of European security, the British chiefs felt 'very strongly' that the fullest American participation in these groups was essential for the success of the 'pact' from both military and political points of view.

The British and American chiefs of staff were both in agreement that the real work (the work which would make defence under the Atlantic Pact a reality) had got to be done in the regions. 'The idea that the work that matters should be carried out with anything less than the full cooperation of the United States seems to us to be quite out of tune with the whole Atlantic Pact conception.' As the chiefs of staff saw it, there were two essentials:

a. That United States representatives should be appointed to take part on an equal footing with the other full members of these three Regional Groups in the Regional Defence Committee, and in the case of Western Europe, in the Commanders-in Chief Organisation under Field Marshal Montgomery.

b. That United States representatives should speak with the full authority of the United States Chiefs of Staff and be authorised to inform their colleagues in the Region of the extent of the United States contribution to the Defence of that Region.

In short, the British and US defence chiefs believed that a failure of the United States to associate themselves with the European regions, on the basis described above, would see the existing Western European organisation 'slowly die'.

The British chiefs of staff further examined the functions of a standing group of the Atlantic Pact military organisation. The primary function of the group would be to advise the defence committee on matters of broad strategic policy and on defence planning problems affecting more than a single region.

The detailed planning would be done within the regional organisations. The British chiefs of staff wanted the standing group to be a purely coordinating body, served by a small military secretariat and based in Washington DC. The American chiefs were of the view that the group should be served by a 'North Atlantic Military Staff', which would have a director. The British ambassador in Washington believed that the Americans wanted the standing group to be the main spring of the entire defence organisation.

Following an earlier meeting between the British and American chiefs, the Americans had declared that they were not prepared to accept full representation in regional organisations, but they would 'participate actively in defence planning as appropriate'.

The British chiefs remained unsure that the Americans would eventually come on board and actively take part in the regional organisations, certainly as far as the two European and Mediterranean ones were concerned. Yet they did believe that the standing groups should press on and be governed by three principles:

a. All detailed planning should be done at the regional level.
b. The authority of the National Chiefs of Staff should be preserved.
c. The views of the British, American and French Chiefs of Staff should be adequately and equally represented.

Their functions were to be:

a. To prepare the overall strategic concepts for approval by the Defence Committee, on which regional plans should then be based.
b. To co-ordinate Regional Plans where necessary.
c. To determine priorities between regions.
d. To advise the Military Supply Board on strategic problems.

The standing group's members would be provided by the national chiefs of staff committees of the USA, UK, and France, so each country's defence chiefs would have a representative. This would be an officer of an appropriate rank to whom they would delegate day-to-day business and its direction. The representative would be of the same rank as the British representative to the joint chiefs of staff in Washington, DC. The other military contributing nations could appoint a representative officer to liaise routinely.

The British chiefs, in line with their desire to see a small military staff and a secretariat, were opposed to the idea of a large combined and integrated military staff. They disliked the latter idea because it would have the potential to develop into something similar to the OKW (*Oberkommando der Wehrmacht*, the High Command of the German Armed Forces of the Nazi era) and in so doing would usurp the functions of the regional organisations. It would also make it harder to set up a combined chiefs of staff function in the event of the outbreak of war.

The representatives of the standing group would also need to be able to convey the views of their respective national chiefs of staff. The British chiefs' conclusions were as follows:

  a. Representation on the Standing Group should be by a member of the Chiefs of Staff Committee of each member nation.
  b. Responsibility for day-to-day business should be delegated to the Head of a Joint Staff mission, served by a small national staff.
  c. These staffs should be composed of representatives of the appropriate staff directorates in Washington, London and Paris, in the form of National Joint Staff Missions in Washington.
  d. A Chief Staff Officer would be required to co-ordinate the work of combined committees formed from the National Joint Staff Missions. He should be subordinate in rank to the representatives of the National Chiefs of Staff on the Standing Group and would need only a very small combined staff.
  e. It would be appropriate for the Chief Staff Officer to be an American.
  f. A Secretariat in addition to the military staff will be required. It would serve the Defence Committee and Military Advisory Council in addition to the Standing Group.

Thus, NATO had arrived, almost—the title of the group was still variously WDU, North Atlantic Ocean group, and Atlantic Pact. A drafting committee met in the morning of 12 September 1949; they sent an immediate top-secret telegram to Sir Oliver Franks, British ambassador in Washington, DC, revealing the outcome of the meeting.

Various representatives of the member states were present. The Canadian representative brought up the matter of 'economic and financial aspects of defence'. He essentially wanted the new organisation to cover financial and economic matters of a more general nature, rather than just those that fell within the sphere of North Atlantic defence. The authors of the telegram to Sir Oliver stated that they had taken the opportunity to say that they had been instructed 'by you' to press for the immediate establishment of a committee of finance ministers.

To this, however, the Americans intervened to either mediate the constitution of such a committee or the establishment of any economic machinery to cover matters going beyond the defence field. They explained that during the passage of the treaty through Congress, they had given congressional leaders an undertaking. This was that no additional machinery would be set up under Article 2 for economic cooperation between the parties in general matters.

The question was not further pursued and was left over until 'tomorrow's Working Party meeting'. Sir Oliver was told by the British side that the way the American representative spoke, it seemed very unlikely that they would be prepared to modify their attitude. There was more—the Belgian and French representatives each brought up new points. The Belgian stated that his government attached 'the greatest importance' to being a member of the North Atlantic Ocean group. A comment from the British followed this note, 'Presumably in view of the large number of countries which have now been allowed to come in as full members we can agree to Belgium coming in as well.'

The French representative requested that the name of the Western Mediterranean Group should be changed to Southern European and Western Mediterranean Regional Planning Group. The Americans and the Italians both said they would support this proposal. The British, on instruction from Sir Oliver, later asked the French representative what the object of his request for the alteration was. He said that the original title of the group suggested that it would only be concerned with planning for the sea and air defence of the western Mediterranean.

The French were also concerned with the land defence of Southern France and Italy. Still the suggestion that Italy should become a full member of the group was something the British wanted to resist. The French reassured that their request for the title change did not in any way represent an attempt to alter the existing planning operations performed by the Brussels powers. The Italians like the Belgians attached the greatest importance to their participation in the standing group. Iceland was given permission to be represented by a civilian member as they had no standing armed forces.

The Belgian, Dutch, and Italian representatives all wanted representation in the standing group while the Portuguese representative stated that his government view was that in addition to the United States, United Kingdom, and France, two other countries should be represented in the standing group, on a rotational annual basis in alphabetical order. The British representative reserved his majesty's government's position on the role to be played by the United States in the European regions. His statement read:

> That the United Kingdom attaches the greatest importance to the exact role that the United States will play in the Northern European, Western European and Western Mediterranean Groups. The United Kingdom representative therefore reserves his government's position on this point.

The Belgian, French, Danish, and Portuguese representatives all joined in and allied themselves with the UK; they likewise reserved the positions of their respective governments on the same point while the Italian representative claimed his government held the view that the United States should be a full member of both the Western European and Western Mediterranean region planning groups. The Dutch and Norwegians stated that by the meeting of the next working party; they would have received instructions from their respective governments to ally themselves with the UK position as well. Finally, the Italian representative stated that his government believed they should receive full membership of the standing group.

The following month, the title of the new defence pact was changed to North Atlantic Treaty Organisation (NATO), and interim measures had now been accepted by the United States for use within NATO in order that information furnished to or originated by NATO committees or groups may be protected according to the degree of security required. Security classifications for information originating from any committee or group provided to or originating within NATO would be subject to the appropriate security grading from restricted, confidential, secret, and top secret. Dissemination of such information would be limited to those countries and within those countries to those individuals whose official duties require access so they could take action as required. Dissemination of classified information was still in an interim phase; an official process was yet to be introduced.

Personnel allowed access to classified information would need to be screened for vetting purposes, by their respective governments to ensure integrity, discretion and judgement. The Standing Group first convened on 10 October 1949, in Washington, DC, to facilitate the swift and efficient work of the military committee. The regional planning groups were composed quite logically as follows:

Northern European Regional Planning Group: Denmark, Norway and United Kingdom (the United States had been requested and agreed to take part actively in the defence planning as appropriate)

Western European Regional Planning Group: Belgium, France, Luxembourg, Netherlands and the United Kingdom (Canada and the United States had been requested and agreed to take part actively in the defence planning as appropriate)

Southern European-Western Mediterranean Regional Planning Group: France, Italy and the United Kingdom (The United States had been requested and agreed to take part actively in the defence planning as appropriate)

Canadian-United States Regional Planning Group: Canada and the United States (Other parties may take part under the same provisions as those for the other groups listed above)

North Atlantic Ocean Regional Planning Group: Belgium, Canada, Denmark, France, Iceland, the Netherlands, Norway, Portugal, the United Kingdom and the United States.

The North Atlantic Ocean Regional Planning Group while made up of all member states except, Luxembourg and Italy, did not mean an equal share of defence planning responsibility for each member. Instead, responsibility was divided along functional lines allocated to the member best positioned to perform the respective defence functions.

The Headquarter for the Northern and Western regions was to be based in London, the Southern European-Western Mediterranean in Paris while the Canadian-US Group's HQ would be in Washington DC.

By December 1949, the navy had completed their review of how to approach the matter of the defence of the Kiel Canal. They concluded that the only 'safe' preparation for a surprise attack would be to have depth charges, a demolition party and about two companies (marines/infantry) *in situ* beforehand. The infantry provided immediate cover while the charges were set to ensure a safe (as far as could be managed) withdrawal thereafter.

A fresh dispute had arisen between the navy and the army over who should provide the two companies to cover the operation and subsequent withdrawal. Neither wanted to do it, and each had the same good reason—they were short of men. At this stage, the junior service was getting involved; the RAF position was that it was important that one or the other of the other two services take up the cudgels and resolve the matter, otherwise the pressing nature of the situation meant that the RAF would have to assign aircraft to deny enemy access to the canal.

Not surprisingly, the RAF fought shy of having to do this because all their assets would, in such an event, be required elsewhere. Therefore, they were anxious not to sell the idea of the canal being attacked from the air. It was also not lost on the chief of naval intelligence Germany that the canal could be seized by an 'inner nucleus' of communist sympathisers, working at either end (lock gates). This in itself would require a sizeable force to deny either end to fifth columnists, even before far more substantial assistance from the Red Army arrived. The British Army commander of the Hamburg district, having claimed all his forces, were already assigned under Operation Congreve, explained that the only alternative he could suggest was to task a Norwegian battalion stationed at Itzehoe. This unit was due to be relieved by a Danish one at the end of the year.

The Hamburg district commander believed that the Danes and Norwegians might provide reliable close protection if 'in the know' and had carried out a peacetime reconnaissance of the area. However, neither could be relied upon for this purpose even under these conditions. The flag officer recommended in view of the strategic importance of the demolition task that a request be considered for a British close protection force. Furthermore, it should be noted that the demolitions could not be started until the force was at the locks and that therefore, the force must be based at or very nearby Brunsbüttelkoog.

As for the ports, they had to be able to take ocean-going shipping, sufficient civilian labour, storage capacity, adequate communications and be able to provide a measure of dispersion against air attack. Relating to this point, the RAF in Germany, keen to modernise, sought a policy change regarding aircraft used to reinforce BAFO, specifically requesting that Tempest and Spitfire aircraft should not be included and that spares for such already held in Germany could be withdrawn and issued to those squadrons still flying these types in the FEAF.

Air staff approval was needed for this, but BAFO were also made aware that should it come to it, Tempest and Spitfire aircraft would not be available if the command's Vampire squadrons, for example, were to become exhausted. There would be no re-supply of any aircraft and the squadrons in question, if wastage exceeded reserves, would have to fold. In the light of the most recent events concerning the USSR, 1949 was a year of constant rounds of meetings largely regarding Operation Congreve—the comprehensive plan to prepare for a Soviet attempt to use military force to extend the communist umbrella as far and wide as possible. The now recognised state of the Federal Republic of Germany would be the principal aim of any such attack, should it come. One such meeting was convened on 10 August 1949, aimed to determine the short term, or indeed, interim plan for Operation Congreve and Air Forces Western Europe (AFWE).

Those attending were relatively junior in rank for such a strategic assessment, the most senior rank present, and the appointed chairman being a group captain. The rest were one more group captain with a mix of wing commanders and squadron leaders. The chairman, Gp Cpt G. G. Barrett, opened by explaining that the purpose of the meeting was to examine the implications of the AFWE's short-term plan, to find out whether the preparations already made for Congreve could fit into it, and to determine what changes and additional preparations will be necessary. Of primary concern was which squadrons were going to reinforce BAFO in an emergency. There was mention of either 33 or 80 Squadron returning from the FEAF or the Odiham Wing deploying to Germany. Nos 33 and 80 Squadrons were equipped with Spitfires and Tempests but if recalled from the Far East would re-equip with Vampire FB5. Yet the re-equipment would only happen if there was time to do this. What this meant was, if there was, ultimately no emergency, they would still have to make do with their Spitfires and Tempests until such time as the Vampires became available.

That being the case, these squadrons were deemed operationally useless. On the other hand, there were revised plans for increased reserve stocks from thirty days of supply to forty-five days. Also, a defensive rather than an offensive role would take priority in the event of hostilities, as such, 75 per cent of bombs and other ground-attack ordnance would be removed.

It was feared that the Russians could mount a surprise attack, under the guise of manoeuvres, in which case they could launch an attack on the Western zones with no warning at all. They could move their mechanised units directly from their areas of occupation in East Germany without moving on the western sectors of Berlin prior to advancing into the zone. The zone referred to the Federal Republic of Germany as distinct from forces based in West Berlin.

There was, despite all, the belief that the Russians accepted that any incursion into the West would inevitably start a third world war. The joint intelligence committee Germany listed a series of likely Russian preparations that if commenced would indicate 'the clear possibility' of a Soviet offensive against the Western sectors. These would include either the extension of standard rail track gauges (as used in the western sector) eastwards or the construction of eastern track gauges westwards. Further clear indications would be a concentration of rolling stock in Poland and Soviet-occupied Germany as well as the assumption of Soviet military control of all railway operations. Ultimately, a clear indication would be the sudden appearance of tank transporters, an increase in personnel levels, and a large build-up of fuel and ammunition on lines of communications, especially west of Berlin.

In terms of air power, the build-up of fuel and ammunition dumps adjacent to airfields were not at all surprising. Interestingly, because of the Soviet mistrust of the Polish Air Force, an indication of preparation for an attack west would curiously be preceded by either the disbandment or transfer east of the Polish Air Force, or a purge of the remaining non-communist elements. There was a particularly high build-up of Soviet air units in Soviet-occupied countries (including East Germany), increased Russian R/T traffic, and all manner of other indicators.

In the event of a Soviet surprise attack, it was expected they could reach the river Wester in seven hours, leaving the British forces little time to affect any kind of worthwhile resistance. This would place Russian forces several miles west of Hanover and several BAOR garrisons (including Paderborn, Lippstadt, and Bielefeld) and very close to the garrisons at Münster and Osnabruck. Units that remained or managed to redeploy east of this line would soon be reduced through weight of numbers and simple lack of preparedness. All ground forces in the Hamburg and Bremen districts and air forces in the Schleswig and eastern Hanover districts would also be overrun.

This amounted to about 35 per cent of the total of British forces available. The 1st Belgian Corps and 2nd British Infantry Division would receive early warning of an attack and could commence a withdrawal across the Rhine before being engaged. The success of the withdrawal would very much depend upon the ability of the Soviet forces to deploy airborne units early enough as well as the effect of Soviet air attacks on bridges and routes to and across the Rhine.

As for BAFO assets, if, as anticipated, the crossing of the internal-zonal boundary (the inner German border) by Soviet ground forces coincided with Soviet air attacks on airfields, few, if any, of the British air forces of occupation's operational aircraft could be flown out of the zone. It was not the advantage of a surprise attack in any case that would aid Soviet forces to prevail, but the significant numerical superiority in numbers particularly in terms of armour and aircraft.

The only course to be considered was to plan for a rapid withdrawal to the Rhine/Ijssel line (where the River Ijssel flows north through Holland from the Rhine to the North Sea), where a defensive line would be established. This meant the implementation of a definitive and well-understood plan and the evacuation at the earliest opportunity of all dependents, families, and civilians.

To effect full mobilisation to a war footing, all BAFO squadrons from airfields in Germany were to re-deploy to airfields in the Low Countries, Belgium, and Holland. Other than the numerical superiority of the Soviet forces, the British weaknesses were, perhaps surprising given the British armed forces standing reputation, a low standard of training due to a high percentage of national service soldiers and airmen at various stages of training; a lack of anti-tank and anti-aircraft weapons; and a lack of operational mobility due to a static administration and shortage of reliable British-driven transport.

Despite the British concerns, the more concerted enemy thrust was expected to be in the American zone through the Eisenach–Frankfurt–Maine belt, combined with air operations to seize the crossings over the Rhine in this area. This was the shortcut route to the Rhine and was not covered by any major obstacles, although a more difficult route. However, it allowed the Russians to outflank a major portion of the British forces and expose their southern flank. The Russians had adequate strength to also conduct powerful thrusts via Helmstedt, Hanover, Ruhr, Hamburg, and Bremen, with subsidiary thrusts against pockets of British/American and other allied forces left behind by the main attack.

At a strength approximate to four divisions and lacking adequate administration, the BAOR had a line of 180 miles to defend, hence the imperative to withdraw all west of the Rhine to take part in establishing a more realistic line of defence. Estimations were that four days was the least amount of notice required to evacuate all dependents; anything less and it was doubtful they could be moved west of the Rhine before Soviet troops arrived.

During this time, the army would re-group and the RAF would also move to bases west. The army's new defensive line would run from Konigswinter to Kampen. A covering force would be deployed and at the time was to consist of the following: Royal Horse Guards; 1st Royal Dragoons; 11th Hussars; 1st Royal Tank Regiment; 1st Battalion, the Rifles Brigade; one battery, 3rd Regiment Royal Horse Artillery (self-propelled); one battery, 10th Anti-Tank Regiment (self-propelled); and a detachment from the air support signals unit.

Their task was to delay the Soviet advance between the Weser and the Elbe; Hamburg district would provide their own covering force for withdrawal west of the river Weser. The 1st Belgian Corps and the British 2nd Infantry Division would each provide their own covering force.

The BAFO would be tasked with providing fighter defence of the Rhine bridges and their approaches, day reconnaissance, night armed reconnaissance, and offensive support to slow up or indeed halt the enemy's advance, provided this did not prejudice the other roles.

Prior to this would be the move to the predetermined bases west of the Rhine while as many facilities as possible at the present bases would be destroyed. The ratification of NATO drew the line in the sand beyond which it was abundantly clear to all that any attack on any member state would be regarded as an attack on all.

Just how comprehensively this would have been honoured is something no one—not even the organisation's strongest proponents—would cheerfully bet a handsome amount of money on. There would be numerous occasions along the road where Soviet military muscle would be used to impose the Kremlin's wishes on the 'near abroad'. NATO could breathe a sigh of relief that none of these poor wretches happened to be legitimate members at the time. Did Western inaction, whenever challenged, embolden the Kremlin each time? Hungary and Czechoslovakia were both subject to a Soviet incursion to quell uprisings against the communist rulers, in 1956 and 1968 respectively.

Shortly after the ink on the parchment was dry, work started on deciding who from which service and which nation was going to head up each of the different posts in the command structure. Each member addressed the state of their own defence arrangements, set about getting their respective assets into a more practical posture, and joined up so that some preliminary form of cohesion was in place.

The BAOR were right on the centre line. Still using the reference 'Western Defence Union', a meeting of minds was held at Fontainebleau on 12 July 1950. The force requirements recommended to meet a Soviet-led intervention west of the inner German border were not light. Field Marshal Montgomery's report noted that sixteen divisions would be needed to meet the initial attack. This seems outrageous, but spread across the board, it is not quite so. Furthermore, *in situ* at the time, no fewer than seventeen divisions plus an additional two from the USA were already available.

The breakdown was an eye-opener. The bulk of the land force would come from France, who supplied thirteen divisions; the UK, two and one-third divisions; Belgium, one and two-thirds divisions; and the Netherlands, one-third of a division. This made 17.3 divisions, along with the two from the States. The UK promised an additional two divisions in reserve.

Altogether the wartime establishment of British land forces in Germany would need to reach 40,000 personnel. On mobilisation, France had a sizeable establishment of twenty divisions, of which eleven were poorly equipped, five were reasonably well-equipped, and four had between 25 and 35 per cent of the equipment they required. The Belgians' total force came to five divisions— one had 25 to 40 per cent equipment, three had little equipment, and one described as reasonably well-equipped, was based in Germany. As for the Netherlands, they had an army of 13,000 personnel making up nine infantry battalions.

They could, if called upon, raise a further twenty-three infantry companies. The Dutch Army had no heavy equipment. All contributing nations, save for Luxembourg, were relying on national service; all had a minimum service length of 12 months. The UK had a set minimum requirement for eighteen months. Training to meet this brief amount of military service had to fit within the overall period of service and therefore was deemed too short to be effective.

The French and Dutch headquarters could only function when reservists were called up. The British noted a 'lack of realism' and an unwillingness to learn from those with experience and an outmoded attitude toward combined operations, or rather cooperation between land and air forces. France also lacked experienced NCOs in their army as at the time, they were deployed in Vietnam in the Indochina War against the Viet Minh. Indeed, the charges of criticism by the British military chiefs against the French armed forces in particular were positively undiplomatic. The report went on to cite a lack of higher direction, no director of training, and no manuals in proper doctrine; it almost patronisingly pointed out that this was being rectified with 'our help' and the arrival of US equipment via aid 'to get matters right'. It was also noted, in contrast:

> Junior ranks are enthusiastic and individual and unit training is on the right lines. As far as Belgium was concerned there was a lack of any kind of length of service in the rank and file and a lack of continuation training for conscripts. Training areas in Belgium were also not surprisingly restricted in size due to the density of the population and level of industrial infrastructure. The Belgian army was said to be benefiting from its association with the BAOR but that there was a bad spirit within the country toward military service. As for the Netherlands, the main weaknesses observed were a lack of officer training instructors and an army which was far too dispersed to support any kind of cohesion in training.

The air forces' position, according to Field Marshal Montgomery, was broadly described as follows:

Until this year the main effort has been devoted to the build-up of Fighter Defence Forces, the functions of which are closely complimentary with those of TAF this is especially true on the Continent where the air defence areas either adjoin or nearly correspond to the combat zones. Some progress has been made towards the requirements of the Air Defence plan, but the position is far from satisfactory. The more important aspects in which progress is not satisfactory include the lack of Night Fighter aircraft and the inadequacy of reserves either for peace or war. Applications for tactical aircraft have been made to the United States under this year's MAP (Military Assistance Programme) but no rapid build-up can be achieved without a big increase in the number of trained technicians and the size of the air force credits.

A copy of a French five-year plan had been given, privately, to the CAS, Sir John Slessor, by General Lecheres. It provided for a frontline figure of 2,189 aircraft plus 756 non-operational aircraft. This proportion of non-operational aircraft was high compared to the UK standard. The plan did not relate to the Western Defence Union but to the perceived productivity output of the French aircraft industry. The figures looked very impressive but were perhaps too ambitious and appeared not to account for the difficulties of manning such a large force.

The new defence force needed to establish its own infrastructure. They needed a new headquarters, communications established, an airfield programme, provision of navigation aids, and an administration process. The financial responsibilities of each of the four main powers was France: £15 million; UK: £9 million; Belgium: £4.5 million; and Netherlands: £4.5 million. The only work started so far was on the new headquarters.

Return of 2nd Tactical Air Force, 1951–52

Owing to the relocation of the BAOR operations room, all WRAF personnel had to be posted away, at least for the short term. The year 1951 brought a revised emergency plan for Germany, which centred around a radical new approach to assets, facilities, and infrastructure, affecting all the main zones of occupation in the West.

First and foremost, BAFO was (as of April) placed under the direct control of SACEUR and therefore became a component part of AAFCE. Then came the next step—the jewel in the crown of the infrastructure plans: a proposal from SHAPE to produce sixteen new airfields and upgrade ten existing ones essentially runway extensions. The original airfield specifications under the Western Union airfield requirements sub-committee allowed for runways of 5,400 feet in length but no communications, no permanent stores other than bomb stores, and a minimum of airfield lighting.

The increases were to include runway extensions to 8,000 feet and increased taxi tracks for which concrete was now specified for the operation of jet aircraft. A small quota of technical buildings—wing and squadron operations rooms and fuel storage—doubled in size to equal seven days of supplies, at the time approximately 500,000 gallons. These measures were being pursued by SHAPE as they now appreciated the very great numerical superiority of the Soviet Russian Air Force. SHAPE's planners took the view that every possible opportunity was to be taken to exploit what technological advantage the 'Atlantic Powers' had.

Efficiency was now needed to equip the airfields with sufficient lighting for day fighters to afford a position to attack Soviet aircraft on the ground at dusk and still be able to return to their own airfields after dark. Permanent new accommodation was to be built naturally, but SHAPE hoped the cost of this would be met separately. There was a reason why billeting was expected to be borne by national funding rather than via SHAPE; it was so each national force could construct accommodation according to their own specific standard. There was a stark difference in the forecast cost of accommodation to be built at US and British airfields.

This was due not to a difference in the scale of accommodation, but due to the fact that the US base/wing strength type had a typical head count of 3,000 personnel while for the RAF the figure was down to 1,300, approximately. A briefing was to be placed before the British representative on the standing group on 20 July 1951.

Here, a bombshell of sorts was dropped: SHAPE reported to the working parties examining this problem that an original estimated cost of £18.7 million would now be increased to £41 million. This was attributed partly to the rise in prices since the original estimates only eight months earlier. Further, an additional £18 million was to be found for accommodation at some airfields. As BAFO was now under SACEUR and given the changing political climate or rather developing political climate, brought about by the new German state, the military posture was to change. Allied forces in West Germany were no longer forces of occupation but contributory forces for the defence of West Germany—such was the now long forecast fear of intervention by Soviet troops or, put bluntly, invasion.

To this end, BAFO had its title changed, as of 1 September 1951, officially to 2nd Tactical Air Force. This was their previous wartime identity, but this time with the remit of the defence of (the British sector of) Germany. The British, Americans, French, and Canadians were wholly responsible for the Federal Republic's defence and security arrangements; the resumption or reformation of a Federal German military force was still to be properly considered. Furthermore, the new 2 TAF was also to take assigned Belgian and Dutch Air Force units into its ORBAT.

This change in structures and titles also presaged a change to the title of the commander in chief BAFO, the chief of the air staff, MRAF Sir John Slessor, favoured a change from C-in-C to air marshal commanding. This was agreed via an interim title: commander in chief 2 TAF was changed to air marshal commanding 2 TAF.

Trivial sounding as it may come across, such matters have to be taken seriously and recognised. For example, court martial warrants would need to be amended or re-issued. Some minor amendments to administrative instructions would be required, this largely amounted to confirming, among the proper quarters, that the financial powers and entitlements of the current commander in chief remained unchanged even if the title had. Yet one key point driving such decisions was that as 2 TAF now formed part of AAFCE, it could not have a commander in chief, as this title belonged to the USAF general appointed to this wider command.

The new TAF naturally married up to the corresponding land forces in the British sector (the northern sector of the Central European region). The army element now became Northern Army Group (NORTHAG) consisting of the British Army of the Rhine together with Belgian and Dutch Army contingents. The Belgian and Dutch Air Force elements were to fall under the Benelux base defence group in the first instance with each respective national force responsible for its own national sector, remembering that the Belgian and Dutch commanders had such specific considerations to address over and above NATO.

The move toward a force of defence rather than occupation as far as the continental forces were concerned was described as likely to be heavily circumscribed. Two of NATO's foremost generals—France's Alphonse Luin (commander in chief allied forces Central Europe), a venerable general with service in both world wars, and the relatively young Lauris Nordstad (commander in chief allied air forces Central Europe) from the US Air Force— wanted to forge ahead with the nucleus of an army group/tactical air force. They also had trouble trying to reconcile the differing views of nation and service, to the idea that their armed forces were to be trained for a possible specific wartime role.

Rather than continuing to oversee the policing of the Federal Republic of Germany, both also noted that the early semblance of NATO, which had the former BAFO at its heart, consisted of just the 2nd Tactical Air Force, which was not fully an 'air force'. It was a tactical air group and it was attached to an army headquarters that had control of what was just a corps. For this reason, the proposal was that the continental forces of Belgium and Holland should now be integrated into the resumed 2 TAF, although this was not expected to be fully formed until 1952. Nothing was clear as to just how far the Belgian and Dutch air forces would fit in.

With the multi-national makeup of the new force, consideration was given to changing the title to 'Allied Tactical Air Force'; the result of this was to have both a 2 ATAF and the RAF element within, still referred to as 2 TAF, which caused some confusion and would be met with a further change in due course. Meanwhile, the Northern Army Group was happy to look ahead to how the land element would look and projected that by 1954, it would consist of two British corps of four divisions each, two Belgian corps totalling five divisions, and a single Dutch corps, assigned to the British element, consisting of four divisions. This was the intended level of deployment, if placed on a war footing, by 1954.

The actual peacetime size of the Northern Army Group would be a single British corps of four divisions, a Belgian corps of two divisions, and either a Dutch division or a brigade. There was also a Jutland land-covering force, consisting of a single brigade each from Denmark and Norway. A further brigade was made available from the Canadian Army, which was embedded with the British corps. This was the established peacetime land defence posture of NATO forces assigned to the northern FRG.

The integration and build-up of the new TAF was very much a work in progress. Roles for the RAF's assigned units were subject to a build up from December 1952 to December 1954. This was part of a wider programme of development for all Allied Air Forces in Central Europe under SACEUR's 'Plan K'. Over this period, 2 TAF was to expect five squadrons to be deployed in the photo reconnaissance role. These units were to be issued with the English Electric Canberra but with an establishment of no more than eight aircraft each. However, the undersecretary of state air, George Ward, wanted just four squadrons assigned one to each group and two to the control of HQ Allied Tactical Air Force. This was to try and find some balance against a proposed additional seven day fighter squadrons. Mr Ward also proposed organising the PR Canberra squadrons into a UE of ten aircraft each. Plan 'K' sought to establish an RAF Germany total figure of 266 aircraft divided into nineteen squadrons.

Four new airfields were to be built for the RAF. These would be the last operational RAF stations to be built from the stage of being nothing more than woods and rural farmland inside Europe. All four were to be sited as far west as possible and would therefore sit along the German–Dutch border. In time, these air bases, sitting in a grouping near to one another, would become known as 'clutch bases'.

First to be flattened in readiness was Wildenrath—in fact, a second choice. The first location chosen was Freialdenhoven. One might imagine, on a jocular level, that the choice was changed to a place name that Brits could get their tongues around more easily. The real reason was because this was valuable beet land, and as of February 1951, the German land government was appealing against the RAF's decision to build the first of their new airfields here. It was, according to the British authorities, the GLG who suggested Wildenrath as an alternative.

When the Germans were first consulted about the project, they had no idea that extensive tracts of valuable farmland would be requisitioned. They were thinking, perhaps more logically, of non-arable land. The RAF accepted the Wildenrath alternative and the AOC BAFO's staff marked out the perimeter, to suit their needs. This perimeter went far beyond the low-value land that the newly elected government intended to offer.

However, the North Rhine-Westphalia minister for food, agriculture, and forestry, Heinrich Lubke, was publicly seen as the official who gave the British the Bonn government's blessing and supposedly wrote a letter officially thanking the RAF for choosing Wildenrath. This was expected to help the situation, so that when the first wave of protests appeared they could say: 'it is the choice of the German authorities'. The RAF also agreed to give up some of the land that the perimeter originally was to go round but with the understanding that it may be required later; the RAF thought that this would be most unlikely. It transpired that Heinrich Lubke's seemingly ready acceptance and cooperation with the British over the selection of Wildenrath was the cause of a great deal of political criticism of Lubke.

A not unexpectedly sensitive issue, there was the equally predictable negative press speculation especially as the new airfield, even with some land given up, would mean the requisitioning of about twenty-five houses affecting thirty-six families. This was a considerable number but with some land no longer required; only four houses and twenty-three occupants in all would need to be evacuated.

Herr Lubke had nevertheless been put on the spot by the British who had made a letter public. This letter, picked up by the German press, indicated Herr Lubke expressed his gratitude to Major General Bishop for intervening on his behalf. This was to urge the senior BAFO officer to settle for Wildenrath as the site for construction, in place of Freialdenhoven. This led to a series of misunderstandings about his actual position, which had led to the vehement political controversy, Herr Lubke wanted to set the record straight. In a letter to the North Rhine/Westphalia commissioner, Major General Alexander Bishop, he stated:

> You will realize that I must lay stress on the real facts of this case being established'. The real facts being that; 'On 16 October 1950, Major General Bishop announced in a press release that an airfield for the training of Allied armed forces was going to be built at Wildenrath in Erkelenz Kreis and that the site had been selected at the request of the German authorities.

On 24 October 1950, the minister president of land North Rhine-Westphalia wrote to General Bishop, stating that Lubke's suggestion that a site at Wildenrath should be substituted for the valuable sugar beet soil at Julich was in respect of woodland of about 500 hectares:

> This was exactly the same size as the site selected by the RAF at Freialdenhoven. The selection of this area would mean that, except for two to three Farmsteads and some few plots of land, damage to agricultural interests could be avoided, as also the vacation of dwellings or localities. Now, however, an area of 800 to 1,000 hectares had been earmarked for requisitioning, and under this scheme a number of at least 12 farmsteads, would be wiped out completely. A substantial number of agricultural undertakings would be greatly hampered regarding their economic management. In addition to this, 42 houses with more than 200 inhabitants would have to be evacuated and their occupants would have to be resettled.

The minister president went on to say:

> I am sure you will readily understand, dear General, that the Land Government is very perturbed at this turn of the matter all the more so because the Press has published your statement that the area had been selected on suggestions of the German authorities.

The minister president then asked the general to take steps to request the size of the airfield be confined to 400 to 500 hectares as originally intended or that the land government be afforded an opportunity of suggesting an alternative site of the same size where the damages would be lesser than with the Wildenrath site under construction.

The German authorities had made other proposals for the siting of the first airfield, all of which had been dismissed each in turn as being unsuitable. The time factor alone was said to have precluded consideration of any alternatives.

A second airfield to be used as a reserve was also planned for Gillrath; this was a NATO requirement. The limitations on Gillrath were objected to by the Belgians due to their own air force's expansion. If the construction of Gillrath was limited to a 'reserve' construction, then infrastructure would be less substantial than if it were built to peacetime scale. The Belgians wanted the latter to alleviate a problem they had with accommodation. The RAF only budgeted for a reserve airfield and proposed to limit their requisition to this requirement, and if the Belgians required more room for accommodation, they should make their own arrangements. Between 1952 and 1954, the four airfields were built and occupied by operational units. During this period, the

RAF was at its most post-war expansive in Germany with all the airfields held as of 1950 still active and the four new bases.

The first two squadrons took up residence at the brand-new RAF Wildenrath, 71 Sqn in April and 67 Sqn in May, both equipped with DH Vampire FB5s. A year later, the second clutch base, Geilenkirchen, opened for business. The first units arriving here in 1953 were ground based—HQ 138 Wing and 25 Wing RAF Regiment. No. 3 Squadron arrived in July that year with F-86 Sabres.

In 1952, there was concern of another attempted blockade. This time, the weight of commitment made by the Americans to the Korean War might mean they would not be able to match the tonnage of supplies flown in during the previous crisis. The idea of the Russians attacking anything in the corridor was dismissed as an act of war and something the Russians genuinely wished to avoid. Attempting to force convoys through on land would be different; the chiefs of staff examined this proposition in 1948 and decided that it was not practical.

The ability of NATO forces in Germany in 1952, to force through convoys by land action, was no different to where they were in 1948. The Russians could halt such action through force of arms and by blowing bridges. It would be impossible for NATO to guard all routes and in any case, they had no treaty rights to do so, meaning any attempt at running the gauntlet as it were could only be embarked upon if there was every reason to believe the Russians would back down, otherwise the likelihood of failure or worse may mean war would follow. With regards to another airlift, it was expected that the Russians would be well aware of the weaknesses of the previous one and its methods, in so far as the centre route was used to maximum capacity and doubtless would be again. This would be dependent on there being no interference over control of the exercise.

Whatever the concerns, the Russians were not expected to use fighters to attack allied transport aircraft simply because this would also constitute an act of war. This point was made with the knowledge that the RAF could not provide adequate fighter escort cover anyway. If the Russians did attempt to do anything to thwart another airlift, it would be by jamming communications. There was no evidence at this stage that the Russians operated on UHF. Still, any radio interference would force the airlift to operate in daylight; even in the best possible weather conditions, this would reduce the capacity to a mere trickle of what it was in 1948–49.

The resolve was that should the Russians attempt another blockade, they would not jam communications. If they did, an attempt to orchestrate an airlift on the largest possible scale would stand the best chance of getting something through and prolong the West Berliners while giving heart during a difficult period. This would also, hopefully, help them to hold out longer even if the supplies were paltry compared with before, and allow negotiations more time to succeed. The single greatest concern was that the effort would have to be maintained, to the point where negotiations either succeeded of failed. In the case of the latter, NATO would have to admit defeat or face war. To avoid either of these awful conclusions, negotiations would have to reach a successful outcome 'fairly quickly'. One option reviewed and dismissed in 1948 was the idea of sending foreign convoys through on land.

This was expected to yield no advantage; the Russians could still block convoys and even blow bridges if necessary. What was considered a net advantage was superiority in nuclear weapons as a likely sanction. The concern of a further Soviet attempt to seal off Berlin resulted in the Bonn Convention on 26 May 1952. This sought to clarify the responsibilities of the three occupying powers and the Federal Republic of Germany, now a democratically governed nation again. The convention agreed the rights of the three powers to station armed forces in the FRG. They also retained the responsibilities, previously held by them, in respect of Berlin and Germany as a whole, including the aim of German reunification and a peace settlement.

The British ambassador to the Federal Republic was appointed to exercise their reserved rights on their behalf. This meant that the British government were responsible for the Western side of the border with the East German state. When it was the British zone of occupation, the BAFO dealt with the Soviet authorities on matters of an international nature that may arise, such as border crossings and violations. The new appointment for the commander of the RAF in Germany—commander in chief 2 TAF—was therefore responsible for all air matters relating to the border, including taking such actions as may be necessary to preserve its integrity.

As the senior RAF officer on the continent, he was responsible for the following:

> Empowered to take precautions for the military security of your forces and installations in the event of civil disturbances which may jeopardise the safety or operational readiness of your forces or endanger their property.

He was also empowered, by a letter from the West German chancellor to the British foreign secretary dated 23 October 1954, under the Paris Agreements, to take appropriate action, including the use of armed force, to protect such forces in the face of imminent menace. Further, with the exception of the protection of her majesty's forces in imminent danger, C-in-C 2 TAF was not authorised to make forces available for the assistance of the German civil authorities without prior consultation with the British ambassador. British rights in Berlin continued to be the responsibility of the British commandant Berlin, who was responsible to the ambassador.

1953

The surge in UK military expenditure in the early 1950s as a result of the Korean conflict had been taken advantage of more generally. The threat from the Warsaw Pact was as clearly defined as it ever would be. The remaining two new airbases under construction were nearing completion and would shortly be ready for operational units to occupy them. It might have been seen in some quarters as an expensive form of aggravating the international climate, but they were deemed to be needed.

The day was coming when the FRG's own military force would be established; they would need their own airfields that would need to be available at short notice. The new RAF base at Brüggen was ready for occupancy by 1 March 1953. An 'opening up party' was formed to prepare the new station for full establishment from 1 May, which became operational just two months later.

There were, not at all surprisingly, outstanding matters to deal with, not least among them an incomplete perimeter fence. Until this was built, the German police and customs officials were given access to the station. On 3 June, a conference was held, attended by Brüggen officers with military, civilian, and customs authorities of both the Netherlands and West Germany. Three days later, the first wholly assigned OC tech wing, Wg Cdr F. C. H. Kirby, arrived on posting from the UK. He took charge of maintenance personnel, hitherto lodged under admin wing, and organised all into the new tech wing ready to fully function by July.

This essentially consisted of unpacking and preparing equipment. Elsewhere, the new field trials were conducted in laying 'Soil stabilised concrete' to the north-west. This involved members of the royal engineers with high-ranking observers from the army. The command fire and rescue officer, Mr S. R. Wood, conducted a check of the station and airfield and found no exceptional risks but did recommend the removal of remaining young trees and undergrowth around the standings in south-east dispersal. This had to be done before jet aircraft could be allowed to operate from there.

Next, an advanced party of personnel of 85 LAA Squadron, RAF Regiment, under the command of Flying Officer B. N. Fowler, arrived. On 15 June, the station received its first SMO (station medical officer), Flt Lt R. W. Ballantyne, on posting from Butzweilerhof. As soon as he arrived, the station's sick quarters were fully opened for business.

All that was needed now was something to enable flying to take place. Wg Cdr G. B. Johns, DSO, DFC, set up his HQ, in the newly completed HQ flying wing building.

The next day, 19 June, a conference was held in the officers' mess, including Sqn Ldr I. D. Bolton DFC, OC 112 Sqn; his attendance presaged the arrival of that unit soon from RAF Jever.

Brüggen's baptism of fire was expected to take place in the forthcoming Exercise Coronet. In preparation for this, various fuels—AVTAG, AVTUR, and AVGAS—needed to be stored and stocks maintained at a minimum or above. Here another teething problem presented itself, the absence of a spur railway. This was included in the station infrastructure but was not yet ready. It was therefore decided to offload the fuel from rail tankers at the Arsbeck Petroleum Depot and convey it to the station 6 miles by road in tankers supplied by the army.

This, alas, proved unworkable as it would further delay the completion of the rail spur by blocking access to it. The solution was to offload from a point on the railway spur at RAF Wildenrath. No. 85 LAA Sqn RAF Regiment began setting up on 20 June and were followed five days later by 89 LAA Sqn, under the command of Flying Officer P. Kemp. This was the process, with sometimes similar obstacles to overcome, at each of the four new stations over the period January 1952 to October 1954.

Another 'clutch base' was already operational—RAF Geilenkirchen had its full establishment and was operating as an element of 83 Group. Ten days later, an operational conversion unit for the new F-86 Sabres opened at Wildenrath to begin local conversion of Meteor and Vampire pilots, prior to re-equipping the squadrons with the American jets.

The 2nd Tactical Air Force adopted a new mission statement in September 1953 to replace the occupation force mindset of the immediate post-war era. The stated role of 2 TAF was, not at all surprisingly, to act in support of the ground forces associated with the British Army of the Rhine. Squadron size was determined as well at sixteen aircraft per squadron and twenty-one pilots with corresponding aircrew (e.g. navigators) as required.

To meet the established level, each squadron was to be supplied with additional pilots over and above the UE. Gradually, they were to be reduced in number until the minimum was reached. However, no further flying hours would be allocated. The annual average for flying hours per aircraft was set at twenty-eight per month, but during the more intense period from April to September, this was increased to thirty-two, while during October to March, twenty-four hours was the set limit. At this rate in a perfect world, each pilot should accrue 254 hours each year.

The nature of the force's overall role of supporting ground forces determined three principal operational role designations with one broken down into two more specific tasks:

> Fighter Bomber
> Tactical Light Bomber
> Tactical Reconnaissance
> Fighter Reconnaissance
> Photographic Reconnaissance

Missing from the list was that of quick response interceptor/tactical air superiority. With the conflict in Korea still in progress, the UK defence budget for 1953 came as a surprise—the increases of the previous three years were going into reverse. On 6 October 1954, the foreign office made a declaration, in light of growing demands, for NATO to maintain a solid defence posture on the continent, Germany being the principal area of concern:

> The United Kingdom will continue to maintain on the mainland of Europe, including Germany, the effective strength of the United Kingdom forces which are now assigned to SACEUR, four Divisions and the Tactical Air Force, or whatever SACEUR regards as equivalent fighting capacity.

What concerned the air staff about the foreign secretary's declaration was what effect it would have on the UK military posture elsewhere as not all of UK's forces were immediately committed to NATO. The RAF's chief concern was the effect on the current deployment to full strength of the Canberra force within Bomber Command. At first glance, it appeared to have no effect on either the Bomber Command Canberra build-up nor the current four squadrons in Germany, already equipped with Britain's new jet-powered bomber.

However, they were concerned about how SACEUR's specific approval would affect the RAF's own plans for variations in 2 TAF's current deployment. The RAF's intention was to reduce the current deployment of 494 aircraft to 466. This reduction was caused by the desire to remove the already obsolescent force of 162 de Havilland Venom AD/GA fighters. However, the 466 figure would be arrived at by the offset plan to deploy a further forty-six aircraft in the fighter reconnaissance role along with thirty-two tactical reconnaissance Canberras and a further forty-eight Canberras in the interdictor strike role.

Bearing in mind the foreign secretary's message, this proposal was thought to adequately address the requirement to maintain 'equivalent fighting capacity'. On the other hand, the net force was to be wound down by thirty-six aircraft and the day fighter force by 116. SACEUR had expressed concern at any significant reduction in 2 TAF's fighter force.

Therefore, the air staff expected the NATO council at the next comprehensive review, due in December, to call for a reduction in the reduction. SACEUR had requested the strike force deployment and this was being funded by US aid under 'Plan K' (Chilver Gap). Therefore, the best that SACEUR could reasonably argue for was the retention of some Venoms. The problem for the air staff was that such retained units would, in time, need to be replaced. As of October 1954, the following figures show 2 TAF establishment strength (the nominal strength) on the continent, compared with the actual standing strength:

	Establishment Strength	Standing
AWF (Meteor)	64	60
SRPR (Meteor)	16	17
Fighter Recce (Meteor)	32	31
DF/GA (Venom/Vampire)	162	157
SRDF (Sabre)	220	211
Totals	494	476

The future planning for RAF assets deployed in West Germany over the rest of the decade proposed to SACEUR was as follows:

	Dec. 1954	Dec. 1955	Dec. 1956	Dec. 1957
AWF	64	64	64	64
Reconnaissance (inc. SRPR Fighter Recce & MRPR)	48	88	88	88
IDF (SRDF)	220	220	264	264
FB/GA/DF	162	64	-	-
AW Interdictors	-	32 (48)	48	48
Totals	494 (464)	468	464	464

The figures in brackets were originally placed before SACEUR before being revised.

The figures above do not include four Canberra squadrons in Germany, as while deployed, they were not assigned to SACEUR. These Canberra squadrons described as fulfilling the 'light bomber' role therefore remained in Germany but still part of the AOC-in-C Bomber Command's orbat. The reason these four squadrons were housed in Germany was there simply was not room back home. The UK was not in a strong position financially and the proposed strength of 2 TAF depended on financial aid from the USA. The amount agreed for the period 1956–57 and 1957–58 was £75 million. There were expected objections to the reduction from 494 to 464; the argument from the RAF would be that the numbers of aircraft are not all and that the loss of 110 fighter aircraft from the command was being offset by the assignment of Canberra interdictor and reconnaissance aircraft.

The RAF had, in 1953, proposed a force of about forty of the new Canberra PR7s. This was to address an earlier request by SACEUR for an increase in the photo reconnaissance role.

It was seen as a terrific step forward, even though the jets were not available at the time. On top of this, the RAF were also proposing to deploy the equally new Mk 8 interdictor strike Canberras. The counter to this was the certainty that the RAF simply could not increase the number of aircraft in Germany overall, so something had to be sacrificed, much to SACEUR's chagrin. The sacrifice was to be cuts to the fighter strength, with the British ministry of defence determined to impose limits of expenditure; they were not going to be able to afford interdictor and PR aircraft and the number of fighters that SACEUR wanted.

Not only would there be reductions in the number of IDF/GA aircraft, but there would have to be a reduction overall due to the complex nature, maintenance and operating costs of the Canberras. The British reduction proposals were made known to SACEUR at a discussion on US aid to the UK. There was no certainty that SACEUR would accept the planned reduction/ restructure of the RAF in Germany.

The end of 1954 brought a review of airfield deployment and consideration over the actual number of airfields required by 2 TAF. At the time, the unit establishment of a fighter squadron in Fighter Command was still sixteen aircraft, as originally determined. In 2 TAF, that number was fourteen, but it was reasoned that this resulted in easier supervision and a lower accident rate—less is indeed more.

The CAS, Sir William Dickson, understood these benefits, but he also made it clear that these altered arrangements did not justify a reduction in the number of aircraft that 2 TAF put into the air. The reduced number of aircraft per squadron did not reduce the need for additional skilled tradesmen and extra squadron equipment such as engine stands and MT equipment. The government raised no objections on financial considerations as far as additional manpower was concerned, as long as the changes could be justified or considered to be right.

The role of the 2 TAF Fighter squadrons were a mix of air defence (day or all-weather/night) and ground attack. This differed from the squadrons of Fighter Command, which dedicated themselves to either the day or all-weather fighter role but tended to be in a wing or group with a dedicated role. In 2 TAF, it was not unusual for a mix of squadrons with different roles and aircraft to be concentrated on a single airfield.

The availability rate of the squadrons in Germany was expected to improve as well, given the greater ratio of maintenance personnel to aircraft. A more radical proposal from the C-in-C 2 TAF was the increase in tour length for aircrew from two and a half to four years—a quite unprecedented length of time. The future composition of the RAF in Germany, proposed in 1954, was agreed by the Air Council then to consist of nineteen day fighter and ground attack squadrons with a UE of fourteen aircraft each and four medium-range reconnaissance squadrons with a UE of ten aircraft each. Furthermore, the number of RAF airfields in Germany would be expanded from nine to eleven.

There was widespread agreement from a practical point of view that less congested airfields were far preferable.

The four new clutch airfields were now complete and in operation; the last, Laarbruch, opened on 15 October 1954. With the remaining airfields, mostly ex-Luftwaffe, in use, the search for eleven bases was done. Time was now approaching, which would see the official forming of the Federal Republic's own armed forces.

At the end of July 1955, the air and war ministries sent working parties to Germany again with the aim of investigating military expenditure. Sir William Dickson notified the 2 TAF commander, Sir Harry Broadhurst, that at the end of October 1955, the Air Ministry working party had completed the review of the expenditure of the RAF in Germany. They accepted that the concept of the tactical air force, clearly embodied in the title, was that it should be mobile, but with resources being ever tighter on top of growing demands in public expenditure elsewhere, maintaining 2 TAF strictly in line with its remit was not going to be possible any longer. 'Requires modification' was the expression used in an air ministry report, that it should only be capable of rapid re-deployment in the first instance to enable it to operate at maximum intensity in the initial phase of operations. SHAPE would need to be brought around to this way of thinking. Additionally, SACEUR had made proposals for an atomic posture that were accepted. Economic limitations prevented 2 TAF from fully implementing them.

The future size and shape of the RAF in Germany would need to be accepted first, but this would alleviate the problems faced once the future force structure was agreed. By this point, the RAF in Germany now had twelve Canberra squadrons to call upon, including the four lodger units from Bomber Command's ORBAT. These were to be disbanded, which would fit in with the rundown of the Canberra force overall. They could either be disbanded at Gütersloh, where they were, or returned to the UK to take the place of other units being disbanded there. The RAF Regiment, the RAF's in-house infantry unit, were also set to lose some of their squadrons.

In November 1955, the working party report on the state of operational efficiency in 2 TAF arrived at several recommendations for making improvements. The manning position was said to have steadily deteriorated according to Sir Harry Broadhurst. Various interim and *ad hoc* measures had been introduced to alleviate manning but to no avail. The situation was such that maintenance of aircraft was poor enough to fail to meet the number of flying hours planned in accordance with the operational training syllabus. While the broad aim of UK defence policy was to make 2 TAF fully mobile, the report recommended being simply capable of rapid redeployment to war stations.

In the first instance, this would be to enable it to operate at maximum intensity during the first phase of operations. This diluted the readiness posture expected by SACEUR, which revolved around the readiness of the future nuclear strike force. The RAF contribution to this would be four dedicated Canberra squadrons, mostly equipped with the new B(I)8 and a smaller number of the B(I)6. SACEUR required that the nuclear-armed Canberra squadrons, when they became available, be on the continent. The RAF Regiment units assigned to 2 TAF were to be 'restructured', which meant reduced. The RAF were also responsible for the provision of a segment of early warning—the radar chain facing the inner German border.

With West Germany's largely resumed status as a sovereign democratic state, it was now administered by its own elected government, taking over from the military governorship of the post-war era. Soon this would mean the resumption (or, more accurately, reformation) of Germany's armed forces, as far as the Federal Republic was concerned. As the FRG was seeing the establishment of its own military forces, it was thought quite logical that the role, certainly of early warning, should be transferred from the RAF and USAF to the new *Bundesluftwaffe*, at least in part.

It was envisaged that a percentage of the manning of the Type 80-equipped GCI stations would be German. The Type 80 was probably the most effective primary long-range control and reporting radar system of the time; it continued to be relied on by the RAF at the early warning GCI station, RAF Buchan, in Aberdeenshire into the 1980s.

Being the most northerly and therefore most prominent mainland early warning station, Buchan was situated to respond to the most likely direction of attack by Soviet air forces that could be expected. There was an ambitious recommendation that the Germans should be able to provide 100 per cent manning by 1957. The air ministry working party thought this was too ambitious given the forecast length of training of Luftwaffe personnel and what degree of depth was likely to have been achieved two years on. In the meantime, the T80 stations were the UK's (and therefore the RAF's) remit.

Indeed, they were regarded as an essential forward line of air defence reporting in respect of Britain's own early warning. In fact, handing the T80 sites over to the Luftwaffe was alluded to as something to be met in full only due to political considerations. This point was tricky—depending on the detailed nature of defence considerations, sometimes political sensitivities demanded ceding greater or complete control to the Germans, and sometimes not, if the diplomatic wind happened to blow in the other direction, as it did over battle flight/QRA duties.

Interestingly, the report observed that matters such as air defence were exactly what led to the kind of political tact that would mean the RAF transferring the air defence radar cover of West Germany to the Germans. Yet the duty of sending fighters aloft in response to an actual challenge to FRG airspace stayed with the RAF/USAF up to the end of the Cold War, even though the Germans operated their own interceptor fighters and conducted practice QRA scrambles. To put matters in perspective here, whatever poll position West Germany was in, regarding the nose-to-nose position of NATO and Warsaw Pact forces, the real continuous challenge to NATO airspace lay further north.

The presence of an RAF air defence element in the FRG was covered under the terms of the treaty. The air defence commitment had existed from 1945 because of the quadripartite agreement; this was a follow-on element of the Potsdam agreement, whereby the four governing nations each took on the role of policing their respective airspaces.

In later years, because matters developed as they did, with no subsequent peace treaty between the FRG and the USSR but instead the emergence of the Iron Curtain, the original post-war agreement remained. This ensured the three Western victors continued to meet the air defence of the FRG. To abandon the role may well place in question other portions of the agreement that were imperative to maintain, specifically West Berlin and the air and land access lanes to it from West Germany.

France withdrew from the NATO defence structure in 1966, to retain full independence over its own forces. For the UK government to withdraw as well would effectively leave the US Air Force upholding the entire commitment, which would doubtless be problematic, at least from a diplomatic position. The British had already compelled the Americans to uphold a portion of the British air defence effort when the RAF withdrew from Jever in 1962. The upshot then was that the Americans, who had less difficulty in maintaining their stated obligations, decided to step in and fill the gap by providing air defence fighters to police the North German/Schleswig-Holstein area. They maintained this commitment until 1994, with the 32nd Tactical Fighter Squadron based at the RNLAF base at Soesterberg, known to the Americans as Camp New Amsterdam.

Financial concerns, as always refusing to go away, were enough to see the Air Ministry concerned about their ability to meet the exercise commitments as directed by SACEUR. They had already convinced the supreme commander to look into the financial implications of the NATO exercise programme for Autumn 1956 and wanted to draw his attention to the current economic pressure and the desire to keep exercise costs to the essential minimum.

Yet the truly worthwhile reductions in expenditure in Germany lay in shape and size. Although it was some years away, the first discernible move toward the 'flexible response' strategy was being mentioned. Toward the end of 1955, change was at hand as far as doctrine was concerned, while the British were having another perennial look to reduce the commitment of 2 TAF's frontline by 1958–59. They were also keen to see a review of NATO's strategic concept as soon as possible, particularly as the process was expected to take some time. On a quite unrelated matter, the standard of living and amenities for personnel in West Germany was also under review. Germany represented something of a dilemma here as with the four new airfields fully operational, a new standard of airmen's accommodation had been reached. The desire was to do all to improve the overall standard and quality of living conditions; the thinking was that it would be a mistake to reduce the general standards in the one theatre where they approached the level, which all wanted to see universally applied. The challenge was to lift standards elsewhere.

The ongoing round of reviews usually resulted in pruning bits off expenditure, particularly in West Germany. Sir Harry Broadhurst, referring to further visits by Air Ministry and War Office working parties, believed that this was a nonsensical exercise. If the aim was to secure substantial savings, then major political and strategic decisions regarding the future size and role of the armed forces in West Germany were the only way that substantial savings would accrue, 'particularly in relation to an era of atomic plenty and the build-up of the German Air Force'.

Other economies would be relatively minor and ineffective, but that any economies made to the RAF must not leave personnel coping with standards less than that for the army, otherwise an intolerable situation would arise. Sir Harry's concerns were further heightened as the suggested economies to be made by 2 TAF were more comprehensive than those offered by the army:

> Our contribution has been offered on the basis that we must make the very fullest cuts (even to the point of making life hard). I am not at all sure that we haven't gone just a little too far but I am prepared in the present financial climate, to let our offer stand.

That the C-in-C RAF Germany would seek to maintain comparable conditions for RAF personnel with the army was not very reassuring given that conditions of service in the army were traditionally a touch more austere. What was not perhaps widely known was that the level of the British military force in Germany was only possible through US aid—not something that the British government, given the trappings of a global power, would be anxious to speak of in public.

Noticeably at the time, the plan for Fighter Command was to increase and improve. SACEUR, perhaps politely, responded by saying that he did not think himself competent to evaluate the relative importance of forces for national defence in comparison with those assigned to himself, but noted that the forces of allied command were deficient in quantity and therefore hoped that some way might be found of increasing the RAF fighter contribution to Germany. His outlook on NATO's defence posture in Central Europe was shortly to receive another British spanner in the works.

5

The Nuclear Option

On 29 August 1949, the Soviet Union successfully tested their first nuclear bomb under the codename 'First Lightning' at the Semipalatinsk test site in Kazakhstan.

At the Bermuda conference in 1952, the US presidential candidate Dwight Eisenhower told the British prime minister that he did not think there would be any 'serious objections' to the United States giving Britain the necessary technical information that would enable British aircraft to carry US nuclear weapons. What would become 'Project E' subsequently came into being in 1954.

In December that year, three United States Air Force Officers visited the UK to discuss the modifications required to allow British aircraft to carry an American-built nuclear bomb. The secretary of state for air, the 1st Viscount De L'Isle and Dudley VC, reported to the prime minister the results of their visit. The report indicated that it was likely that RAF aircraft would be able to change back and forth between carrying American and British bombs, this being desirable. This visit was preliminary to Project E, which referred to the assistance with nuclear weapons within NATO and is best described as 'nuclear sharing'.

By April 1956, Air Chief Marshal Sir Thomas Pike, deputy chief of the air staff, sent a letter to the deputy chief of staff operations at the USAF headquarters in Washington, DC, Brigadier General RT Coiner, advising that the RAF were progressing fairly well with the engineering aspects of fitting American nuclear weapons to RAF aircraft. They had reached a state where a full trial installation on various marks of Canberras would soon be completed. They would then be able to plan what proportion of the Canberra force they would be able to use in this role. The cost in man hours had proved to be more extensive than originally envisaged, and on the Canberra, the B2 mark would require somewhere over 2,000 hours of work each. However, the B(I)8s were proving much easier and it was expected to have a few of these ready by the end of the year.

Trial installations were to continue with the V-bombers, but Pike really wanted to press on with the coordination of operations and long-term logistics planning. There was a degree of anxiousness to tie the project in with the use of British nuclear weapons. The policy agreement, initially, was to modify all Canberra B(I)6s and B(I)8s. This totalled 150 aircraft and would support a front-line availability of 100.

As for the foreseeable future, there was concern that too many would be made ready only to find that a pending defence review cut the numbers. There was an expectation that the Mk 6 and 8 Strike Canberra UE would be cut from 100 to fifty with some PR jets thrown in. The preferred deployment in this case would be to withhold all B(I)8s from Germany and the Middle East bases and use them as an emergency reinforcement reserve instead. As for 2 TAF and the Middle East, nuclear-armed B2s would have to suffice for the foreseeable future.

To ensure against further shortfalls, the RAF were authorised to order 200 Honeywell LABS sets. Some would be fitted to some B2s to give them a low-level capability, using British bombs. Following a meeting between the Foreign Office and the Ministry of Defence in July 1956, the prime minister was urged to approach the US president to test his reaction to a public pronouncement on Project E, at the time highly sensitive information. The rationale behind a public acknowledgement was that there would inevitably be a leak of information in either country.

1955 was the year that the RAF V-force deployed its first squadron on an operational footing. No. 138 Squadron formed at RAF Gaydon at the beginning of the year and was equipped to carry the 'Blue Danube' bomb. This was a step forward in improving the survivability, for the moment anyway, of the RAF crews tasked with carrying the bomb eastward. This was if relations between east and west had broken down to the point where reliance on nuclear weapons was seen as indispensable.

There was a great deal of concern now that Armageddon was just around the corner, but that if nuclear weapons were exchanged, it would probably be as a result of an attempt to neutralise (ironically) a developing military situation or as a form of blackmail in an attempt to exploit a perceived moment of compromise or military weakness which could then escalate. I would not begin to suggest which scenario would put which of the two military powers on which side—Warsaw Pact or NATO.

The posture between the two is what came to be termed 'MAD'—mutually assured destruction—because no one could, under the circumstances, envisage the opportunity for a more restrained response from either side, or a less costly outcome. With atomic and hydrogen bombs being stockpiled on both sides, all the world had to go on historically was the last month of the war in the Far East, when the bombs dropped on Hiroshima and Nagasaki. Each side feared the other resorting to nuclear weapons to gain an advantage and deliver a knockout blow from which the opponent could not recover.

The development and stockpiling of 'the bomb' meant each side was capable of inflicting such considerable harm simultaneously that no advantage would be gained. Instead, the situation would develop so quickly with a very early transition, if not a pre-emptive strike. The outcome would be reached in short order, and it would be appallingly grim. NATO had a solution to this fearful future, which had school children practicing nuclear drills in classrooms in America by ducking under their desks upon the teacher's command. That was to provide an order of gradation from the firing of the first 7.62-mm bullet through to the first hydrogen bomb. The solution was more nuclear bombs, but little ones carried by smaller aircraft. This was the initial step toward what eventually became known as 'flexible response', but at the time, the aim foremost was to provide a radioactive hole for the strategic bomber force to fly through. These aircraft would be launching from East Anglia and Lincolnshire essentially, or wherever they were dispersed to. The radioactive hole would be created by the tactical nuclear bomb carriers operating from West Germany.

To meet this change in NATO policy, high-performance jet aircraft were to be relied upon to carry the 'tactical nuclear strike' but as a stage in escalation. The RAF in Germany were perfectly placed to take on this responsibility; they would have a deeper reach than UK-based squadrons and ironically, or perhaps not, would be less susceptible to a pre-emptive strategic strike from the USSR. The logic here was that the Russians would be less anxious to drop nuclear weapons early on across the very continent they wanted to bring the benefits of Marxism to. They did not want to place themselves so close to a radioactive wasteland, so went the theory. It is important to remember that the Kremlin, certainly Stalin, who passed away in 1953, never believed communism would conquer the world through all-out war, nuclear or conventional.

Both sides feared the other's hidden intentions. The Soviet president could not rest knowing that the larger chunk of Germany was in the grip of capitalism, which may give rise to nationalist hegemony yet again. The West knew what Russia feared and in turn feared what they might one day try to do about it, if only through impatience or even through a simple miscalculation or misunderstanding.

The Kremlin were always ready to try and force the situation with gradual pressure, such as blockades and internal pressure. The Russians and the Americans were not averse to military arm twisting, if they thought it would get them anywhere. There was a subtle difference—the western powers following the debacle of Dien Bien Phu would find themselves propping up various powers, against communist incursions in faraway lands. This prompted growing discord at home, the classic defining example being Vietnam in later years. The Kremlin would never tolerate unrest in its satellite nations, such as the revolution in Hungary, which lasted two months in 1956, before the Russians crushed it with force; allied relief flights were involved again, this time to no avail.

The range of strategic targets were quite wide and far afield. Plans for nuclear attacks on the Middle East were drawn up. Strikes on mountain passes were included as well as on Soviet forces and airfields in Southern Russia. The UK bomber force would take on a share of these tasks. Many hundreds of targets were identified; all would have to be destroyed in short order. This was the strategic response and by this stage, time would be of the essence—retaliation had to be of the shortest order.

While in the preliminary stages, it was impossible to determine the division of targets between the British and Americans; the RAF determined that they would need no fewer than 400 nuclear warheads, most of at least 1-megaton yield, though this was looking forward somewhat. As for the tactical requirements, before the phrase 'flexible response' was doing the rounds, UK requirements were based on the urgent need to neutralise the enemy air forces supporting the WP armies.

It was therefore vital that there should be adequate and timely nuclear support for the Northern Army Group (NORTHAG), which, from 1956, formed not only of the BAOR together with assigned forces from Belgium and Holland, but northern based units of the new *Bundeswehr* (Federal German Army). When fully formed, the German units became the 1st German Corps.

The Americans (V and VII Corps) and *Bundesheer* units (2nd and 3rd German Corps) in the southern half of the country formed CENTAG (Central Army Group). These units were joined by a Canadian division, which typically retained a single armoured brigade based in theatre at Lahr with the divisional HQ. It was upon NORTHAG that the responsibility fell for the defence of the Low Countries, Schleswig-Holstein, and ultimately Denmark and the Baltic exits (the narrow water running through the Danish straits out to the North Sea). The air elements included 2 TAF and US 3rd Air Force together with the Belgian and Dutch air elements and soon to be assigned units of the Luftwaffe.

The aim of the tactical strike squadrons was the destruction of Soviet airfields within the range of the tactical air force. In so doing, this contributed to the survival of the United Kingdom, by denying advanced bases to the enemy's strategic air force and his light bomber force. Heavy troop concentrations would also count as targets for the strike squadrons. This relied upon, above all, an all-weather capability to be fully available to SACEUR. The RAF could present two aircraft that came within a country mile of meeting that requirement, the Canberra and the new Javelin, the latter still to be introduced into frontline service but on the eve of operational service. The RAF were prepared to promote the all-weather capability of their aircraft as superior to that of any of the fighter bomber aircraft of the United States, which SACEUR was relying upon for this role.

The F-84G Thunderjet and later the F-84F Thunderstreak were the strike aircraft of choice for not just the USAF European Command but (by the end of the decade) the strike wings of the Belgian, Dutch, and Federal German Air Forces. All tactical strike aircraft initially carried the Mk 7 nuclear bomb. There was a further nuclear strand here being advanced by the army—nuclear artillery shells and the introduction to both NORTHAG and CENTAG of 'Honest John', then 'Lance', battlefield nuclear surface-to-surface missiles. This immense fire power further added to the tapestry of the central region's small nuclear weapons.

The deployment of land-based nuclear weaponry was discounted by the RAF as unnecessary and inferior to the great versatility, range, and flexibility of the tactical air force. In 1955, the Red Beard warhead was regarded as the best possible device for delivery from either a Canberra or (as was then mooted) a Javelin. The wider deployment of tactical nuclear weapons outside of Europe was also pursued. It was an accepted doctrine that nuclear weapons were the best way to limit any build-up of Soviet forces and subsequent operations in the Middle East. Thus, tactical nuclear ordnance was an essential element of any forward strategy in that theatre. The 2 TAF was to have a force of about 120 Canberras and/or Javelins.

Assessing specific targets and matching their allocation to certain units was as impracticable for RAF Germany as it was for the new growing strategic medium bomber force. For the tactical RAF force, 250 Red Beards were considered the minimum requirement. This was not an overestimate; it was viewed as an understated figure and that more may likely be needed. For this, the United States were again to be relied upon.

In September 1956, the RAF operated what was called the 'long term force', consisted of Canberra B(I)8, B(I)6, and B6 aircraft. All were to be modified with a bomb carriage known as Type E. Some of the associated equipment was to be purchased from the USA and would be fitted to the bomb bay of each of the LTF Canberras.

Modifications would be applied to fifty-two B(I)8s, twenty B(I)6s, and seventy-nine B6s. This was costed at £1.2 million—to carry out the modifications in house. The bomb release units defined according to the type of use was based on whether the jet would be used to air toss the bomb or lay down the weapon in the traditional manner. For this, 180 LABS M.A.2 units and 168 aero 61b bomb release units were purchased, all at a cost of $850,000. Some 180 T.145 control boxes and 165 bomb carriers, all made in the UK at a total cost of £142,000, were produced.

An estimate of the man-hours required to carry out the work varied according to the model of Canberra—for the B(I)8s, the estimate was 1,000; the B(I)6s, 2,000; and the older B6s, 3,000 hours. Not surprisingly, the priority was to modify the B(I)8s—the cheapest and most reliable of the three. A trial installation on a Mk 8 had already been carried out—trials on a B2 on behalf of the Mk 6s were in progress, and the results were expected by January 1957.

Defence Minister Duncan Sandys wanted to know the views of his cabinet colleagues on proposals about to be put to him concerning 2 TAF and BAOR. What he was looking for were proposed units for disbandment; this was not as such anything to do with the much reported and highly significant 1957 White Paper proposing the replacement of fighter aircraft with an all-missile defence screen.

Sandys was responding to the outcome of a NATO conference agreement in Paris. The cuts to the UK force in Germany were justified simply on cost savings and nothing else. A reduction of aircraft in RAFG from 460 to 278 by March 1959 was being suggested by 2 TAF. This should reduce the equivalent expenditure in *Deutsche Marks* from £12.2 million to £8.6 million. The RAF wanted to make the case, 'if politically possible', to highlight spending on more important areas. What was particularly difficult about these cuts was how it affected the set strategy, and it was hoped that the ministers would understand this. Any reductions had to take into account the growing importance of the overall contribution to the nuclear deterrent; the provision of a nuclear capability in the Canberra force; and the expectation that the new Federal German Air Force would take over remaining continental air force duties.

The Bomber Command force was to be reduced from a UE target of 240 to 200 or less, together with the expected reductions in Fighter Command, all of which were being called for by Duncan Sandys. He had yet to make the infamous announcement heralding the end of the manned fighter, as he thought would happen.

The build-up of the new German Air Force had been delayed until 1959 or later, and SHAPE, while welcoming the nuclear capability for the Canberra Force, did not consider that any of the reductions elsewhere justified the reduction of forces declared to NATO below the level of the most recent UK review. The UK review determined 2 TAF should retain 460 aircraft, which Sandys now wanted to reduce considerably. In fact, the defence minister had not yet made a firm decision on numbers but was due to make a statement to NATO on the subject.

Britain was still in the somewhat embarrassing position of relying to a degree on US aid and the post-war political psyche of constant whittling away attitude (developed from the constant self-reassurance that there were endless amounts to be shaved off) toward our own defence interests. This was not going to strengthen the British negotiating position with the Americans.

With plans being revised downwards again so soon after the recent review, the proposals coming around the corner might well prove something of a shock. Savings had already been made earlier in the year; much had been made in administrative areas, to wit, greater use was made of German civilian staff on RAF stations in place of some RAF personnel. They were cheaper and more productive than servicemen because they had no extraneous duties. The cost *per annum* was £100 less than an airman.

This policy had to be reversed as high employment in West Germany was reducing the pool of manpower, and further civilianisation of 2 TAF made the command less mobile, which was of course very much at the core of its existence. When 2 TAF was created in the Second World War, it was for the very purpose of battlefield support, whenever and wherever. Some room for manoeuvre might have been found in the loss of the four warehoused Canberra squadrons—102, 103, 104, and 149, equipped with the earlier B2. These were to be disbanded in August 1956 along with a base closure—that of Faßberg—in January 1957.

Still the defence minister sought further cuts over the next four years. Also, all the antecedent Luftwaffe bases currently operational with the RAF would close bar one. The four clutch bases would remain. Before 1956 ended, fifteen RAF officers were drawn from squadrons, groups, command headquarters of Bomber Command, and from 2 TAF; they had all completed a course, under USAF instruction, on toss bombing. This was about the handling and qualities of the US Mk 7 bomb to be carried by Canberra aircraft of both Bomber Command and 2 TAF units. The fifteen officers were regarded as the initial instructors in this technique.

After October 1956, no more had been trained. Early in 1957, Canberra crews would commence training to employ the toss bomb technique, using the LABS sight equipment purchased from the United States. Courses were also conducted within squadrons assigned the strike role in addition to the OCU courses. There was no security element involved as the LABS system could and was expected to be used in conjunction with a British bomb.

The first modified aircraft was expected to be delivered in February. By the end of August 1957, some modified Canberras were in service with 2 TAF. The number of squadrons equipped with these aircraft would increase over the next nine months. Six RAF stations were involved—four in Germany and two in the UK. Aircrews received regular training in the new LABS technique. The modification of all aircraft was expected within the nine-month period. On the other hand, work was progressing at a slower pace on getting around to building the associated infrastructure required.

At this late stage, there had been public acknowledgement that RAF aircraft, other than the V-Force in Great Britain and in West Germany, were to be armed with nuclear weapons. Nothing had been made public about the extensive role the Americans were playing. The more the situation progressed, the more people became involved, making a security leak more likely especially as the buildings to accommodate the weapons and 'personnel' to guard them would soon start to materialise.

That the Americans were to provide the weapons, and under which arrangements, was still sensitive information. While the British government were minded to make either a joint or unilateral declaration that this was the case, the US president vetoed the idea for political reasons at home.

Among the kind of questions the RAF envisaged being put by the press were whether the arrangement with the Americans meant that the UK had insufficient nuclear weapons produced at home or that we were cutting back our own production, if there was a corresponding arrangement for US aircraft to carry British weapons, and whether fighter aircraft would carry nuclear weapons. There were defined points on which no information would be given:

    a. The length of time the USAF engineering team had been in the UK.
    b. Information of any sort on the weapons i.e., size, weight, yield, etc.
    c. Information on the number of aircraft converted.
    d. The location of the aircraft being adapted and the places where adaptation was being carried out.
    e. Information on the planning and execution of the project as a whole.
    f. Information on the detailed work involved in adaptation.
    g. Details of the air or ground training programmes.

Set performance parameters were established for the LABS manoeuvre—an approach speed of 434 knots and a 3.4-*g* rotation of the nose if carrying the US Mk 7 bomb. This weapon weighed 1,650 lb. The parameters also applied to both the Red Beard (2,000 lb) device and the 25-lb practice round equally.

These parameters were queried in respect of the 2,000-lb bomb and the 'forward toss'. The claim was that 420 kts would be a sufficient approach speed. The approach speed was to remain at 434 knots as there would be insufficient time to increase speed from a forward toss release manoeuvre if, at a late stage in the bomb run, it became necessary to change to an over-the-shoulder delivery. The over-the-shoulder manoeuvre was known by pilots as the 'idiot's loop', perhaps for obvious reasons; this is where the aircraft pulls through the vertical, half-loops, then rolls out, having reversed direction, away from the bomb trajectory.

The pilot was required to apply full power before rotating the nose in the forward toss as both his hands needed to be free in order to pull back on the control column to pull the necessary '*g*'. A&AEE Boscombe Down analysis advised that the pilot would have no reference to mark the point where the pull up would begin. Therefore, they offered to conduct a short trial to determine whether the navigator could provide the datum for the power-on point and relay a verbal countdown to the pilot using a simple stopwatch. The over-the-shoulder profile faced no such problems as a visual reference would be available—that would be the target itself.

In April 1960, a meeting was held at RAE Farnborough to determine the introduction of the Red Beard bomb and the standard of preparation of the Canberra B6 in the nuclear role. The RAF armaments department also questioned the accuracy of the LABS technique, given the likely variation in thrust obtained between different aircraft. There was certainly variation between the two different-sized bombs—US B7 and the heavier British Redbeard. Standardisation in training was essential but for aircrew to be current in the practice of deploying both weapons would be a greater advantage.

The air staff considered as late as July 1960 fitting LABS instrumentation in Canberra T4s issued to the strike/interdictor squadrons in both Germany and the Middle East. This would allow for fully comprehensive instruction and supervision to be afforded in LABS training. The difference with the situation up to this point was that it was only possible to assess a pilot's ability to perform the LABS manoeuvre in a T4 based at Bassingbourn without any comparison with the instrumentation in the operational aircraft.

A check ride was possible in the operational B(I)6, which had an occasionally unused third seat, but this was far from satisfactory. In the case of the B(I)8, because there was no third seat and the fact that the pilot sat in a separate fighter like cockpit with a water droplet canopy, no checks on these pilots' standards could be made.

The T4s, it was stipulated, would not be armed for operational use, simply be fitted with the instrumentation. The requirement was to equip six T4s with LABS equipment—four would be based in Germany and two in the MEAF. This concern arose partly from a fatal crash involving a B(I)6 of 213 Squadron based at Brüggen, while practising the LABS manoeuvre on 10 May 1960. The crash was caused by rivets coming loose in a section of the elevator. Specifically, these were rivets in the connecting sleeve of the torque tube assembly in the elevator spring tab mechanism. This assembly section was exercised in the LABS practice and more heavily so than in any other roles/manoeuvres. One of the fractured rivets showed signs of fatigue and so LABS practices had been suspended.

By July, the suspension had been lifted. The cause of the crash had been resolved to the absence of a stop pin from the tab-operating lever. When properly in place, it would not be possible to over -stress the riveted joints. As the stop pin restricted movement, the pilot was prevented from 'applying destructive *g* loading accidentally'. Before this incident, there was already concern, raised by what was now RAF Germany, about the stresses encountered through operating Canberras at low level.

There were doubts about whether the Canberras could be maintained and remain reliable until such time as its intended replacement, the TSR2, was available. The VCAS, Sir Edmund Huddleston, ordered a full examination be made into the long-term implications of the Canberra under 2 TAF operating conditions and its repercussions on the requirement for a replacement aircraft. Bomber Command had determined back in 1958 that there would be no LABS or low-level navigation training carried out on 231 OCU at Bassingbourn. Instead, teams of instructors would train with the BCDU, while attached to the operational squadrons. All training was to be carried out using aircraft fitted with tail plane aerodynamic modification and fatigue meters. No. 2 TAF were consulted, and a pattern was concocted consisting of seven stages:

a. Dual low flying exercise: 1,000 feet initially, lowering to 500 feet then 250 feet AGL. Speed, 250 kts initially increasing to 350 kts IAS. Type: Canberra T4. Duration 1.5 to 2 hours.

b. Dual manoeuvre demonstrations and practice: 5,000 feet AGL, 350 kts IAS. Type: Canberra T4. Duration 1 hour.

c. Solo manoeuvre practice: 5,000 feet AGL, 350 kts IAS. Type: Canberra T4. Duration 45 minutes.

d. Map reading exercise: 2,000 feet AGL, 300 kts IAS. Type: Canberra B6. Duration 2 hours.

e. Map reading exercise: 1,000 feet AGL, 300 kts IAS. Type: Canberra B6. Duration 2 hours.

f. Dual manoeuvre practice and check: 2,000 feet AGL, 350 kts IAS increasing to 420 kts IAS. Type: Canberra T4. Duration 45 minutes.

g. LABS Demonstration: 2,000 feet AGL. Speed for manoeuvre, 420 kts IAS. Type: Canberra B6. Duration 30 to 45 minutes.

1958 brought the operational declaration of the first nuclear-armed Canberra squadron in Germany. HQ 2 TAF stated a requirement for specially designated training areas to be assigned for the execution of LABS manoeuvres. Initially, these manoeuvres were flown using existing low-flying areas when flying under VMC (visibility minimum conditions) rules. When IMC (instruments minimum conditions) rules applied, the danger area at Nordhorn bombing range was used, and manoeuvres were also carried out using GCA (ground control approach) surveillance at the squadrons' respective home stations.

These procedures sufficed during early training in the LABS role but there were now disadvantages as all low-level training sorties were now planned and flown as LABS attacks. The disadvantages were as follows:

a. Collision risk when carrying out the LABS manoeuvres in low flying areas which were open to all aircraft.

b. The use of Nordhorn bombing range (the only range available in 2 TAF) for LABS practices reduced its availability for practice bombing sorties.

c. The concentration of all high-speed, low-level exercises in one small area would lead to numerous complaints from the German authorities.

d. The use of GCA search radar for LABS surveillance was undesirable and detracted from its normal task.

e. The airfields were not in low flying areas and low-level approaches couldn't be made when the equipment was being used for LABS practice.

6

The 1957–1963 Restructure

At a briefing for a visit by Air Secretary Sir Theodore McEvoy in May 1961, he was informed of the current structure of the RAF in Germany and how it was planned to look by the end of the decade. The command was due for a review in July. An example of the current posture and how it was due to be transformed was explained using RAF Laarbruch as an example. Laarbruch was as typical an RAF station in Germany as any. Situated just 20 miles from Arnhem, Laarbruch was the most northerly of the four clutch stations along the Dutch border. The base had the kind of establishment in operational terms that was typical of all four clutches. The line-up of the day included a light bomber squadron (Canberras), a photo-reconnaissance squadron (Canberras), and a night all-weather fighter squadron (Javelins).

Laarbruch was described as a long-term RAF station. Having said that, it was already established that the fighter squadron would be withdrawn at the end of 1962, but that the Canberra squadrons would remain until 1968 when they would re-equip with TSR2—such was the level of confidence held by all that the TSR2 would make it to the front line as planned.

On 1 January 1957, RAF Faßberg was vacated by the RAF; Oldenburg and Celle were also handed over to the Luftwaffe by the end of November. After the cuts of the post-Korean War era, matters had not properly settled down before the ramifications of the typical off piste thinking that blights British defence policy from time to time started to get in the way of settled long-term planning.

This time, the radical approach came from the defence minister *in situ* in early 1957. Duncan Sandys announced what amounted to the end of the road for the manned fighter. As this was a government pronouncement, it was doomed not to be and quite predictably so, but a decision had been taken and problems were afoot. The proposed system to replace the 'manned fighter', the ground-launched guided weapon, was destined to become all but non-existent within five years of reaching the high-water mark of deployment.

So, the 'manned fighter' would live on, but in nowhere near the numbers maintained at the time of Sandys' announcement to the house in April 1957. This came just three months after he had taken up his appointment. Much has been said in public about the infamous Sandys Review, and indeed, it can only be surmised that the long-term effect was to all but wreck the British Aerospace industry, seeing many companies shut up shop. Various military aircraft projects at various stages of development were lost forever. As for the RAF, the numbers were staggering—Fighter Command had contracted, in terms of operational squadrons, from forty to five between 1957 and the end of 1965. The promised missile squadrons generated to offset the loss of the fighter force (or bulk of it) reached the pinnacle of readiness with ten squadrons by 1963, then over the next two years were eroded down to a single unit.

This rate of reduction was offset to a degree by the ending of national service, which undoubtedly impacted more heavily on the army. Save for the loss of bases along the banks of Suez, the RAF lost no commitment anywhere else of any significance. The navy and the marines suffered least of all from the ending of conscription as they had managed to continue to rely almost exclusively on volunteer regular recruits. There was something about national service that more than suggested that rather than provide a surfeit of trained military personnel, it produced a volume of young men in uniform for all manner of menial demands rather than a genuine force expansion.

However, any loss of existing units still impacted on the level of available manpower, which was already in decline. Those services obliged to take them found increasingly that an excess number of non-skilled labour presented something of a bugbear rather than an in-depth capability. The loss of aircraft and skilled long-serving personnel amounted to a serious problem.

Aircraft were also getting more complicated, development was jumping forward, airframes were getting both sleeker and heavier, and jet engine performance was coming on in leaps and bounds, meaning procurement was taking longer. This demanded that a break of some kind needed to be applied to the numbers. Like-for-like replacement was taking a much bigger bite out of the RAF's and navy's budgets. The reduction in fighter squadrons was most severe; it also included many of the tactical units. Ground attack and reconnaissance aircraft in support of ground forces—a vital component— almost vanished from within 2 TAF. This latter point is something that appears to have not been considered by the review.

The ground-attack capability of those fighter squadrons that were so equipped could not be replaced by anti-aircraft rockets. A total of thirty-two tactical squadrons on eleven stations equipped 2 TAF as of 1 April 1957, comprising thirteen Hunter squadrons, five still equipped with Venoms, five with Meteors, seven with Canberras, and two with Swift FR5s. In addition to this, each squadron usually had an assigned 'Hack'; this was usually a Meteor T7 or Vampire T11 for each of the fighter units and a Canberra T4 for the light bomber/reconnaissance squadrons. The Hacks fulfilled the requirement for acting as a run-around—drop people off, collect stuff, and fulfil other domestic requirements.

The 2 TAF units themselves filled the full-spectrum tactical requirement and were an imperative asset as far as any attempt to try and slow a Warsaw Pact advance was concerned. What they brought to the party simply could not be replaced with ground-launched missiles. One theory for such a drastic move was the cost of the RAF's expanding contemporary nuclear deterrent—the V-force.

This was a serious flaw and contributed to the notion that the logic of mutually assured destruction was accepted, partly on cost grounds, by Sandys, and therefore the government, as the only reliable philosophy as far as how to confront an attack across the inner German border was concerned. The logic was that neither side would dare risk it. This flaw in defence thinking was eventually addressed through flexible response, but MAD was certainly mad and the likes of the Sandys Review likely contributed to the possibility of a strategic nuclear exchange by removing a tier of containment that might just work before such a stage was reached.

This so often foments wider scepticism when holes in policy are so obvious. A possible by-product was the move toward accommodating the new Federal German Air Force, who were quickly moving back into the air bases that the RAF moved into at the end of the war. In March 1958, RAF Wunstorf was handed over to Luftwaffe *Gruppe Nord* (Air Force Group North) as part of the build-up of the new West German Air Force. It may be worth noting that 'Luftwaffe' literally translates as 'air weapon', though it is the accepted term for what in English is referred to as the air force. A German public notification declared:

> Since the 7 April 1945, for almost thirteen years, the flag of a foreign power has been flying at the Air Force station Wunstorf. We, who have been through those first fateful hours, have not forgotten the day when British and American Tank units marched into the town and fast fighters and bombers appeared over the aerodrome in the morning light of the 7 April 1945 and attacked everything they could see. The weather then was just as cold as it is this March. From that very day the aerodrome has been occupied by British Troops.
>
> Soon a few men and women found work with the Royal Air Force, but for the rest of the local population the camp was just 'Taboo'.

At the beginning it was understandably quiet, but during the weeks of the Berlin airlift there was no end, both in the air and on the runway, to the noise of four-engine bombers landing and taking off.

Then came the jets and whined so often that it became unpleasant. But this noise, of course, is common to any airfield.

On Monday the bad dream came to an end. The Royal Air Force gave the camp back to the Deutsche Luftwaffe.

Yesterday we were informed of the parade and the Station Commander, Sqn Ldr CAA Davis expressed his thanks to the people of Wunstorf and the neighbouring countryside as well as the clerks and labourers working for him.

Yesterday morning at half past eleven, the actual handing over ceremony took place. In attendance at the parade were Landrat Meyer, Oberkreis-Direktor Dr Homann, Burgermeister Weintzek, Stadtdirektor Dr Neuhoff, Burgermeister Seehausen und Gemeindedirektor Kirschmann.

While Guards of Honour of both the German and Royal Air Force, further training units of the German Air Force and a Band from Münster under the direction of Hauptmann Schnade marched on in front of the large Hangars, Group Captain Brown from No. 2 Group, Royal Air Force, spoke a word of thanks and emphasised the good liaison which has existed between the British and the local German population. In the last few weeks, during the formality of handing over, there has been a friendly co-operation between both nations. He wished the Deutsche Luftwaffe at Wunstorf all the very best in the future.

For the Germans *Oberst* Jackisch answered and said that the handing over of Royal Air Force Wunstorf meant a further step in the re-building of the Deutsche Luftwaffe. He further expressed the wish that the excellent co-operation between both nations would continue and would help in the strive for world peace. He wished the members of the Royal Air Force good luck in their new postings.

Then the Union Jack came down from the flagpole and the order 'Hoist the Flag' rang out. Amid the sound of the German national anthem the Black, Red and Gold flag with the Black Eagle was hoisted up on the flagpole.

A march past of both guards of honour ended the parade, which was watched by some British families, who are soon to depart Wunstorf, and many German clerks and labourers.

The senior German Administration Officer at German Air Force Wunstorf is Major Ahrens. *Hauptmann* Seegers, as the first German Officer at Wunstorf has done the preparation for the handing over.

For the last fortnight recruits have been trained on the camp and further to that a repair unit is stationed there for the maintenance and repair of vehicles and aircraft.

The outgoing station commander, Sqn Ldr Davis, in his own farewell address, made mention of the 'Red Barrel club' started in the sergeant's mess four years earlier. This was a fundraising endeavour, the principal aim of which was to raise money to buy Christmas presents for the disabled children in the Anna Schrift home in Hanover. The club had in the intervening period raised £700, and Sqn Ldr Davis noted his wish to see this continue under the station's new/resumed management: 'May I be so bold as to hope these children will continue to receive help from this station'.

Nos 11 and 266 Squadrons were the last two operational units at Wunstorf. They both left on 16 November 1957, following which Wunstorf became the master diversion for RAF stations in North Germany. Sqn Ldr Davis also mentioned Wunstorf's role as the main despatching airfield during the Berlin Airlift.

This handover ceremony and exchange of goodwill took place from 1957 to 1961 at several RAF stations, which once were Luftwaffe stations and were, essentially, all becoming so again.

Wunstorf followed Faßberg, both going to the Luftwaffe in 1957. Later that year, Oldenburg and Celle were also handed over. Another of the former occupation stations, Wahn, was under continued pressure by the now elected federal German government to increase civilian use by 1957. An increase in civilian use was permitted by 2 TAF, in so far as military air operations and aircraft safety were not compromised. The request from the Germans was very much driven by Wahn's additional role as the official airport for the new capital, Bonn.

The current level of civilian activity permitted was inadequate from the point of view of the government. Matters were coming to a head when a letter was sent from 2 TAF to RAF Wahn, advising that the Germans were going to increase the amount of civil air traffic, including regular services from KLM and Swissair. They further took the quite strident view that any repercussions on military air traffic would, in their view, have to be accepted. As the military use of Wahn was primarily a NATO concern, 2 TAF had referred the letter to AIRCENT; later AAFCE; the situation was also reported to the Air Ministry.

The German chancellor, Konrad Adenauer, also contacted the British ambassador, suggesting that the time had now come where military use of Wahn should be terminated and that its future lay in bilateral talks between British and German experts. The British ambassador passed the German letter to the Foreign Office, who were of the view that the British should not enter into any proposals that would adversely affect the efficiency of any of the squadrons in Germany, except under the auspices of NATO.

In the meantime, 2 TAF sought urgent advice on what was becoming an urgent situation—the Germans had agreed to these additional scheduled services without any proper consultation with the RAF, and they were due to commence imminently. Temporary arrangements had been made under Foreign Office and embassy oversight to limit the amount of traffic in the meantime, to acceptable levels, but 2 TAF needed guidance as to their precise standing with the German authorities.

Plans were not yet set for the RAF to yield Wahn to anyone, but the occupants were quite prepared to give up the airfield providing adequate facilities were found elsewhere to house the two squadrons, 68 and 87. One of the suggestions to arise during negotiations was the allocation of a block during the day for civil movements. Wahn was the most southerly of all the RAF airfields and sat just 15 miles from Bonn. This was a better solution than looking around for somewhere else to billet the squadrons. SACEUR had already been made aware that the RAF would be looking to cut their numbers after the end of 1957.

The two squadrons moved from Wahn in July that year, which effectively ended RAF operations here with the last RAF personnel leaving in 1958. The rapid draw down of RAF stations occurred with such short order—in some cases, some RAF personnel at home on leave were notified not to bother returning to their unit. The remaining—mostly 2 Group bases: Alhorn, Jever, and Sylt—were all handed back to the Federal German Air Force by the end of 1961. By this time, just a single former *Wehrmacht* air base remained in RAF hands—Gütersloh. The remainder were the four bases on the Dutch border.

The scale of the post-war RAF, taking account of the number of other operational commands from the UK to the Far East, clearly possessed a quite impressive inventory. It is easy to understand how successive governments, both Conservative and Labour, had wrestled with the UK's still widespread military commitments across the world following the war. No. 2 Group disbanded on 15 November 1958; all remaining units transferred to 83 Group.

The structure of NATO also took another step forward. The 2nd Tactical Air Force became the RAF contribution to 2nd Allied Tactical Air Force. The new element encompassed the Belgian and Royal Netherlands Air Forces along with elements of the Federal German Air Force and the United States Air Force, of the latter, essentially UK-based tactical squadrons. As of 1 January 1959, 2 TAF, as the RAF in Germany continued to be referred, was retitled Royal Air Force Germany (RAFG).

The cuts announced in 1957 largely affected those fighter units primarily assigned to day fighter duties, essentially the Hunter squadrons which also doubled up in the ground attack role alongside the Venom squadrons. Fighter Command bore the brunt of the cuts. The other victim was, as expected, the British aviation industry. Many projects in the pipeline with various aircraft manufacturing firms were destined never to advance beyond the draftsman's board.

What was left, in fighter terms, were the Gloster Javelin and the English Electric Lightning. Neither, especially the Lightning, was particularly versatile with regards to close air support (ground attack). The former was already operational with Fighter Command and already under threat from the radical re-structure. The Lightning was to escape the scythe being sufficiently far enough developed but would be reduced from the planned numbers. For all the faith in surface-to-air missiles, the forecast for deployment of the Lightning still promised more than the total eventually delivered. The RAF in Germany did not see any surface-to-air defences beyond the Bofors guns until 1970 when 25 Squadron moved across from RAF North Coates to Brüggen, from where operational Bloodhound missile flights were deployed to Laarbruch and Wildenrath.

By 1960, the government was being urged to withdraw all remaining fighters from RAFG. By December that year, the Foreign Office contacted the Air Ministry claiming to have a very strong case for postponing the withdrawal. There were a handful of arguments cited, chief among them was that it was essential to maintaining good relations with the federal government in Bonn; there was also the introduction of a new pre-planned operation to respond to any further attempts by the Russians to close the Berlin air corridors.

On 12 May 1960, a new operational procedure titled 'Jack Pine' came into effect, which relied on NATO fighters based in the Federal Republic to confront, if necessary, Warsaw Pact fighters while escorting allied transport aircraft up and down the corridors. The British were not initially committed to any such plans, expecting to remove their last fighter aircraft in the short term; the final redeployment of RAFG squadrons was to be completed in 1961. In the interim, the political climate soured and instead, two all-weather fighter units and one day fighter unit would be retained in accordance with the following re-structure:

(a) All Weather Squadrons (Javelins)
1. The two all-weather Squadrons to be retained are, No. 5 at Laarbruch and No. 11 at Geilenkirchen.
2. No. 3 Squadron at Geilenkirchen and No 87 Squadron at Brüggen to be disbanded as soon as possible after 1 January 1961.
(b) Day Fighter Squadrons (Hunters)
1. No. 14 Squadron to be retained at Gütersloh.
2. Nos 4 and 93 Squadrons at Jever and 20 and 26 squadrons at Gütersloh, all to be disbanded as soon as possible after 1 January 1961.
(c) Fighter Reconnaissance Squadrons (Swift FR5s)
1. No. 2 Squadron to be re-deployed from Jever to Gütersloh in the first quarter of 1961.

2. No. 79 squadron to be retained at Gütersloh.

(d) Transfer of senior Squadron number plates

1. No. 59 squadron (Interdictor Strike Canberras) at Geilenkirchen, to become No. 3 strike squadron with effect of No 3 all-weather Fighter Squadron disbandment.

2. No. 79 FR squadron to become No 4 FR Squadron with effect of No. 4 Day Fighter squadron disbandment.

The disbandment of the two Hunter fighter squadrons at Jever would then leave that base free to be handed over to the Germans. This would need to wait until autumn as Gütersloh's runway was being resurfaced and the bolthole airfield for the squadrons was Jever. Despite NATO's central region being reinforced with the *Bundeswehr* (Federal Armed Forces) from 1956, as far as any contingency planning for West Berlin went, German participation was still being resisted.

The British Foreign Office, and presumably their counterparts in the USA and France, had received an official request from the federal government to be included in the Berlin contingency planning. The UK defence committee had so far forbidden any approach at any level from the Bonn government for facilities in relation to Berlin, even if such rejection had a negative impact. There was a suggestion now that the ruling was too strictly interpreted and that a modified view would better serve.

If 'Jack Pine' were to be implemented, in the near future, then RAF Gütersloh would need to be used to launch tactical fighter operations. However, Gütersloh was due to close for several weeks for repairs and the next most suitable airfield was at Celle, which had since been handed to the Luftwaffe. Under the circumstances of the time, it was not absolutely necessary for plans for the use of Celle in such an emergency to involve the Germans. Yet while they were not expected to raise objections should the operation order for 'Jack Pine' be given, it made such plans even more tentative should any reaction be ignored.

On 2 November 1960, a meeting of the defence council concluded that upon implementing Jack Pine, a mobile radar unit would need to be deployed close to the East/West border. Celle was the chosen destination for such a unit. This would require communication lines between Celle and the early warning radar station at Auenhausen, which would need to be put in place by the German authorities. Further, the idea of involving the German forces in any future Berlin crisis had not been dismissed by the chiefs of staff entirely. The procedure envisaged using German (as distinct from NATO) airfields, navigation aids, and communications circuits, if plans for another Berlin airlift, and air access agencies, were to be enacted.

By 1961, the situation with the Warsaw Pact was seeing an increase in tension. This was largely focused on the air corridors once again, and NATO's resolve to keep them open. It certainly was a hairy situation, bearing in mind what was at stake should it be mishandled. The RAF alone had all four of its planned squadrons armed with B7 bombs; they were deployed one squadron per clutch base—3 Sqn at Geilenkirchen, 88 at Wildenrath, 213 at Brüggen, and 16 at Laarbruch. Each flew the Canberra B(I)8, save for 213, which had the B(I)6; each was tasked to provide tactical attack bombing sorties as required, but with the dual role of blasting a radioactive hole in any Warsaw Pact invasion, should it be deemed indispensable to do so.

It was important not to follow a foolhardy course of action. Psychology always played a part in the game of chess between NATO and the Warsaw Pact. The signals and how they were interpreted by each side all contributed to the fine balance of not giving the impression of changing to a war footing while avoiding the impression of supine concession. Therefore, peace was again in greater peril—swords were drawn and pointing straight at the Berlin air corridors, connecting West Berlin's airports with West Germany.

Soviet awkwardness over the use of the air corridors resulted in the RAF expanding the size of the two Javelin squadrons in Germany. No. 5 Squadron at Laarbruch was to have its establishment of twelve Mk 5 Javelins increased to sixteen as of 24 August, and the twelve Mk 4 Javelins of 11 Squadron, at Geilenkirchen, expanded with the addition of four Mk 5 aircraft. There remained 14 Squadron with Hawker Hunter F6 day fighters at Gütersloh. These Hunters were due to be removed by the end of 1962, but circumstances now suggested they could stay on while the situation remained what was described as sterile. The Three Powers agreed:

> Tripartite plans will be prepared for the direction of military forces in a manner which will make it unmistakeably clear to the Soviets and the German Democratic Republic that the Allies are determined to maintain unrestricted access to Berlin by any means considered necessary.

Should there be any attempt by the Warsaw Pact forces to threaten or shoot down an allied aircraft, whether civilian or military, operating to and from West Berlin, the allied powers 'may' conduct tactical operations to regain unrestricted access.

Specifically, what this meant was transport aircraft would continue to operate within the corridors in accordance with existing procedures. At the same time, French, British, and American fighter aircraft would be available to fly directly, or indirectly, in support of such flights as required at the time.

Support by tripartite fighters was to be restricted initially to the Bruckeburg–Berlin controlled corridor. This was the central corridor and the one most favoured by all flights simply as it was the shortest. The tripartite fighters were expected to fly within this corridor to carry out escort duties. It may be noticed that as well as the Luftwaffe, Belgian and Dutch air force units were not affected by this order.

West Germany until the 1980s would continue to rely on other NATO allied fighters to react to peacetime challenges to their airspace in accordance with post-war controls on German military operations in peacetime. Belgium and Holland were in effect responsible only for their respective airspace. Indirect support was to consist of maintaining fighter patrols constantly near the mouth of the corridors, ready to fly to the aid of any transport aircraft; this would be to intervene by flying up the corridor to ride shotgun. British fighters would ordinarily picket the mouth of the central corridor while the French and United States air forces took responsibility for the southern Frankfurt–Berlin corridor. If weather conditions and or enemy jamming were evident, the French and American aircraft would concentrate on the central corridor. The more detailed instructions governing escort operations would only be issued on the point of such escorts proving necessary. The aim was to force the Soviet air forces in East Germany, and the that of the GDR, to allow unheeded access or risk war.

The British element of the operation was given the unclassified reference 'Sharp Lance', which, despite being unclassified for reference purposes, was classified top secret as to its actual meaning.

The French Air Force committed 25 F-100D Super Sabres to the operation, deploying these aircraft from Reims to the USAF base at Spangdahlem, while the US Air Force made twenty-five F-100C available at their Bitburg base. The British contribution at the time was Javelins and Hunters drawn from Nos 5 and 14 Squadrons, operating from Gütersloh. The RAF element ultimately fell under the command of C-in-C RAFG but more directly, the station commander at RAF Gütersloh was the tactical commander. The American commander, C-in-C USAFE (commander in chief United States Air Forces in Europe), would exercise control through the Jack Pine command post, which was set up at the US 17th Air Force combat operations centre at Kindsbach.

The RAF radar station at Auenhausen would be the principal provider of any necessary GCI. All allied aircraft were monitored and directed by Auenhausen. The usual accepted shortfall in available aircraft was 30 per cent; for the units assigned to the corridor escort, it was 20 per cent. With 5 Squadron being based at Laarbruch, should this operation be put into practice, two Pembroke twin-prop-powered aircraft would be positioned at Laarbruch to support the deployment of 5 Squadron personnel to Gütersloh.

Callsigns in Use for Corridor Operations

Jack Pine Command Post	Sea Hawk
Auenhausen CRP (Control & Reporting Post)	Backwash
USAF Wing	Stale
RAF Tactical Wing	Light up
RAF Transport Wing	Answer
FAF Wing	Mazurka
Emergency	Mayday

By Christmas, the decision was taken to deploy Firestreak-armed Mk 9 Javelins from 29 Squadron based at RAF Leuchars. This irritated many, specifically those of the Germany-based Javelin squadrons, whose earlier Mk 4 and 5 versions were armed only with 30-mm Aden cannons.

The ongoing climate with Germany being a flashpoint seemed to have a negative impact beyond what could go wrong. The constant, if varying, tension may have driven the Air Ministry/MOD and RAF to fight shy of any long-term investment in West Germany. The clear logic leant toward the likelihood of the continent going up in flames at any minute. Combined with the usual heel-dragging and bureaucracy (endemic in western democracies, to a lesser degree in the USA) over defence investments, the long-term plans for the RAF in Germany were not particularly promising anyway.

So, despite the pressing demands of the situation, the RAF still felt it could not commit to an extensive building programme on its remaining five operational air bases (Jever was handed to the Luftwaffe in 1961) in Germany due to the uncertainty of the extent of the long-term deployment. They did not expect to still have the five bases in the country by 1968. They wanted certainty until at least then, before committing any funds to building upgrades and starting new projects.

So much was marred by the lack of clarity and information at the time, that the principal long-term programme—the future basing in Germany of potentially the most advanced and capable strike aircraft that had escaped the cull of 1957–61, the TSR2—was now being affected.

The TSR-2 was a supremely advanced design, even though the first prototype was yet to fly. With the Canberra still the sole aircraft with which RAFG would retaliate with nuclear weapons, the TSR-2 promised a quantum leap in every aspect of performance and capability. The tensions were perhaps, as is well-publicised, at their height in the early 1960s. RAF Laarbruch, as a typical example, had put in place plans for the evacuation of all the operational personnel, simply known as 'Project E—Evacuation'.

In certain circumstances, the evacuation of Laarbruch by personnel of 5 Detachment (USAF maintenance personnel) and a unit called 6 Tactical

Depot Squadron were a particular concern. In the event, OC Tech Wing was to arrange for a thirty-three-seater coach with assigned driver, together with twenty-six 3.5-ton trucks with drivers, all to assemble at the special storage area. This commitment was to take absolute priority. The station provost officer was to arrange for a security escort for the convoy. In the case of an airlift evacuation, security guards were to be positioned at the special storage area as required by OC 5 Detachment. If the evacuation was to be made by road after all, then OC Admin Wing was to ensure that the airmen's mess prepared packed meals for at least sixty personnel for twenty-four hours on receipt of the order to evacuate.

OC 5 Detachment would command all involved in the evacuation. The plan was tested on 2 October 1961 with the implementation of Exercise Quick Train; all of 2 ATAF were involved. The exercise assumed the detection of a large-scale attack with little warning. All 2 ATAF units were to implement their plans for general alert 'R/Hour', which meant they were to launch all aircraft with pre-allocated tasks at the outbreak of hostilities. They were to bring the remainder of aircraft to the highest state of operational readiness with aircraft armed and, where possible, aircrews in their cockpits.

Exercise Quick Train very much set the pace for the future of NATO exercises and came to typify life on any operational RAF station at home and abroad. However, the epicentre of all such activity would be north-west Germany, where time to react was at an absolute premium. No one knew what was going on for sure until personnel arrived at their duty position. It never encouraged any degree of complacency that most exercises were instigated in the early hours of the morning to ensure everybody was at their 'best'.

Quick Train became typical in so far as the form of execution of the order went. On receipt of such, the duty operations officer was to follow a set procedure, starting with a broadcast over the station tannoy and the sounding of the station alert hooter. In addition to this, an ambulance and a fire tender were to drive around all the messes, singles' accommodation, and married quarters, sounding their sirens. In later years, verbal messages were broadcast through a loud haler and, in some cases, recorded messages on the station tannoy system—'alert, alert, this the station alert, all personnel are to report for duty'. This would continue for over an hour with a warbling siren or tone in between. Speakers were positioned in all messes and accommodation.

The vehicles were not to be driven at more than 10 miles per hour. The order meant exactly that—'all personnel to report for duty' officers with wartime appointments were to report to these posts. This was not necessarily restricted to officers as there were NCOs and junior ranks as well who may have some off-piste location to head for. For example, the author was to make his way from Spadeadam in Cumbria to Whitehall to join the MOD CCTV staff.

If the alarm sounded while flying was in progress, Air Traffic Control were to recall all aircraft airborne on normal peacetime training missions. Any aircraft under sector control would be ordered to return by the sector controller; this is largely likely to have been the case with interceptors on GCI sorties. Flight plans for standing or automatic sorties assigned to 16 and 31 Squadrons (in Laarbruch's case) were to be completed and issued to the movements section at operations. Aircraft were to be equipped and 'armed' as for their normal war mission. For the Canberras of 16 Squadron, this would mean with the Mk 7 bombs.

No. 5 Detachment of the USAF were to assist 16's personnel; for the purposes of the exercise, drill purpose rounds (also known as 'shapes') were used. Those aircraft on battle flight—essentially 5 Squadron and QRA for 16 Squadron—were to remain so as they fell inside what the Americans refer to as 'real world'. For the purposes of the exercise, all of 5 Squadron's available aircraft were to go to telebrief scrambler; a maximum of six of their aircraft would be scrambled for sector control, while any more aircraft launched would be brought under sector control as consoles became available. What this means is the Javelins would be assigned to the direction of a ground control intercept officer, the plan being for six to be allocated in the initial operational task.

The scramble of any further aircraft would have to wait until an additional controller at the GCI station became available. Although not based at Laarbruch, more Javelins from 85 Squadron, present at the time of Exercise Quick Train, were also to go to standby on the telebrief scrambler. This required crews at cockpit readiness. Once ordered off, 85 Sqn's jets would be brought under close control by the sector GCI.

Nos 16 and 31 Squadron aircraft were to taxi to the end of the runway and await launch instructions to attack their pre-designated targets at the discretion of the station commander (in the case of 31, the targets would be the subject of pre- and post-strike reconnaissance). Wing, squadron, and unit commanding officers were to use their own private transport, otherwise coaches were to report to the officers' mess and various identified barrack blocks, to collect all squadron personnel to drive all to their respective squadron locations. Reports were to be fed back to ops, on the response time of each.

Live QRA strike crews responded to such exercises, which in the future would be Tacevals and Minevals. After checking in with operations, they would cross the loading pan, taking the live target folders with them. They then checked into the USAF guard post, where they contacted ops again, to inform them they were returning to the QRA quarters; they then did so and checked in a final time from the QRA quarters.

After their walk-on part in this spot of theatre, the live QRA crews took no further part in the exercise. The composition of NATO Allied Forces across

West Germany was (by the end of 1961–beginning of 1962) consolidated. The formation of NATO's central region air element was now composed of the 2nd and 4th Allied Tactical Air Forces. By this point, No. 2 ATAF included the northern half of the new *Bundes Luftwaffe* and the American tactical air elements based in the United Kingdom. The 4th Allied Tactical Air Force was the southern element; this was composed of USAF units based in the FRG and southern-based German units.

The southern air force also included the 1st Canadian Air Division, later 1st Canadian Air Group, the deployed element of the Royal Canadian Air Force. In 1962, with two squadrons per wing, 1 CAG deployed four wings—the first and second were based at Marville and Grostenquin, both in France, and the third and fourth in West Germany respectively at Zweibrucken and Baden Sollingen. Each was equipped with an AWI squadron operating CF-100 Canuks and a squadron of F-86 Sabres. By 2 March 1964, the RCAF in the north-western European theatre in both France and West Germany began replacing these with Lockheed C-F104 Starfighters, all armed with nuclear weapons. Eventually, all eight RCAF squadrons were armed with the C-F104. The maintenance unit for the Canadian CF-104s was located at Prestwick airport in Ayrshire, Scotland.

Together with the corresponding land force elements, Northag and Centag, this largely remained the structure of NATO's Central European Force. This is the essential peacetime military posture that stood sentinel against any likelihood of a Soviet-led Warsaw Pact incursion into north-west Europe, at the time. There would be ongoing changes to the posture before the end of the Cold War. Danish and Norwegian forces formed the essential elements of AFNORTH (Allied Forces Northern Europe). The Royal Marines were predominantly assigned to reinforce Norway in the event of hostilities developing here. Various Royal Navy, RAF, US Navy, and US Air Force elements were assigned to AFNORTH with similar contributions from the FRG, Netherlands, and Canada, with Iceland playing its part as a strategic location. HQ for AFNORTH was at Kolsas near Oslo.

AAFCE had their headquarters at the US airbase at Ramstein; they were the only purely air force command element in Nato, existing due to the heavy air presence in the central region. AFCENT moved its HQ to Brunssum in the Netherlands. All were under the command of SACEUR, based in 1961 at the NATO HQ in Paris.

This was the reporting structure of three of four principal commands within NATO. There remained AFSOUTH headquartered in Naples. Finally, there was SACLANT (supreme allied commander Atlantic), whose headquarters was at the US naval station at Norfolk, Virginia. SACLANT's responsibility covered the essential length and breadth of the Atlantic—from the Arctic Circle south to the Tropic of Cancer and from the East coast of the USA across to the west coast of Africa and Europe.

However, the principal concern over north-west Europe invariably centred around the Federal Republic of Germany. This is where the bulk of military personnel and hardware was concentrated on either side of the Iron Curtain; where the Kremlin's concern was concentrated and therefore that of NATO; where the bulk of both sides finished up in 1945; and where the main thrust of a Soviet-led attack would come.

The Russians remained convinced that the West posed a continuous military threat. The likelihood of a Fourth Reich, regardless of the oversight of the United States, to the Russians was most likely. West Germany by the end of the 1950s was experiencing the early promise of the *Wunderwirtschaft* (economic miracle). The country was now a model of democracy and tolerance, with an enviable industrial output to boot. This served in no way to ameliorate Soviet wariness; instead, the concerns of the USSR were that a strong West Germany would pose more of a future military threat. It made no difference to the Kremlin that West Germany was a model of liberal democracy in the post-war years, even though this was the reason for the strengthening economy. A strong Germany was not the Kremlin's fear, rightly or wrongly. To be brutally frank, the Kremlin wanted all of Germany under full Soviet control to hand over everything in war reparations. That West Germany and West Berlin, by no small miracle, resided in the western sphere of influence upset the Russians after the cost they had paid in blood in the Second World War, especially given that Germany reneged on the peace treaty signed in 1939.

The old argument posed that it was subjugation of Germany in defeat in 1918, imposed by the victors of the First World War, which in part led to the dreadful privations of the depression of the 1930s. This in turn paved the way for the prominence and rise of national socialism. However true this may have been, it was never likely to convince the old men in the Kremlin that circumstances would never develop along similar lines again.

Apart from the resurgence of Nazi Germany, the capitalist system could not be trusted not to take a sympathetic approach to fascist stirrings. This was at the heart of East/West relations—capitalism *v.* communism or democracy *v.* communism. So went the thinking east of the Iron Curtain. What has never been properly understood is that along with the acceptance of the commercial markets in all western democracies, the western democracies embraced varying degrees of liberal socialism, West Germany certainly not least among them. Such progressive attitudes were not a feature of Soviet socialism.

The RAFG restructure was all but complete by the end of 1961. The end of the fighter squadron cull had been reached as well, essentially. The air defence element of RAFG had been boiled down to two all-weather squadrons (5 and 11 Sqns with Javelin Mk 4s and 5s), both to be based at Geilenkirchen and one day fighter unit (14 Sqn with Hunter F6s) at Gütersloh. A letter from the director of operations, air defence, in April 1962 described the fighter situation Germany as 'sterile'.

Firestreak-armed Javelins had been deployed from UK bases since September 1961, but the director of ops was concerned that the deployment was endless, showing no signs of the deployed units being withdrawn. The prospect of the commitment continuing indefinitely was causing concern to Fighter Command. This thorn in Fighter Command's side would continue; 'gun only' armed fighters were no longer acceptable to SACEUR with respect to Jack Pine. Re-equipment of RAFG's interceptors was the only solution, yet the three squadrons of RAFG were to be withdrawn by the end of 1962 and were therefore withdrawn from 2 ATAF's orbat.

Fighter Command's seven Javelin squadrons were reduced to six effectively due to modifications to the Mk 9R aircraft, to carry long-range tanks and to the ongoing Germany deployment. Additionally, both a Hunter and a Lightning squadron were each assigned an aerobatics team commitment through to the end of the summer; realistically, the figure was four.

There was some expectation that two UK-based squadrons equipped with Mk 8 Javelins, both due to disband in the first half of 1963, would instead be used to replace the remaining Javelin units at Geilenkirchen. On the face of it, this was the best solution as SACEUR would get two permanently stationed missile-armed interceptor squadrons instead of just one on detachment. This was a plus, of sorts, for Fighter Command—they were losing two squadrons anyway (although earlier than planned) but would see this offset by the end of the long-term deployment.

Then there was the question of conversion. The Mk 4/5 Javelins currently *in situ* were fitted with AI.17 radar sets, while the Mk 8s were fitted with AI.22—a development of the American AN/APQ.43 radar and Firestreak. These were significant changes as the Javelin OCU had recently disbanded, meaning there might be a requirement for a training programme. These concerns were considered the counter argument—that the two squadrons could not just move to Germany and replace the older units. There was also the need to plan to accommodate the later version Javelins on a permanent footing in Germany.

It was not expected that a straight transfer of the two Mk 8 squadrons would be all there was to it. In the end, while this plan was not followed verbatim, any worries about a quick transfer were managed with few teething problems.

The RAF's tradition of preserving the oldest and most illustrious squadron numbers gave rise to proposals to renumber three Canberras squadrons—213 as 5, 80 as 11, and 88 as 14. In early 1962, this proposal was based on the notion that the Javelins were to be replaced by Lightnings but would be withdrawn ahead of this. The eventual outcome was that two missile-armed

Mk 9 Javelin squadrons—25 and 33—were to disband in the UK; their aircraft then were to be deployed to Germany. These aircraft would be renumbered 5 and 11.

Further to this, 213 and 80 were recognised as 'standard' squadrons, granting them a degree of sympathy when ordering the disbandment of units. So, the renumber of these two was cancelled; it also made it easier to renumber the Javelins from the UK. Meanwhile, 88 not being blessed with the same degree of traditional privilege—not having the pedigree of a 'standard' unit—meant its colours were destined for St Clement Danes in London, this being the final location for the laying up of squadron flags.

Following a long and continuous service with an illustrious history, 14 Sqn had the honour, upon relinquishing its Hunters, of living on with 88's Canberras. The old jets got a quick makeover—the Yellow Snake insignia disappeared and the 'Winged Crusader' with his cross of St George appeared on the fins instead. This meant that 14, 80, and 213 were, under the circumstances, allowed to survive; a different unit was to disband, to preserve those with seniority and notoriety.

By October 1962, the two Mk 9 squadrons transferred from Leuchars and Middleton St George to Germany were duly re-badged/repainted. This did not prevent the disbandment of the Mk 8 squadrons in 1963. Forward planning now placed two Lightning squadrons, which had not yet formed in the UK, from their home base at Leconfield to Geilenkirchen. As such, extensive works were afoot at Geilenkirchen to provide sufficient up-to-date support facilities for Lightnings. These facilities were expected to be ready by December 1964.

Up to this point, the units based at Geilenkirchen followed a similar pattern established at most RAFG airfields—tactical strike/attack squadron and two interceptor units, instead of (in the case of the other clutch bases) a tactical reconnaissance squadron. Thus began a move to a more concentrated role at each base. The new facilities at Geilenkirchen were to include an 'electronics centre', a new building to house a Lightning flight simulator, Firestreak storage, and servicing facilities. The Lightnings were not to move until all was ready.

In the end, just one of the two squadrons, 92, moved to Geilenkirchen at the end of December 1965. Earlier, in September, the second squadron, 19, moved from Leconfield direct to Gütersloh.

As the Federal Republic of Germany was still acclimatising as an independent sovereign state (still living with a small degree of oversight from the wartime allied powers with respect to West Berlin and defence of its own airspace) with its own armed forces, there was some difficulty experienced in accommodating the allied armed forces in their new posture of reinforced defence, as well as the new *Bundeswehr*. The RAF had been approached by the government in Bonn with a view to accessing the storage facilities at RAF bases. Space for training and storage was at a premium. The Germans were looking for 10,000 to 30,000 sq. metres of covered depot space and were hinting at such space being made available under the control of the RAF's 431 Maintenance Unit located at Brüggen. To achieve the necessary cost reductions, the RAF had absorbed a freight handling outfit, No. 86 Movements Unit, into 431 MU; the upshot of this meant no spare room.

The Germans also requested space to store 300 to 600 tons of ammunition and in this regard were hinting at the four clutch airbases as well as 398 MU based at Duren, located between Aachen and Cologne. Room was tight here as well, but again, to economise, a British field hospital originally located at Melsbroek in Belgium was now co-located with 398 at Duren. In any case, the Duren option was quite impossible as regulations determined that ammunition and bombs be stored in categorised groups, meaning simple quantity of munitions had little to do with space available, as no explosive stores could be mixed. As it was, the RAF had insufficient room for their own operational stores on the clutch airfields due to SACEUR's strictly applied safety regulations on bases that housed Project E sites. Project E referred to the provision of nuclear weapons from the USAF to the RAF until such time as Britain was able to produce enough nuclear bombs to become self-sufficient.

Most of the bombs the RAF had stored for use by the units at the clutch airfields were stored at Duren, where capacity had been reached. In 1962, the West German Air Force had regained control of all its former airbases from the RAF, save for Gütersloh.

No storage space had been available here for the RAF, but since the Germans had resumed command of these airfields, they had managed to obtain some 10,000 cubic metres of storage. Maintenance facilities were also sought for F-104 aircraft that the new Luftwaffe were fast equipping with. None of the operational RAF airfields had either spare capacity or the facilities for the F-104 or any American aircraft for that matter. RAFG was described as having contracted as far as possible while still being able to carry out the operational role tasked by SACEUR.

Right: Clearing up, RAF bomb disposal unit preparing to blow up a pile of Luftwaffe 50-kg bombs, *c.* 1945–6. (*Air Historical Branch*)

Below: British and American aircrew, both military and civilian, involved in Operation Plainfare take a break in one of the Malcolm clubs; these were said to be of a better quality than the more familiar NAAFI-run junior ranks clubs. (*Air Historical Branch*)

Temporary canteen for personnel set up at RAF Wunstorf during the Berlin Airlift. (*Air Historical Branch*)

Not to disparage the NAAFI's long and distinguished service to HM Forces, this is a NAAFI wagon providing tea and rolls to personnel during the tense months of Operation Plainfare, 1948–49. (*Air Historical Branch*)

Avro Yorks of Transport Command on the apron at RAF Gatow in West Berlin, 16 September 1948. (*Air Historical Branch*)

Aerial photo of RAF Celle, *c.* 1949. At least seventeen USAF C-54 Skymasters (candy bombers) are dispersed around the airfield. Five RAF Avro Yorks can be seen near the hangars while nearer the foot of the picture, a couple of C-47 Skytrains. Such was the operational tempo during the Berlin Airlift.

Meteor FR9 of 2 (AC) Squadron with animated discussion between air and ground crew, 16 October 1951. (*Air Historical Branch*)

No. 2 Sqn Meteor FR9 gets airborne on a training sortie, the role of armed reconnaissance, which 2 (AC) Sqn had long specialised in, was vital to RAFG's ready posture. (*Air Historical Branch*)

A Venom FB1 of 11 Squadron with ground crew at RAF Wunstorf, 18 May 1953. Their Venom FB1s concentrated on tactical air support. (*Air Historical Branch*)

No. 11 Squadron pilots at Wunstorf, pre-sortie briefing, May 1953. (*Air Historical Branch*)

Start up. (*Air Historical Branch*)

Venom NF2 belonging to 33 Squadron, based at Driffield but visiting 2nd TAF, *c.* 1955. (*Peter March*)

No. 4 Sqn Hunters on APC (armament practice camp) at RAF Sylt near the coast, May 1956. A powered target drone is being prepared in the foreground. (*Air Historical Branch*)

North American F-86 Sabre F Mk 4s from 20 Sqn on the apron at RAF Oldenburg, *c.* 1954. (*Air Historical Branch*)

Unknown image of WRAF personnel on parade, *c.* 1955. (*Air Historical Branch*)

Canberra B(I)8, the first RAFG-deployed aircraft to carry nuclear weapons. Unlike later wholly British-designed aircraft, the Canberra was armed with US B7 and B43 bombs. (*Peter March*)

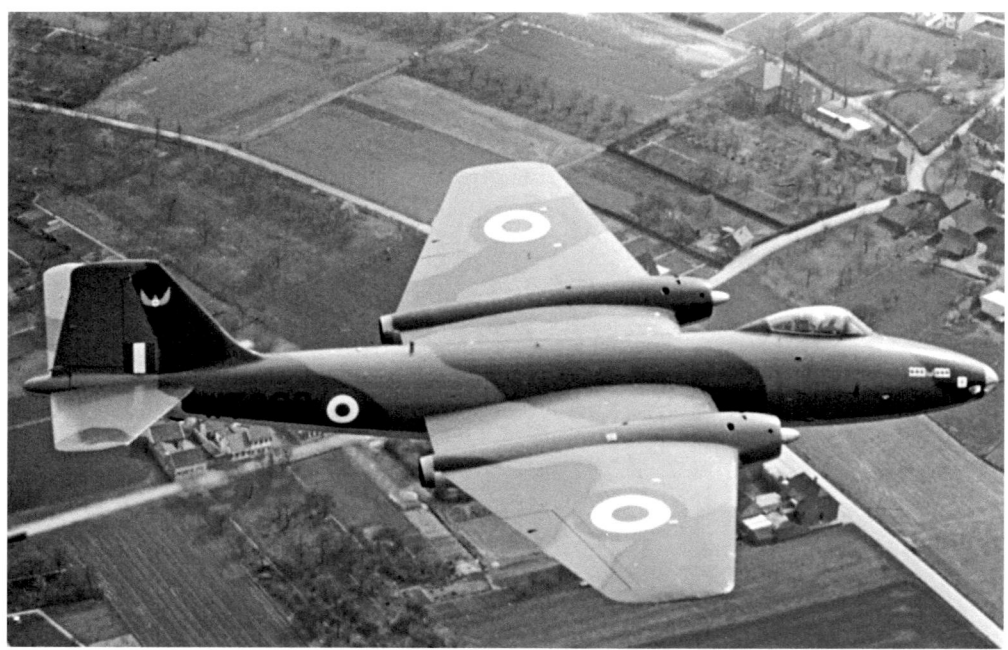

No. 14 Squadron Canberra B(I)8. The squadron took over the interdictor strike role from 88 Sqn in 1963 following a far-reaching restructure of operational units in order to give way to an all-missile force, a short-lived exercise that was abandoned after a brief period but not before a widespread disbandment of squadrons. (*Peter March*)

AOC's annual formal inspection at Bruggen, 10 June 1955. Air Vice-Marshal Ronald Lees takes the salute before station personnel; the F-86 Sabres are from 112 and 130 Sqns, and the LAA guns, either side of the dias, are from 55 Wing, RAF Regiment. (*The National Archives*)

During the AOC's annual inspection of any RAF station, near enough everywhere receives a visit and formal preparations are made; here it is the turn of the airmen's mess. The officer stood immediately behind Lees looks terrified that the catering sergeant is answering the AOC's questions with a little too much candour. (*The National Archives*)

A visit to an RAF regiment's LAA Bofors gun crew, the young chap on elevation appears to have his Mk 3 Helmet on back to front. The AOC's annual formal inspection means everything gets turned upside down. The visiting AOC never has time to inspect everywhere, but there is always the chance he will depart from the CO's prepared itinerary. (*The National Archives*)

AVM Lees inspects senior NCOs. (*The National Archives*)

Following the anti-communist student-led revolt in Hungary, started on 23 October 1956, the resultant crisis brought Transport Command aircraft staging through West Germany again. A 30 Squadron Vickers Valetta loads up at Wildenrath with emergency supplies to be delivered to Hungarian refugees escaping the Soviet-led backlash. (*Air Historical Branch*)

No. 118 Squadron Hunter based at RAF Jever. Both were victims of the 1957 cuts to the RAF's operational strength, with the promise of ground-launched missiles to offset the losses. (*Peter March*)

Hunter FR10, 4 Sqn, rapid turn-around at Wildenrath, during Exercise Royal, May 1963. (*Air Historical Branch*)

Above: Javelin FAW9 of 5 Squadron with air and ground crew at RAF Geilenkirchen, April 1963. (*Air Historical Branch*)

Left: Javelins of 5 Squadron at Geilenkirchen in formation with aircraft from 33 Sqn in November 1962; the latter were being changed to 5 Sqn and moved from Middleton St George to Geilenkirchen. (*Air Historical Branch*)

Above left: Aircrew walk from a 5 Sqn Javelin at Geilenkirchen, April 1963. (*Air Historical Branch*)

Above right: Canberra Mk 8s of 14 Sqn at RAF Wildenrath around 1967. (*Air Historical Branch*)

Above left: B(I)8 crew walk from their charge at Wildenrath, June 1967. At this time, it was still hoped that the cancelled TSR-2 replacement, the American F-111, would replace the aging Canberras. (*Air Historical Branch*)

Above right: NATO Exercise hosted at Wildenrath, 14 Sqn B(I)8 alongside F-104Gs, fulfilling the strike role for the Bundes Luftwaffe, June 1967. The F-104s here are from the Nörvenich-based JBG31 (fighter bomber wing), also on apron, with Mirage III all-weather interceptors of the French Air Force. (*Air Historical Branch*)

No. 19 Sqn Lightning F2s. Their supersonic charges arrived at Gütersloh at the end of September 1965, to relieve the Javelins at Geilenkirchen of the air defence role. (*Peter March*)

Battle Flight from 1962, known as 'QRA' (quick reaction alert). There are two Lightnings at Gütersloh armed, fuelled, and ready in their purpose-built QRA shed. (*Peter March*)

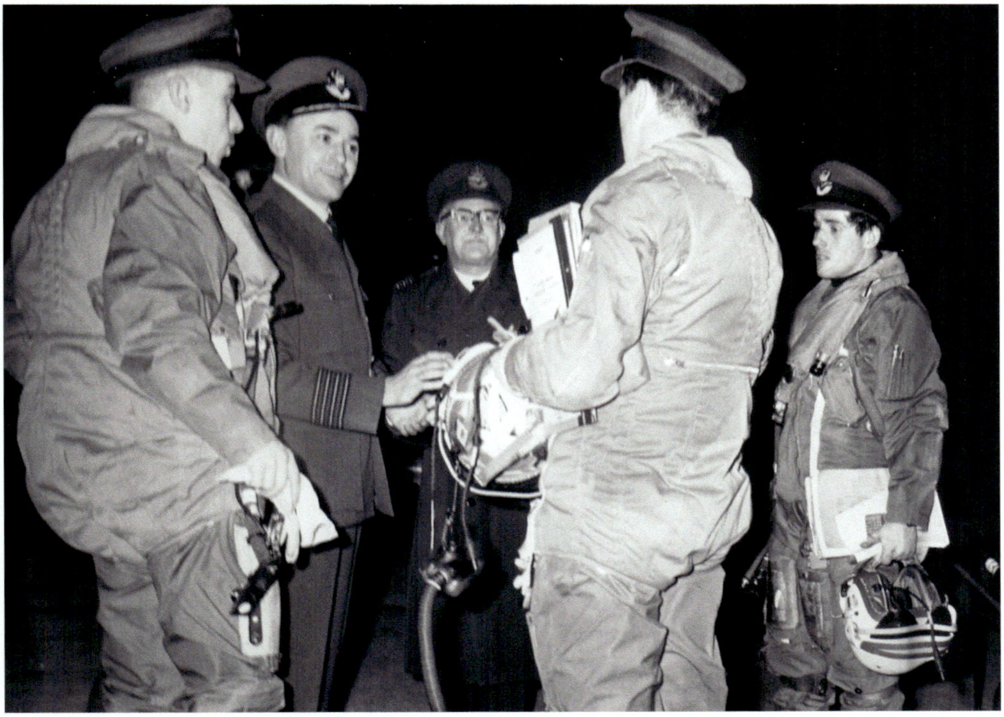

Group Captain William Hedley, station commander, RAF Geilenkirchen, welcomes Squadron Leader Joseph Gilbert, OC 92 Sqn, December 1965. The squadron had just arrived on posting from RAF Leconfield. In the background is Wing Commander G. R. Hadfield, STO. The officers to the right are unidentified, but are almost certainly two of 92 Sqn's pilots. (*The National Archives*)

No. 92 Sqn deployed from Leconfield in East Yorkshire to Germany shortly after as 19 Sqn. Initially, 92's Lightnings settled at Geilenkirchen, later moving to Gütersloh in January 1968 when the former station closed. (*Adrian Balch*)

HRH Prince Philip meets 16 Sqn Canberra crew at RAF Laarbruch during a visit, December 1968. (*Via Hugh Alexander*)

Ceremonial parade at RAF Laarbruch, with 16 Sqn Canberras in the background, April 1969. The reason for the occasion is not known but was probably the AOC's annual formal inspection. (*Via Hugh Alexander*)

Station formation flypast; the occasion was most likely the AOC's annual formal inspection. The lead eight aircraft are B(I)8s from 16 Sqn; the four jets at the rear are PR7s of 31 Sqn. (*Via Hugh Alexander*)

Visit to RAF Bruggen diving club by Air Chief Marshal Sir John Grandy, chief of the air staff, October 1967. The senior officer with the moustache is Air Marshal Sir Denis Spotswood, Grandy's future successor. (*Via Hugh Alexander*)

No. 20 Sqn Harrier GR1s deployed into the field during a tactical exercise, *c.* 1974. (*Peter March*)

Early shot of a 2 Squadron Phantom FGR2. This unit moved to Laarbruch to re-equip with the Phantom continuing the tactical reconnaissance role; note the recce pod on centre line. (*Adrian Balch*)

Left: Photograph taken in 1981 showing a 3 Sqn GR3 in camouflage hide during exercise with possibly an RAF officer in Mk 3 NBC kit. (*Air Historical Branch*)

Below: Panavia Tornado GR1 of 14 Squadron; despite its troubled gestation period in the 1970s, this aircraft provided RAFG with its most effective strike platform before the end of the Cold War. Following further defence cuts, the last Tonka's out-of-service date was brought forward from 2024, with the last pensioned off in 2019. (*Peter March*)

Harrier GR3 of 4 Sqn. It is unclear if this photo was taken on a NATO airfield dispersal or at a hidden deployment location; the jet itself is clean apart from a centreline pod and guns and preparing for vertical lift off. (*Peter March*)

Harrier from previous photo now airborne using 100 per cent thrust vectoring. (*Peter March*)

Officers and pilots of the recently reformed 2 Squadron, with one of their new charges, *c*. August 1976. (*Via Hugh Alexander*)

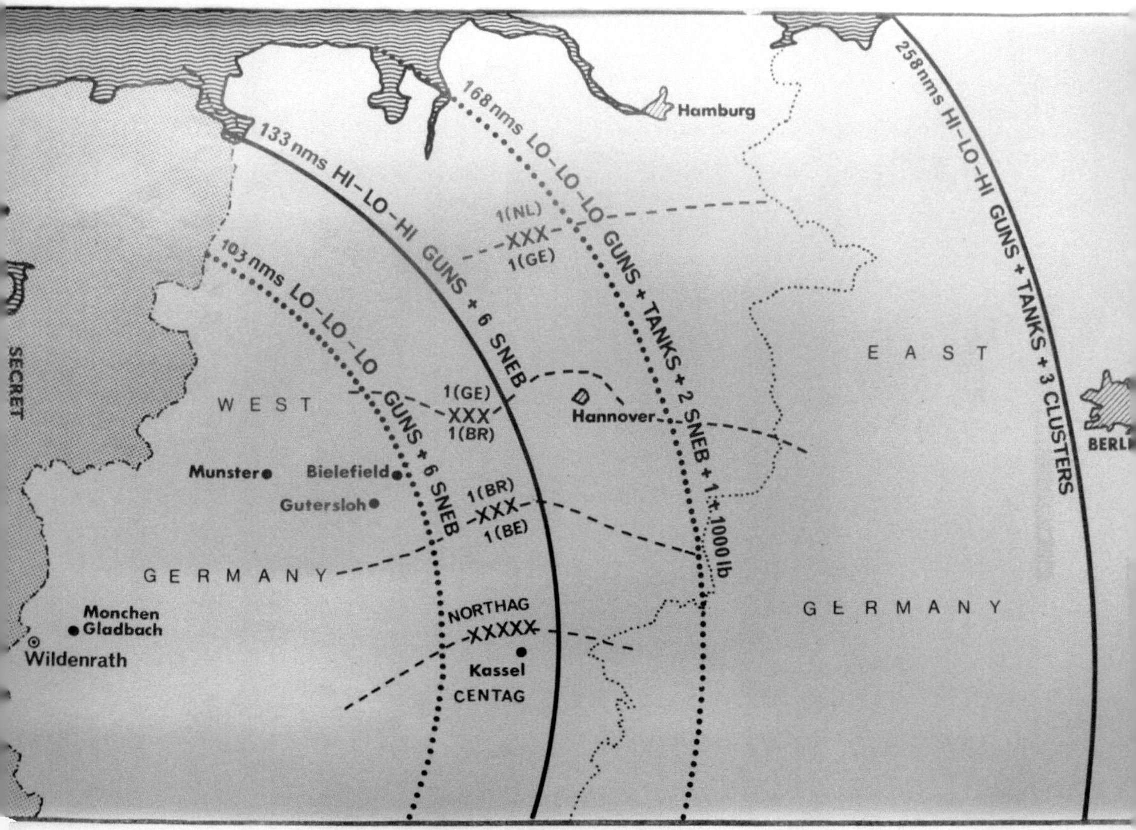

Chart showing range of Harriers, if operating direct from Wildenrath, under differing configurations. (*The National Archives*)

A Phantom in the newer, toned-down grey colour scheme. (*Tony Paxton*)

Newly issued 2 Squadron Jaguar GR1s lead a pair of outgoing Phantoms, *c*. 1977. (*Peter March*)

During the mid/late 1970s, RAFG units re-equipped and redeployed again. As the Jaguar replaced the Phantom in strike and reconnaissance roles, the latter in turn replaced the Lightning in the interceptor and tactical air defence role. No. 19 Sqn Phantom is at low level. (*Adrian Balch*)

Another aspect of the 1970s restructure saw the Harrier force upgraded to the GR3, with the bottle-shaped extension of the nose cone, which housed the new laser rangefinder and uprated Pegasus engine, adding another 1,000 lb of thrust. This aircraft of 3 Sqn is using its much-publicised party-piece—thrust vectoring. (*Peter March*)

No. 20 Sqn Harriers during routine operational training on the flightline at RAF Wildenrath, *c.* 1975. (*Peter March*)

This Lightning F2A waits on QRA in standby shelter during a detachment at RAF Bruggen, August 1970. (*Air Historical Branch*)

No. 20 Sqn Harrier in its natural cold war environment, in the German countryside. The two 30-mm Aden gun pods are noticeable under the fuselage. (*Peter March*)

Again, a Harrier in its hide—a camouflaged, sheltered clearing at a location in any useable environment outside the airfield. Deployment of the Harrier force to forward secret operating locations (as secret as any military forward position can be) had to be established at the earliest opportunity to meet what would be an overwhelming Soviet assault across the inner German border. This could happen under any circumstances and could take NATO, to a degree, by surprise. It would be a Soviet invasion as East German forces, essentially to avoid having to confront their fellow countrymen, would be assigned to the attack on Denmark. The deployment of the Harrier force, therefore, had to be in place as early as possible. (*Peter March*)

No. 92 Sqn Lightning F2A in earlier natural metal finish with decorative squadron markings. (*Adrian Balch*)

No. 92 Sqn Phantom. The American jets were transferred from the strike role to replace the Lightnings in the air defence task. (*Adrian Balch*)

No. 16 Squadron (the Saints) Buccaneer—an early photograph showing the underside still painted light grey instead of the wrap-around dark grey/green adopted from 1977. (*Adrian Balch*)

From 1968, 19 and 92 Squadrons upgraded their Mk 2 Lightnings to Mk 2A standard, two 19 Sqn aircraft, after the upgrade, appear to be climbing just after pair take-off. (*Adrian Balch*)

No. 19 Sqn Lightning F2A landing at Gütersloh. The aircraft has the forest green upper surface scheme introduced from about 1973. (*Adrian Balch*)

No. 17 Squadron Phantom taken around 1974, by which time the Sepecat Jaguar was beginning to replace the Phantom in the UK. By 1976, after a brief association, 17 Sqn re-equipped with the Jaguar; many thought this a retrograde move. (*Adrian Balch*)

No. 14 was the first RAFG squadron to re-equip with F-4 Phantom; after all the trouble with TSR-2 and F-111 projects, the arrival of the Phantom, together with the Buccaneer, represented a truly quantum leap in performance and relative survivability for those tasked with the nuclear strike role. (*Air Historical Branch*)

Arriving in Germany at the same time as the F-4 Phantom, the Buccaneer Mk 2 was viewed as a poor consolation by the RAF, following a disastrous decade looking for a Canberra replacement. However, they found they had a most capable aircraft on their hands and very much equal to the task. These aircraft carry the markings of 15 Sqn. (*Air Historical Branch*)

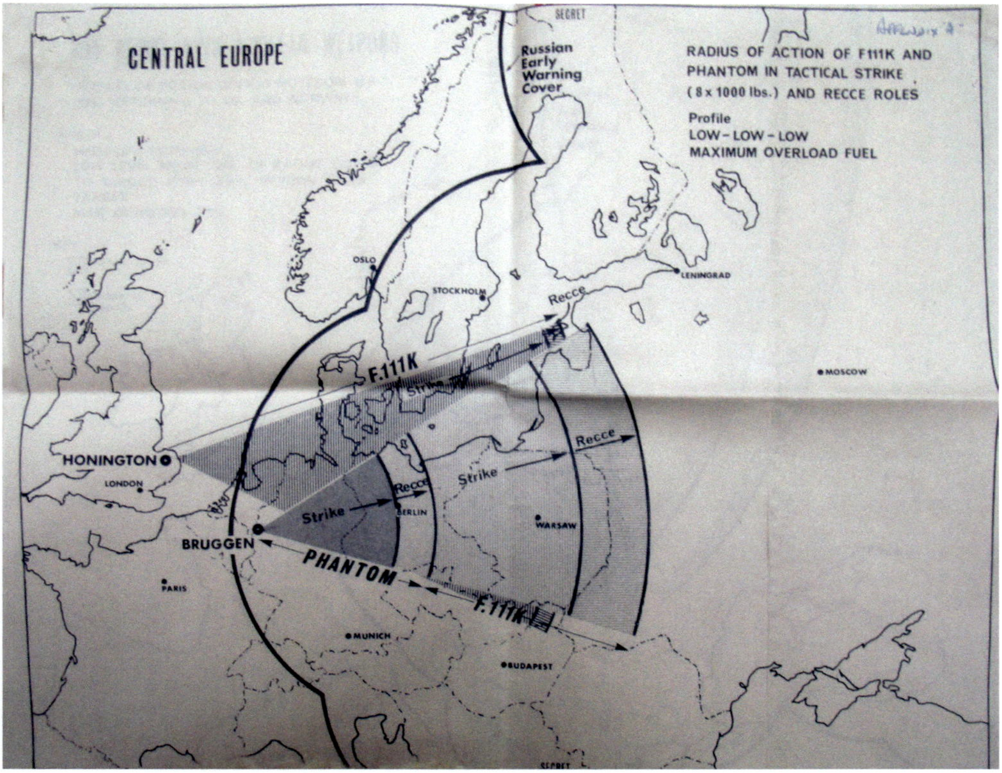

Chart showing the comparison of the same aircraft tasked against Central Europe from East Anglia and north-west Germany. (*The National Archives*)

Fasching parade through a German town—an annual festival every February. (*Tony Hawes*)

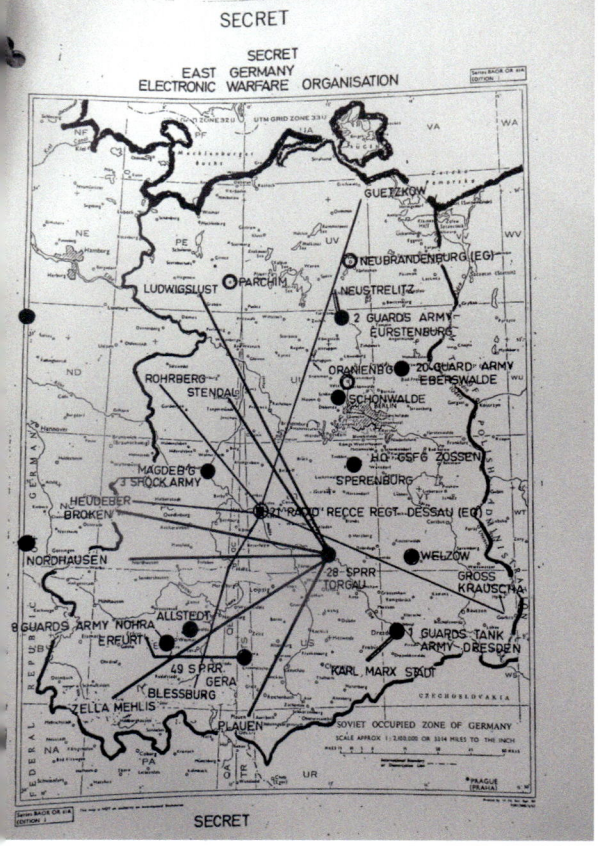

Above: No. 17 Sqn Phantom returning from the range. Bruggen-based Phantoms were armed with the US B43 bomb. (*Adrian Balch*)

Left: This map of East Germany is intended to show the location of Soviet electronic communications intercept stations. However, it also gives a clear idea of the positioning of the GSFG (group of Soviet forces Germany) order of battle. (*The National Archives*)

Soviet electronic intercept site Zella Mehlis. Eavesdropping on all manner of communications was a vital component of Cold War routine military activity. (*The National Archives*)

Brocken Soviet communications intercept site. (*The National Archives*)

No. 2 Squadron was the last unit in RAFG to convert to the Tornado. This looks like a rather scintillating flypast by one of the new charges with two retiring Jaguars—a GR1A and a T2A—over or alongside Laarbruch Air Traffic Control, 8 February 1988. (*The National Archives*)

Panavia Tornado GR1 getting airborne in full afterburner, as evening appears to be encroaching, to head off on a live sortie over Kosovo, 1999. (*Air Historical Branch*)

7

The Canberra Question (TSR-2 and F-111 Cancellations)

The first-ever jet bomber in the free world was already overdue replacement as a light bomber/tactical strike aircraft, even in July 1958 when the first squadron in RAF Germany was declared operational in the nuclear role. There was a potential outstanding replacement that would have set the clock forward many years and a home-grown product to boot, but, however much at hand, the new tactical bomber for the RAF may have been, it had to get past Westminster. First, a bone of contention, especially for the other services and a headache for the air forces of the world, was the rate at which aircraft performance was improving and how it was offset by the rate at which the unit cost was increasing. Logically, the leaps and bounds in airframe and engine performance, coupled with further leaps and bounds in avionics technology, meant leaps and bounds in financial outlay.

Range did not necessarily get better with new types, but in the case of the TSR-2, range was double that of the Canberra. Some degree of progress in performance was very much expected at the time but when comparing the Canberra with the jet expected to take its place on the front line, the contrast revealed a staggering step forward in all respects.

Whatever the loss to the RAF's fighting capability and the British aircraft industry over the preceding years, this was one aircraft project that survived while at such an early stage of development.

For the RAF, four of its operational commands needed a replacement for their own ageing, outclassed, and vulnerable Canberra bombers. There was little hope of ground-launched missiles being relied upon for this role. These were seen more and more as the blunt instrument completely devoid of versatility that it was. Back in the UK, Bomber Command made some inroads to replacing the V-force by deploying loaned American Thor IRBMs, which reached their full flourish with twenty squadrons—just as with the Bloodhound surface-to-air missile, and similarly, its lack of flexibility rendered its use final and irretrievable. Bombers can always be recalled; yet once a missile is launched, it cannot be recalled, and there is no self-destruct button. So, reliance on manned aircraft carries inestimable value in such high-stakes brinkmanship. The understood reason for the cancellation of Thor was, however, its obsolescence courtesy of ICBMs.

The Thor squadrons were deployed at twenty bases, mostly surplus wartime airfields, with three missiles per squadron. So, sixty nuclear Thor IRBMs were sited across much of east England from 1959; they were all operational by April 1962. They were all gone by September 1963.

The Canberra was an aircraft that was quickly overtaken by faster, more agile designs operated by other NATO air arms. The old jet stood a poor enough chance of delivering a bomb anywhere, never mind sufficiently deep into the Warsaw Pact. It had enjoyed not much of a heyday in the nuclear role; even before 1960, the Canberra desperately needed to be replaced.

As the 1960s dawned, the Canberra was still in widespread service and in a variety of roles but essentially as a light bomber and reconnaissance aircraft. In the latter, the Mk 7s and 9s were enjoying a greater deal of success in the high-altitude recce role, mapping routes and targets for Bomber Command and RAF Germany. Cyprus and Singapore also deployed Canberras with the option to carry nuclear weapons. They also had the benefit of the high-altitude services of the reconnaissance Canberras. In the strike role, the aircraft was at far greater risk. The strategic strike was fully UK-based and in 1962 carried by the V-force—the Valiant, Vulcan, and Victor.

RAFG had the Mk 6 and 8 interdictor Canberras deployed one squadron a piece at each base apart from Gütersloh. Alongside were the three reconnaissance squadrons and two small squadrons of Hunters for low-level tactical reconnaissance. The new design that promised salvation was the TSR-2 (tactical strike reconnaissance). Its survival as far as 1960 might owe something to it not being an air defence fighter—the real target of Sandys' missile obsession. This design soaked up most of the redundancy across the UK aircraft industry regarding military projects. It has often been described (or derided) as the first aircraft designed by a committee as opposed to a team headed by a chief design engineer. The likeness to a town hall committee came about as various characters came on board from their own cancelled work and proceeded to make their own recommendations.

On 16 September 1957, the eight UK aircraft manufacturing companies had a meeting with the Air Ministry's permanent secretary, Sir Cyril Musgrave, who accepted the recent white paper had cast doubt on the aviation industry, but he wanted to draw attention to G0R.339 (government operational requirement). This was a large-scale project. The government was not looking to award the contract to meet this requirement to a single company—instead, two or three firms, or a cluster around a lead firm, was how the project would proceed.

This was government pressure to amalgamate ultimately two project teams—English Electric and Vickers—which took the lead. Sir Cyril had implied that the government expected there to be enough work for three or four different project design teams, but if the companies could not come to an agreement on this, the government would make a selection. BAC was the result; this was effectively a nationalised aerospace company and they took over as sole design contractor. The government thinking was, such projects were going to become more costly and complex and the way to address this was to bring the best in various disciplines under one lead group. This meant the amalgamation of several aviation firms into one—BAC, known today as BAE Systems.

The air staff expected it would meet the requirement not just to replace the Canberra in the tactical nuclear role, but the V-force in the medium/strategic nuclear role. What was indispensable was the specified performance that the aircraft would be capable of. TSR-2 (or whatever aircraft got the job) would need to be able to operate at a considerable distance behind enemy lines. Aircraft operating from Brüggen and Laarbruch would be expected to attack targets that, if hit, would seriously disrupt the progress of Warsaw Pact forces fighting through West Germany and elsewhere. Targets considered vital would include, but not be restricted to, marshalling yards, bridges, and airfields. The requirements were very exacting; in addition, the successful candidate would need to be able to reach supersonic speeds at low-level, by day and by night, indifferent to the most shocking weather conditions. To cut to the chase, a contract for the full development of the TSR-2 was placed with BAC in October 1960.

More specific details followed. The proposed design would be able to reach 725 knots at sea level (Mach 1.1) with a high-altitude performance of Mach 2.25. The engines had already been identified; these were the Bristol Siddeley Olympus R22 Turbojets (augmented) and a virtually unjammable navigation system that was impervious to weather. TSR-2 would be an integrated weapons system able to carry a wide variety of both conventional and nuclear stores. The all-weather capability essentially referred to the delivery of nuclear munitions. Conventional weapons would not be deployed unless the final stage of the attack could be done visually, determined by the accuracy required. The new plane would be able to alternately carry a reconnaissance pod, also fully effective in all weathers, day and night, and would be able to operate from smaller airfields, allowing rapid deployment at instant notice with all support equipment air transportable.

In the conventional role, it would carry 8,000 lb of bombs, 2-inch rocket packs or cluster bombs, or up to four AJ 168 ASMs (Martel), which were under development at the time, primarily for Blackburn's NA.39 Buccaneer, for the Royal Navy. In the reconnaissance role, the recce pack would carry line scan cameras and a sideways-looking radar, which would be unaffected by the weather. For nuclear strike, two weapons—likely WE177—would be carried.

No. 35 Reconnaissance packs were to be purchased to meet that role. The aircraft based in Germany would be assigned such roles as part of SACEUR'S atomic strike plan. Elsewhere, they would be assigned such tasks in the Near, Middle, and Far East, in support of the UK's interests and treaty obligations.

As for survivability, TSR-2 would be 'viable against the most sophisticated defences'. This would be particularly pertinent regarding the RAFG-based TSR-2s. Most ground-breaking of all, TSR-2 carried what was still being referred to in slightly more aspirational terms as 'all-weather low flying capability', later referred to as 'terrain following radar (TFR)'. For all these attributes, in comparison with the type it was essentially going to replace, the range of advantages were startling. The Canberra had a radius of action of 570 nautical miles, even if a return at high-level was assumed. Therefore, the existing Canberras on German bases were unable to reach certain targets, which were on SACEUR's atomic strike plan. The TSR-2 offered a radius of action of almost 1,000 nm able to reach all designated targets in the hi-lo-lo-hi sortie profile, even those situated inside what was described as 'Metropolitan Russia while still avoiding the hazardous high-level portion of the return flight over enemy territory'.

The proposed new wonder jet would cope with weather conditions anytime day or night with such a greater degree of navigation and bombing accuracy, well outside of the Canberra's capabilities. A further advantage would be the ability to change targets mid-sortie over hostile territory, again a feature as familiar to the Canberra as to the Avro Lancaster. Among the strategic targets this tactical aircraft could hit was Moscow. Such a target would be within the range of TSR-2s, even if operating from bases in the UK, with a return high-level route to either Norway or Turkey. A wider range of targets would be available to the Germany-based squadrons.

As of 1960, the forecast for getting the first nuclear-armed squadron declared operational was expected by the end of 1967. Preceding this, there would be six pre-production models delivered to the Bomber Command development unit. The build-up of squadrons would then continue expecting to achieve full deployment in both the UK and West Germany by April 1970. Completion of squadrons deployed to the NEAF and FEAF was forecast for April 1971. Conversion training was to be the responsibility of 237 OCU, which would be based at Coningsby.

All was worked out in fine detail; training of maintenance personnel would be carried out at Hemswell, still a serving station at the time and a base for the Thor IRBM. In keeping with the usual form of introducing new and particularly advanced aircraft, crewmembers on their second tour were the least familiar who would be selected to go through the OCU and form the first squadrons. For all the trepidation of getting to grips with such a beast, the RAF were hopeful that by 1970 and before the final squadron was declared they would be able to select crewmembers on their first tour and *ab initio* types straight from advanced flying training who were yet to complete a conversion course onto any operational type. For prospective TSR-2 pilots, there would be a lead-in training period where whatever the pilot's background, they would become acquainted with the Hunter. The use of the flight simulator would be very much to the fore thereafter, both on the OCU and continuing onto the operational squadrons.

At the time all of this was being proposed, not a single airframe existed and the actual design study and costing were yet to be arrived at, with consideration being given to a dual (two-stick) training example. Low-level flying training was, naturally, to play a major part in crew training, and Goose Bay in Canada was the chosen location, should opportunities for fulfilling realistic training sorties in Europe and North Africa prove unsatisfactory. A special projects department headed by an air commodore was to be formed within the RAF to monitor the developmental progress of the prototype and to coordinate the timely and economical introduction of this highly advanced weapon system into the RAF.

The TSR-2 was expected to meet such a set of expectations that the conglomerate of bodies involved, having brought the aircraft to the prototype stage and meet its development targets, proved that the design committee approach on this occasion worked. Overseeing matters from the customer side was a new high-level formal gathering called the RAF special projects committee. This was placed under the control of the chairman of the controller of aircraft at the Ministry of Aviation, with representation from the Ministry of Defence. The latter had the wider remit of keeping an eye on the development of not just the TSR-2 but the HS681 (future transport) and the P1154 (supersonic Kestrel/Harrier).

Including the six pre-production airframes, 158 aircraft were expected to be ordered. A further breakdown saw 106 aircraft assigned to the frontline squadrons while the OCU would have an establishment of seventeen. Squadrons and their total establishment would be as follows:

	Strike Sqns/UE	Reconnaissance Sqns/UE
Bomber Command	2/24	1/8
RAF Germany	2/24	2/16
Near East Air Force	2/16	1/8
Far East Air Force	1/10	

In May 1960, the unit cost of each pre-production TSR-2 was put at £5.2 million; by October, that had already gone up to £5.3 million. The production models were set at £2.8 million each. Research and development costs, at the time, were put at between £250–270 million. Progress was made in the years ahead under the government of Harold McMillan, but an atmosphere of pedestrian enthusiasm seems to be the best way to describe the government's approach. Most notable of all was the limp response to the healthy enthusiasm of the Australian government, who were itching to secure a purchase of TSR-2s to replace their own Canberras. This saga is described in detail in *Fading Eagle*.

The upshot of the political infighting and lack of unity of purpose was mixed messages from the British side, especially with Lord Mountbatten, the chief of defence staff, who was quite biased in favour of matters maritime. He is said to have produced from his pockets three toy Buccaneers and a toy TSR-2 at select meetings with the accompanying line 'three of these for one of these'. It was Lord Mountbatten's contention that the Buccaneer, a naval strike aircraft, could meet the measure of the mooted TSR-2, or certainly that three Buccaneers would provide a wider range of flexibility than just one TSR-2 for the same cost, even though TSR-2 was starting to show promise with the first prototype flying and the second ready by September 1964.

October that year took a turn for the worse for the project's prospects. The incoming Labour government of Harold Wilson, with plans for significant increases in public expenditure, meant that the most advanced and potent strike aircraft of its time was under greater threat. It was neglected under the previous government, but the new one would cancel TSR-2, promise to replace it, and then cancel the replacement. TSR-2 would have placed the RAF, indeed NATO, at a considerable advantage in presenting a formidable response to any likely Soviet-led Warsaw Pact incursion westwards, and it was about to be lost through a mix of a lack of political commitment, vacillation, and undue favour to overseas competition, which did what was left of the British aerospace industry immense harm.

The results of the general election on 15 October 1964 were already being anticipated, and a paper was prepared two weeks earlier entitled 'Briefs for new Ministers'; the emphasis was placed on cost. A mistake to be corrected early on was the inclusion of research and development costs for the Buccaneer, AJ168, and P1154, but the essence of the report was to compare the nearest rivals to TSR-2—the Buccaneer, the General Dynamics F-111, and the F-4 Phantom II. At a meeting on 1 February 1965, the Cabinet was provided with a memorandum from the defence secretary, Denis Healy. This provided some comparisons between the TSR-2 and F-111A, the latter also known at the time as the TFX.

At this meeting, the cabinet chose to defer a decision on the TSR-2 pending receipt of further information on comparative cost and performance between the TSR-2 and its American rival. Eager now to secure orders for the TSR-2, BAC had offered a fixed target price in the hope that if the eventual cost was lower, the balance would be accrued as profit to them. This probably was not the best way to protect the project against US competition. If, however, the eventual cost was higher than BAC's target, they would accept responsibility for bearing losses up to a maximum of £9 million. Any amount over this, they expected the government to sustain—or rather, the taxpayer.

Based on this, a purchase of 110 F-111s against a similar purchase of TSR-2s would yield a saving of £280 million. It would also mean a dollar outlay equivalent to £500 million including interest charges of about £70 million. This amounted to a saving on sterling expenditure but would increase the deficit on the balance of payments. Overall, it would be a net loss.

Wilson's cabinet believed that announcing the cancellation of TSR-2 together with the budget would impress upon the British electorate the government's resolve 'to secure genuine economies in defence expenditure'. It is a curious position to take, to assume such a disregard for the status of the national defence posture would carry public support, as if the electorate regarded every penny spent on defence as a penny lost to anything else. In isolation, it was thought that a strong case could be made for its cancellation simply because it was too expensive. The new government had already cancelled the other two leading military aviation projects—HS-681 and P-1154—and found it easier than it imagined to absorb redundant labour as a result.

The cancellation of TSR-2 together with the purchase of F-111s as a replacement did worry the politicians that they would be open to the charge of becoming unduly dependent upon the United States. Despite the relative ease with which P-1154 and HS-681 were dealt with, industrial harm and redundancy pay outs were expected at a substantial cost to the taxpayer. On top of this was the reputation of American aircraft companies for aggressive marketing overseas and attempts to frustrate sales of UK-built aircraft to US airlines, a market in which British aviation was particularly prominent at the time.

Harold Wilson personally believed the TSR-2 project to be too expensive and this alone was the case for cancelling it. Yet apart from the reasons outlined about the cost of redundancy and yielding to American sales pressure should the F-111 be purchased instead, it seemed unlikely that the resources saved from cancellation would offset even half the £500 million cost in US dollars for the American jet, which would have to be met.

A decision on which to opt for, if either at all, was put off for the immediate future thanks to an ongoing defence review—that instrument by which government gets to take an axe to unpopular, inherited, or unwisely started programmes, or indeed, chooses to do the opposite. To keep the unwise and inherited programmes and take a blunted axe to existing military formations instead has been the form in present times. Until the review was complete, Wilson believed he could not be sure that such an aircraft as the TSR-2 or F-111 would be needed at all. He was, though, reluctant to cancel overseas orders for the TSR-2 such as they were, unless an alternative aircraft was available. In terms of home-grown designs, there was no other aircraft to turn to if the TSR-2 was to be abandoned.

So, an option to purchase the F-111 was established but crucially avoided any commitment to buy beyond a limited number. The cabinet would need to decide if the overseas commitments were such that a substantial purchase of F-111s would prove indispensable. In that case, Wilson was willing to hang onto TSR-2 for about two to three months, despite the further cost accrued.

A memorandum from the defence secretary, Denis Healy, was later placed before the cabinet, which included a draft public announcement. Healy said that in order to secure the fixed price option on the F-111, Britain would have to commit to a minimum purchase of ten aircraft. Healy's news came after the cabinet discussion on the matter, by which time the US had withdrawn the offer. Instead, the US government offered to accept an option agreement whereby the British would not be committed to purchasing any aircraft but would have to place a firm order for ten aircraft before 1 January 1966. They would then have the option to purchase up to a further 100 aircraft and need not place the order until 1967.

Another fixed price was offered if the total order was between seventy and 100 aircraft. An order of fewer than seventy would mean negotiating the cost of the research and development element of the fixed price, which may well include a small increase in the price. The US authorities would still be prepared to accept the waiver of 50 per cent preference rule when the option was signed, though they would not recognise this by administrative effect, meaning for example, an American buy of British equipment if a firm order for F-111s was agreed. The option then was assurance that the government could buy the F-111s on the most favourable terms, should they choose to do so. What is more, the government need not make a decision until 1 January 1966, by which time the review of overseas commitments would be complete. There remained concern about the impact cancellation of the project might have on commercial aircraft sales abroad. Should TSR-2 be scuttled, it would likely damage the reputation of the wider British aviation industry.

On top of this, the idea of picking the F-111 would only compound any lack of confidence that could develop. The effect on the balance of payments would outweigh any financial advantage given a large order for F-111s. There was nothing to be gained by losing the homespun aeroplane. All this though had to be stacked up against the Labour government's overriding political aim—substantial savings in the defence budget. Cancelling the TSR2 would yield economies in the defence budget, although to go down this route would leave the country owing more money, even though the defence budget would be set at a lower level.

At the expense then of a further burdening of the balance of payments, the government's priority was to lessen the defence budget. The impact on the aircraft industry would, given the weakened state of the economy, be offset by redistributing manpower from here to other areas of industry propped up by further investment and subsequent growth. The government were further reassured about going down this path by the rate at which they would have to pay back the cost of the F-111—over five to ten years. By this time, it was expected that the government's policy on wider economic investment would see fruition in the form of improved competitive efficiency in Britain's industrial output.

This was not the end of the matter. Lord Mountbatten had worked very hard to discourage any further pursuit of the TSR-2 project and worked equally hard to dismiss the F-111 by faithfully continuing to tout the shorter-range, slower, and less capable Buccaneer, albeit the Mk 2 version. The Buccaneer was designed to provide low-level strike and attack against what were dubbed 'sore thumb' targets—that is, prominent targets that were relatively accessible.

Lord Mountbatten's lobbying began to bear fruit; the government increasingly wanted to look at a third option—the idea of choosing the Buccaneer, and developing it, to fulfil the TSR-2/F-111 requirement instead. One positive outcome was that it would be cheaper. The government certainly warmed to this idea as it would avoid the need to make an opening commitment to purchase an initial ten F-111s.

The Buccaneer was, with the best will in the world, a lesser aircraft, and this was made fully aware to those upon whose shoulders the decision lay. As was noted at the time, 'even a much-developed version of the Buccaneer would be much inferior in range and payload to the TSR-2 or TFX/F-111'. It was suggested that this could be offset by the increased use of the navy's carrier-borne Buccaneers. Harold Wilson was certain of two things—the TSR-2 programme was not going to be completed and it was not going to be cancelled in favour of an order for 110 F-111s. There were three options he was prepared to consider:

1. to cancel the TSR-2 and take no action over a replacement.
2. to cancel the TSR-2 and secure an option on the F-111 along the lines described by the Secretary of state for Defence.
3. to postpone any decision until the review of our overseas commitments showed whether we should have a requirement for this type of aircraft.

The third option was his preferred route. This meant not cancelling the TSR2 just yet, to avoid being left with the F-111 as the sole option, should such an aircraft be required, which would also mean to become unduly reliant on the United States and incur a heavy dollar expenditure. The vacillating did not cease here as to keep the TSR-2 programme ticking over while waiting for the results of the review would see a possible fruitless £1 million wasted every week with further indecision likely to cause further postponement.

The balance of the cabinet's opinion was in favour of course B. Before a final decision could be made on this course of action, confirmation of an agreement with the United States would need to be reached. The government would seek an agreement with the USA avoiding any commitment to buy a single F-111 initially. Once such an agreement was reached, the announcement of the TSR-2's cancellation in the chancellor's 6 April budget speech was considered possible. It was also thought to be a good idea for the defence secretary and the minister of aviation to hold a press conference later the same day where the decision could be more fully explained, and a prepared statement issued. Despite the certainty that the TSR-2 was for the chop, the press briefing was to allay such fears that this was being considered:

> It should be made clear that the requirement for an aircraft of this type and the possibility of meeting such a requirement in other ways were being kept open pending the outcome of the current review; the purchase of the TFX (F-111) was only one of these possibilities and the option had been concluded as a form of insurance.

So it was that the TSR-2 was extinct before it got anywhere near the RAF. Not only was the TSR-2 lost, but the F-111 would never find its way onto the RAF's inventory either. The prime minister, Harold Wilson, did entertain the idea of continuing the TSR-2 programme with a view to research; he was thinking particularly of the then mooted supersonic transport, already known as Concorde. The commercial aircraft used the same power plant as the TSR2. On the military side, it would also help BAC retain what personnel they could to work on the Anglo-French 'Advanced Fighter Variable Geometry' project.

In the commons on 14 March 1967, the undersecretary of state for defence, Royal Air Force, stated that two-thirds of no more than fifty F-111s would be based operationally plus the OCU at Honington with the rest based in the Far East, while the nuclear strike force in Germany was to be reduced to accommodate an increase in tactical support aircraft; also, the Anglo-French AFVG was to be the core of the RAF's long-term aircraft programme. What was odd about the idea of deploying a much smaller number of F-111s only to the Far East was the government's policy on the Far East—we were pulling out.

The F-111 had other enemies within the establishment of the day, not just Lord Mountbatten and elements of the government, but the 1st Viscount

Head; he was quite concerned about the navy's new landing craft and other expeditionary assault equipment when addressing the House of Lords in 1967:

> Take the Royal Navy landing craft as an example. Nowadays, these inter-Service matters should be taken clean out of the Service Estimates. Things like helicopters and landing craft should be put in a special category of their own. Otherwise, they will be squeezed out by these F-111s, about which I should like to say something but there isn't time.

The 1st Viscount Head was a former army officer and Conservative MP; he would have found a great deal of sympathy with those army officers of decades later, such as General the Lord Richards, battling to make the case for a binary shift toward equipping the armed forces to engage in counterinsurgency wars.

Another situation to cause concern in 1967 was the government's threat to withdraw the RAF from Germany. This was seen as an attempt to pressure the Bonn government into offsetting losses sustained by the pound sterling through the exchange rate as a result of maintaining British Forces in West Germany. The Bonn government were still obliged at this stage for 'occupation costs' and offset payment agreements, but the cost essentially fell to the UK Treasury. The basing of allied forces on West German soil was, in 1967, more adversely affected as a result of the rise in the strength of the *Deutsche Mark* and its impact on the pound.

However, pressure may not be the correct view to take. There were ongoing discussions between Britain, West Germany, and the United States in early 1967 to resolve the issue of exchange rate losses to Britain. One Tory MP, Mr Jock Bruce-Gardyne, asked the defence secretary, 'are preparations now being made for rehousing up to 20,000 or 30,000 troops and their families from Germany? If not, does not the chancellor of the exchequer's statement last weekend about balancing the exchange costs amount, as he said, to an idle bluff?' The loss to sterling was mostly a result of the UK government's devaluation of the pound to try and boost exports.

This threat was given a date—1 July 1967—after which the withdrawal of RAFG units would commence unless the West Germans were prepared to offset exchange rate losses. The government was challenged by Tory MP, Victor Goodhew, in parliament as to how such a serious threat could be made while the situation with the Soviet Union remained, there being no reduction in the Warsaw Pact Forces.

> No one in the RAF can be expected to feel that a withdrawal from Germany is a sensible move now, only a year after being told that our ground forces were just sufficient to cope, provided that they were given additional air support.

The government were told, ahead of any defence review, by Mr Healy on 13 April, that the country did need a tactical strike and reconnaissance aircraft and that the case was irrefutable if the country was to retain the capability for military action alone, in any part of the world. What was also admitted was that no standard of performance or minimum number of aircraft had been decided; this was a rather more complicated issue for the government to find an answer to, so the ongoing defence review was referred to. This would decide how many aircraft would be required and what their performance would be. The defence review was going to answer the comprehensive question of what was needed.

All facets were to be examined, then the findings of the review would determine the capability required, then relate, for example, what type of aircraft would best meet the threat and the likely geographical theatres that would have to be operated in. Healy carefully avoided mentioning specifics.

Conscious of the criticism of sceptics, the prime minister made clear, 'The case is not an open and shut one and any suggestion that this study is a façade is wholly unfounded'. Wilson's problems were not just with political opposition; he also had internal discontent as the Labour party's left-wing section remained in the wings. Dormant for now, it was claimed they had been placated largely due to the change in the US/ NATO doctrine from mutually assured destruction to 'flexible response'. Flexible response, the policy of meeting all threats with an attempt to contain that threat and prevent escalation, was first proposed by President Kennedy to avoid relying on an overwhelming nuclear strike in the forlorn hope of annihilating the other side. However, this change was not adopted by NATO officially until 1967; in 1965, the policy of relying on strategic nuclear retaliation early on, as though survivable, still held. That said, it was aircraft like the TSR-2 that made flexible response a far more feasible option. The Wilson government had in the meantime assuaged the in-house left wing by promising to renegotiate the purchase of Polaris missiles. This they failed to do, and the submarine-launched missiles were ordered.

On 2 May, the minister of state for foreign affairs, Lord Chalfont, clarified the claims about withdrawal from Germany—a single brigade and a single RAF squadron (both unspecified) would be re-deployed to the UK, having already come to the earlier conclusion that another RAFG airbase was to be abandoned. According to the under-secretary of state for the RAF, the base closure was for a separate reason to the matter over the foreign exchange costs, but due to the government drive for defence economies as a matter of course. The most pressing concern for the commander of the RAF in Germany in 1967 was to plan the future of its strike element, which was no longer the F-111. Instead, in answer to questions from Victor Goodhew on 31 May, Merlyn Rees, under-secretary of state for defence, RAF, stated:

The Canberra squadrons in Germany will, in due course, be withdrawn without direct replacement, but some of their tasks will be allocated to the ground attack Phantom squadrons from 1970. In addition, United Kingdom based F-111s and V-bombers would be available to SACEUR in emergency.

Goodhew still asked about the AFVG (a joint project with France to build a new, high-performance fighter) as the Canberras were not expected to fly beyond 1970. Rees said, 'We have made arrangements for the replacement of the Canberra in other ways before the advent of the AFVG'.

Looking around, there was little to be re-assured about in terms of maintaining the *status quo*, least of all any chance of improvements or expansion. The story of other commands at home and overseas was significantly bleak.

AOC-in-C RAFG communicated his relief to Whitehall that his command was apparently spared the butchery planned for everyone else. He had been in receipt of a scaling down plan—'Plan Q'—but was under no illusion about the continuation of the RAF on the continent being under the spotlight. If the British government looked to make another expenditure saving on the ever-growing *Deutsche Mark*, cuts would be inevitable. The defence white paper made no commitments here one way or the other, but the Germans were already making clear that they were not going to spend any more on 'offsets.

Negotiations here lay with Sir Frank Roberts, HMG ambassador to Bonn. AOC-in-C RAFG Air Marshal Sir Denis Spotswood was expecting this to at least result in a one-sixth saving in expenditure to be found anyway, which he viewed as illogical. Sir Denis maintained that beyond the 1970s, the RAF in Germany would be very small—a relative comment. Even so, this was the principal worry of RAFG's senior officers.

The RAF had other commitments and assets assigned so they could not be counted as additional resources for RAFG. Sir Denis determined that the RAF contribution to 2 ATAF was the smallest of all contributing nations. That strength was expected to halve in the 1970s. The comparisons would then be as follows:

German Air Force (North)	166 Aircraft
Belgian Air Force	140 Aircraft
Dutch Air Force	133 Aircraft
RAFG	68 Aircraft

If the British government still expected to retain command of 2 ATAF, something would need to be done to bolster the RAF/UK image on the continent. One suggestion was to allocate to the commander 2 ATAF control over some UK-based squadrons in an attempt to strengthen his credibility.

Plan 'Q' was the name for the planned gradual rundown of squadrons; the B(I)6 Canberras of 213 Sqn based at Brüggen were an early casualty. No. 213 Sqn were to rundown by half over a six-month period between 1969 and 1970. The gradual contraction was expected to encourage an erosion of efficiency, impetus, standards of supervision, and anything else that develops when a unit has a much-reduced status and faces certain disbandment. Therefore, there is a risk to safety through the unintended consequence of a staged running-down of a squadron; it will have a greater effect on moral as opposed to a whole squadron disbandment.

The same fate awaited the Canberra PR squadrons that were set to rundown from three to 1.5, then one squadron. The B(I)8 units were to run down in similar fashion to 1.5 squadrons by September 1970. The expectation was that the last of the PR Canberras would go six months before the first F-4 Phantom PR squadron (there was only going to be one) formed.

The makeup of RAFG was certainly going to be radically different in 1972 compared to the way it looked in 1967, but it would not be smaller, and it would be far more heavily armed. However, that was not how it was expected to turn out; what was expected was a cull and that was not desirable for operational and NATO reasons.

In 1967, to the staff of RAFG, there was only an understanding that from 1970, the Canberra strike squadrons would not re-equip in theatre, but that new squadrons would re-equip in the UK and be posted out, and so were requesting details of how this was to be affected, as soon as possible. They needed to know so that they could start juggling squadrons and bases.

The year 1967 was, despite the expressed relief of Sir Denis Spotswood, a difficult one for the RAF in Germany. The Wilson government's commitment to maintaining the posture was under pressure from the desire to offset the foreign exchange costs. Suggestions that the fighter squadrons could be maintained in the UK and re-deployed at short notice simply missed the point of the Bonn Convention (1952) and the Paris Agreement (1954); this meant making fighter aircraft continuously available and at a high state of readiness, capable of carrying out patrols and intercepts routinely during peacetime. This function was always carried out through an all-British chain of command, from C-in-C RAF Germany through to the crew of the fighters themselves. The French commitment had already been withdrawn due to de Gaulle's decision to end France's military commitment to NATO.

Regardless of any faithful intentions to re-deploy fighter aircraft during any tense political period, the commitment by the RAF to this duty would be removed, while still committed to NATO in full, leaving the QRA commitment solely with the USAF. Attempts to avoid or reduce costs ironically meant there would be a penalty in terms of sterling expenditure if the three PR Canberra squadrons were withdrawn too early—the opposite of what was intended.

There was also the operational and administrative inconvenience incurred by early disbandment, largely because RAF Stradishall, the destination for the obsolescent aircraft, would not be able to receive them before August 1968. It seemed the MOD expected that the PR squadrons could disband by the middle of that year. What was particularly distasteful to the staff of RAFG at the time was the Ministry of Defence line in the proposed cuts that 'The Ministry of Defence consider such a reduction acceptable in present circumstances'. What was particularly irritating was the insinuation that the MOD spoke with the blessing of the chiefs of staff rather than their political masters. It was also noted that plan 'Q' had a distinct army ring to it.

Approaching Christmas 1967, the devaluation of pound sterling coupled with a heavy public spending programme to meet the cost of increasing social, health, and welfare costs forced the government to seek £800 million in economy savings. The F-111 now had a huge metaphoric target painted on it.

That same month, British newspapers were speculating on yet another military aircraft project joining the farrago of those thus far cancelled for reasons of economy and a belief that something else could be found to do the job cheaper. This time it was the cheaper option that faced press critique, hence even the Labour-supporting *Daily Mirror* carried a centre page spread showing the line of projects cancelled since 1965. The *Financial Times* reported that the cost of the F-111K reached £425 million. The *Financial Times* rightly observed that any change to the planned deployment of F-111s would take time for the full impact to show. The time spent in negotiating an extrication from the contract with General Dynamics could take months. In the meantime, the Canberra squadrons in Germany were to go soon. Even without restrictions on airframe stress, which was of particular concern given that RAFG aircraft spent so much time at low level, the Canberra was very much out of date when placed alongside its contemporaries within 2 and 4 ATAFs—the F-104, F-100, and F-4. All possessed a superior performance in all but combat range yet none of these could hold a candle to either the F-111 or the aircraft it was advanced as the cheap alternative to, the TSR-2.

The publicly played-out concerns of the defence chiefs, not least the CAS, Sir John Grandy, and his predecessor now chief of defence staff, Sir Charles Elworthy, were by no means understated. There were worries about what prospects were heading down the track for the new year. The pink sheets reported, 'all three services fear that if the axe should fall again it will reduce to a dangerously deficient level, the forces' ability to carry out the tasks assigned to them'.

Denis Healy suggested any further cuts should 'stem from a new revision of commitments', to which he was not opposed in principle. Subject to review, almost certainly meaning further cuts, were the military commitments in the Far East, Persian Gulf, and Western Europe—in other words, everywhere.

This threw up more confusion and had some opposition MPs growing in frustration over what was going on, given the proposal to withdraw HM forces from east of Suez and concentrate instead on the European theatre. The fifty F-111s were simply a stopgap until such time, although when this prompted questions in parliament, Mr Rees gave an unclear answer, saying that surely an aircraft costing £2.1 million is going to last beyond 1975: 'These 50 aircraft in their various roles are bound to go on for at least 15 years'.

He further stated that the F-111 was purely for tactical strike and reconnaissance roles (the government wanted to place emphasis on the reconnaissance role) and that the remaining V-bombers would be the stop gap; the F-111 would go on long after the AFVG had replaced the V-bombers. The F-111 would go on as the tactical land-based replacement for the navy's carriers. Victor Goodhew again challenged the viability of so few F-111s, asking, 'With a force of only 50 of these aircraft, 10 of which are for training purposes in the United Kingdom, it is unlikely that more than 20 will be operational at any one time?'

Merlyn Rees replied 'nonsense'. When pressed by Goodhew, he stated, 'that the figures which have been in use today and in recent debates are wildly wrong'. The AFVG, jointly developed with France, was now expected to be the Canberra replacement for RAFG. Victor Goodhew described the proposed deployment of F-111s as like scattering a small handful of F-111s around the Far East like penny packets.

The first F-111As were being delivered to the USAF, but the first F-111K for the RAF had already rolled off the production line, with the first RAF unit to form in 1969. Economically, the MOD were concerned that the cancellation of the F-111K could result in cancellation by the Americans of the credit arrangements for other aircraft orders from the US, such as the C-130K Hercules and the F-4 Phantom, thus putting them at risk also. There were also the people who were dismissive of the need for the F-111 at all and who could wield some influence. Yet *The Financial Times* reported that the need for an advanced reconnaissance aircraft of the F-111 type was accepted suggesting that it would be difficult for the UK to abandon it altogether.

Again, *The Daily Mirror* had something to say:

Today the RAF is even more dangerously ill-equipped. In the fat years before Labour's 1964 election victory, the future seemed set fair for the RAF. They had the promise of the most advanced and potent air force in the world. The TSR2, a tactical strike and reconnaissance plane was to be the spearhead. The Hawker Siddeley P1154, a supersonic jump-jet able to leap into the air from no more than a clearing, was to back it up. The Hawker Siddeley 681, another vertical take-off aircraft, independent of concrete runways, was to be the transport plane for the world's finest air force. But the writing was on the wall even then. The Tory regime still in power knew that Britain could not really afford these aircraft. Before the end of 1964 the Government had changed. The P1154 and the HS681 were dead. TSR2 took a little longer, but in the spring of 1965, it too died.

Further, *The Daily Mirror* claimed that if the order for F-111s was cancelled 'without at the same time renouncing Britain's Far East commitments, there is every chance that Mr Healy himself will resign'.

This last line from the same editorial proved the very opposite of what was alluded to—Healy never resigned, the Far East was abandoned, and the F-111 was very much cancelled the following month. There was some suggestion that Healy would have argued for either the retention of F-111 at the expense of the Far East defence responsibilities, or the other way around, but his argument was that the disappearance of one negated the need for the other. To argue that if one goes it would be a resignation case unless another major commitment was lost into the bargain is a curious way of fighting your department's corner, but the logic was that without the Far East commitment, then no need for the F-111, though this did not consider the Near East and Germany.

The Daily Mirror finally referred to a press interview in September with a senior RAF officer responding to the purchase of American C-130 Hercules in place of the home-grown HS-681:

Air Marshal Sir Tom Prickett said bravely; 'This is just the aircraft we wanted'. It was a classic instance of putting a bold front on the inescapable. Because the transport the RAF wanted was the jump jet 681. And today the RAF is growing tired of putting a bold front on things.

To the right of the argument, Air Commodore E. M. Donaldson, air correspondent at *The Daily Telegraph* wrote, 'Mr Wilson has been warned in the strongest possible terms that he can expect the most serious repercussions if he cancels the order for 50 F-111 swing-wing bombers for the RAF.'

Donaldson then claimed that along with Healy, Air Chief Marshal Sir John Grandy and MRAF Sir Charles Elworthy were reportedly prepared to fall on their ceremonial swords. Donaldson had been told this by senior defence officers and others. While very much appreciative of all new aircraft he could get, Sir John Grandy was not prepared to have his response to the cancellation of F-111 predicted by anyone:

The RAF have pressed on, indeed they neither have nor could do otherwise, but they have been tremendously heartened at the prospect of, at last, new equipment.

The way in which the C-130s (and these aircraft only started going into service last July) were used in the not inconsiderable Aden evacuation operation in November shows what new equipment means. This operation, in the time, could not have been met with the old equipment. It is this kind of 'new look capability' which all our long-suffering crews are so looking forward to in their different roles. Demise of the F-111, from this point of view alone, would be a setback of great magnitude. Not only for the crews of the present generation of strike aircraft, but for all our crews who have so effectively and loyally sustained our operational efficiency in ageing aircraft. You may be able to make use of this point. Needless to say, this minute is in no way inspired by the infuriating and damaging stupidity by Donaldson today in *The Telegraph* which I have only just seen.

This was part of a minute sent from CAS to Denis Healy on 22 December 1967. December passed to January and Wilson made his decision—the F-111 was to go. The AFVG was also abandoned following the withdrawal of the French government; their reason was cost. Thereafter came fears of runaway costs inadvertently caused by a lack of enthusiasm for a diminished purpose, bringing an end to it. There was also the suggestion of a rift between the air staff and the defence secretary, to which Wilson responded:

Talk of betraying the Air Staff is nonsense. It is also deplorable practice trying to suggest that there is some split between the air staff and the secretary of state on this issue. The air staff are most conscious of the need to get value for money and to get the most out of the inevitably limited financial and other resources which can be made available to them.

Come January 1968, the cancellation of the F-111 was announced. With the AFVG ended as well, there was now an imperative to replace the Canberras of RAFG. The Canberra tactical bomber wing at Akrotiri in Cyprus was to be replaced by deploying two Vulcan squadrons from the UK. As for Germany, root and branch reform for both the strike and reconnaissance squadrons was soon to arrive. The answer to the question of finding new platforms to deliver the principal role was just around the corner, even if it was the third choice of RAFG. The other headache that never went away was the continuing responsibility of the RAF in West Germany for quick reaction air defence of the north of the country.

By February 1968, the RAF were proposing to buy twenty-six Mk 2 Buccaneers; they had not identified a need for any Mk 1 aircraft. They were hoping for initial deliveries to be made between 1969 and 1970.

RAFG were to get their Canberra replacement, the Buccaneer S2 and the Phantom. The latter was subject at the time to a decision to allow funds to modify British nuclear weapons for fitting to the American aircraft. The British bombs were being modified for use on all British aircraft. Without this programme, the original advice was to fit US bombs to both the Phantom and the F-111. In the meantime, no accurate assessment of the cost of US bombs could be made while work was still being carried out to enable the ejector release unit on Phantoms to be capable of allowing British bombs to be used satisfactorily. In any case, the number of British bombs, purchased for use by the Phantom, would be limited as more than half of the aircraft would be used in the conventional ground attack and reconnaissance roles. Harriers had also been ordered but were subject to delay due to a dispute over the price tag.

RAFG was about to lose one more base before consolidating for the rest of the Cold War. Gütersloh, doubtless for its forward position, was not picked to be the base to go. Geilenkirchen was deemed surplus to requirements, or rather needed to be sacrificed, to help manage public spending targets that the government had set itself.

The last RAF operations ceased here as of 21 January and the West German Air Force moved in during March. Ironically, Geilenkirchen is the last former RAF base in Germany that has continued to the present as an operational NATO airfield, having been home to the NATO AWACS force since the early 1980s. In between the RAF leaving and the AWACS force arriving, the German *Flugkörpergeschwader Zwei* (FKG 2; in English parlance, Missile Wing 2) made Geilenkirchen their home. This outfit was kitted out with the Pershing 1b surface-to-surface missiles and carried a tactical nuclear warhead. The warheads were overseen and maintained by the US Army 85th Field Artillery Detachment, but active control remained with the German Army, who would be launching the missiles in the event of rising tensions reaching such a stage.

Air Vice-Marshal L. M. Hodges, then ACAS Ops, chaired a meeting on 26 January 1968 to discuss the modification and conversion programme for Lightning aircraft based in Germany. He opened the meeting by stating his concern about the problems of RAF Germany's Lightning force, especially the maintenance of an adequate fighter force during what was to be the upgrading of all the Mk 2 Lightnings to Mk 2A standard. This upgrade would be quite extensive, involving the construction of a camber along the leading edge of the main wings and an enlarged squared-off fin tip in common with the Mks 3, 5, and 6. The F2A would also be able to carry the Red Top missile and would have an enlarged ventral fuel tank. This would include essential fire modification.

As all the aircraft for upgrade were fully deployed at Gütersloh, 92 Sqn re-located here following the relinquishing of Geilenkirchen. There was concern over the loss of aircraft during the upgrade. The upgrade/conversion was scheduled to begin that year at RAF Leconfield near Hull. RAFG suggested that to minimise the impact on available aircraft, the upgrades should be conducted at Gütersloh, hence the reason for the meeting. A total of thirty-one Lightnings were involved, and command RAFG had advised that they would need twenty-two; the official bare minimum had been set at twenty-one jets. This would be required to allow Gütersloh to draw on enough airframes to meet SACEUR's generation requirement should a transition to war be embarked upon.

This made sense certainly, but it was argued that it would be quicker to complete modifications at Leconfield; this was regarded as safer given the Lightning's fire-prone history. At Leconfield, the engineering equipment required was already to hand; to carry out the modifications at Gütersloh would require a party of fifteen engineers to be deployed and would result in an expenditure increase for RAF Gütersloh with the increased head count. The increased expenditure was both questioned and seen as unjustifiable against the greater availability of aircraft (which only might be the case) during the refit. The counterpoint might take longer, given the movement of personnel and engineering equipment. Instead, it was settled that Lightnings from the UK would reinforce Gütersloh, if necessary.

The conversion programme was planned to be complete by March 1970, up to which point a single Lightning per month would be converted to F2A standard. With thirty aircraft to upgrade, a full UE of twenty-four aircraft was expected to have been reached by the end of 1969. Regardless of the arrangements to upgrade the Lightnings, the cancellation of the F-111 after the TSR-2, placed the RAF strike force in Germany further behind, leaving the force at its least effective and, with the loss of Geilenkirchen, at its smallest size, since 1950.

The Canberra force was still scheduled to run down but would now live on to 1972. A radical redeployment of the RAF in Germany was already being planned around the contingency brought about by the Canberra/TSR-2/F-111 fiasco. On 16 March 1970, the size and number of aircraft in RAF Germany was debated again in parliament, and again Victor Goodhew, MP and former RAF officer, warmed to his favourite subject, the TSR-2. The new C-in-C RAF Germany, Air Marshal Sir Christopher Foxley-Norris, had recently given a speech at the Royal United Services Institute, in which he had defined the threat from the Warsaw Pact and the RAF's reduced state.

Victor Goodhew challenged Healey again over the present climate and asked which aircraft had been selected to replace the F-111 and the AFVG. Having raised the question of replacing Canberras in Germany with some regularity since before the previous year, Goodhew described Healey as being keen not to answer the question. Goodhew was a keen proponent of defence interests and considered the government's 1966 defence review to have been 'notorious'. He referred to a passage from the review:

The key to the deterrent power of our Armed Forces is our ability to obtain early warning of an enemy's intentions through reconnaissance and to strike at his offensive forces from a distance in case of need. This role has been assigned to Canberra aircraft since the early 1950s; this aircraft cannot safely continue after 1970.

He wanted to know how, if that was the state of affairs in 1966, it was to be explained that in the 1970 white paper, the Canberra force in Germany was being extended until it could finally be replaced by the new Phantom and Buccaneer squadrons. 'What do the government mean by "extended"? Do they propose to go on hoping, or have they done something to make sure that the aircraft can fly safely?'

Goodhew was playing the political opposition man, as all do. The situation was well in hand, but nothing could move faster than the logistics of getting serviceable airframes to the bases in Germany. The more demanding task was to work up the air and ground crews, to fly and maintain the new jets to a satisfactory standard; this would be no mean achievement. Yet events were already ahead of the Canberra—not only were preparations underway to deploy Buccaneers and Phantoms, but the new aircraft would be deployed on just two bases, not four, but with an increase in strength by one squadron.

8

The 1970s and Flexible Response

On 29 August 1949, the USSR signalled an unmistakable change in its relations with the West—it could claim to be a nuclear power, having conducted a 'secret' detonation test. This in turn led to the apt acronym—MAD.

Up to this point, the only chance to halt the overwhelming conventional forces of the USSR from sweeping the much more limited forces of the NATO aside and forcing a new Dunkirk along the Channel coast would be strategic nuclear retaliation. NATO—in effect, the United States and, on a smaller scale, the UK—would not be able to prevent such an outcome any other way, and it would mean prevention at extreme cost, such was the expected outcome.

The idea of MAD was applied after 1949 as it was seen as the stage we would rapidly get to, with the USSR now similarly armed, but what really exercised concern in the West was the likelihood of a pre-emptive nuclear strike by the Soviet Union. It was seen as equally, or even more, likely than a massed conventional assault on West Germany, through into south-west Europe. This would very quickly reach the stage of a strategic nuclear exchange as was feared. It was not that NATO was not likely to halt such an attack with conventional weapons. It was the concern that the Kremlin may consider it viable to cripple the West's nuclear retaliatory ability prior to sending masses of troops forward to mop up once the air cleared. It was also the case that the Kremlin and other Warsaw Pact governments regarded us in very much the same mistrusting way.

Thus, it was that a change in military doctrine was around the corner, after years had been spent building up the nuclear strike force to enable the chance to take a surprise swipe at the other side, the second they were off guard.

President John Kennedy is credited with the replacement doctrine of 'flexible response'; in fact, the USA has since claimed it never advocated the MAD doctrine, certainly not exclusively. The use of tactical nuclear weapons theoretically allows for a graded and controlled escalation, which, at any point, could present the opportunity for a cessation of hostilities. Yet given the destructive power of just tactical weapons, certainly in the numbers available, the notion of a limited nuclear war has always been a forlorn hope.

1967 is seen as the year that the change in doctrine was adopted, suggesting NATO conventional forces could credibly be relied upon to contain a Warsaw Pact advance. Realistically, no one could see a conventional victory or stalemate.

Flexible response did not mean the nukes were not to be forsaken, not for a second, but a move toward a more realistic balance or rather rational response to any likely military threat.

It was in fact widely accepted that NATO would be the first to resort to such a level of escalation, again almost certainly due to the much smaller conventional defensive posture of NATO forces. The TSR-2 and F-111 brought the chances of flexible response working, if only because of their greater survivability and accuracy. The 1970s saw a period of much-needed refurbishment of the RAF contribution to 2 ATAF. The delay had been brought about, in part, by the vacillation of the preceding six years and the extensive removal, from the RAF in Germany, of conventional tactical fighters, some six years or so before that. The future deployment of the RAF in Germany would provide a sturdier, more formidable force to reckon with. In April 1968, future planning of the RAF deployed element in Germany was to lose yet another station, one of the clutch bases, taking the total down to three, this after having just lost Geilenkirchen.

Laarbruch was being lined up for the chop. The reason for Laarbruch being likely to close first surfaced in 1965, at the behest of RAFG; the factors were as follows:

> That although Laarbruch was considered to be the most modern RAF base on the continent with the best dispersal and located outside of controlled airspace, its retention would have meant the use of either Brüggen or Wildenrath by the West German Air Force, which would have led to air traffic control problems.
>
> Considerable administrative benefits were seen in the retention of RAF Brüggen and Wildenrath through co-location and cooperation. For example, maximum flexibility in the use of married quarters and schools would be achieved. These benefits would have been lost if Laarbruch was retained and one of the others given up.
>
> At the time (1965) it was thought that the F-4 Phantom would be deployed on more than one airfield, in this case the best solution would be Brüggen and Wildenrath given their close proximity to one another thus permitting the building of only one electronics centre and only one flight simulator, therefore these two stations were very much in favour.

Further, the air trooping terminal at Wildenrath precluded this base from closure.

The type of building required by the composite MU existed only at Brüggen.

The situation changed again as Wildenrath was now to become the base for the Harrier. As of April 1968, 'irrevocable work' was shortly to commence. Long-term planning still expected Laarbruch to close by the end of 1975 with no more than eight squadrons deployed on the remaining three stations.

There appears to have been an attempt to save all the clutch bases from the Treasury axe. One suggestion was made that to squeeze as many as thirty Phantoms onto a single base would result in congestion; the number of 30 was the original planned deployment, but this was to increase with the 'nothing east of Suez' policy being pursued by the Wilson government.

The proposal for a second Phantom base was put forward by Air Marshal Sir Denis Spotswood in March 1968. The CAS, Sir John Grandy, was not quite so sure that the case could be made. Thirty aircraft on a single airfield could not in all honesty be described as either congestion or even concentration. The specific airfield in question was Brüggen, where, as Grandy pointed out, twenty-five Canberras currently resided. There was also concern about the UE of ten aircraft per squadron proposed for the Phantom.

There was light at the end of the tunnel, though. Grandy could not confirm but was able to advise that with the end of substantial RAF assets being based in the Far East, at least as was being planned, then the air staff were lobbying to have an additional ten Phantoms assigned to Germany, thus being able to make the argument for a third air base on the Rhine. With one RAF station only recently gone and now another about to follow suit, RAFG was, some might have wondered, disappearing without any real sense of strategy. Were the RAF to either abandon the continent or at least consolidate itself?

Grandy's further case put to the government was that any financial savings in closing down Laarbruch could well be accrued by savings on reduced preparatory work at Brüggen. Most pertinently, the idea of placing all the Phantoms on a single base rendered them operationally vulnerable. Delaying full deployment was also being advanced to offset the financial drive to close Laarbruch. More good news for Spotswood was around the corner following the order/cancellation debacle of the 1960s, as an unconfirmed deployment of twenty-four Buccaneers and twelve additional Harriers was being talked about. If this all went ahead, it would certainly save Laarbruch from closure.

The 1970s began just as the RAF in Germany was taking steps at last to upgrade its frontline assets, most urgent of which was to pension off the Canberras. An easy analogy here had they been deployed in anger, as expected, against targets east of the inner German border, would be with the Fairy Battles of the RAF Advanced Air Strike Force deployed to France in 1939. The Fairy Battle was a light bomber which was decimated following the Phoney War period (1939–40). When engaged against enemy targets, they were shot down at an alarming rate. After 1940, they were withdrawn from operational use.

The venerable Canberras never met this test, but why were none of the nimbler American types relied on as an interim? Even though some of those with which comparison could be made themselves were not best suited to the daunting task bestowed upon them either, but the smaller faster jets (such as F-104s or F-100s) would logically stand some fleeting chance of surviving the near impenetrable Soviet air defences.

Back in September 1968, early after the cancellation of the F-111, the RAF moved toward the long-term consideration of what the makeup of its Germany command would be looking like well into the 1970s. Being proposed by the new C-in-C, Air Marshal Christopher Foxley-Norris, was draft plan 'R'; this called for an addition of twenty-four Buccaneers, twenty Phantoms, and twelve Harriers together with specific upgrades to three of his stations— Brüggen, Laarbruch, and Wildenrath. This presented no major concerns to the air staff and MOD, but there was expected to be some awkward questions arising from the Treasury.

The long-term forecast meant there was every justification for operating four air bases in Germany until 1974–75. The planned force could be deployed on just three bases thereafter. It was already expected by that stage that the Jaguar, which flew as a prototype for the first time only a couple of weeks earlier on 8 September, would have replaced the Phantom in what was still then only expected to be used in the 'ground support role'; the Phantom in turn would have replaced the Lightnings in the air defence role. The total force number of aircraft was expected to fall from 124 to 104.

Not perhaps all that surprising, Laarbruch expected to be closed was one of three listed for maintenance work. There were other concerns about plan R; the ground forces involved were expected to decline in number and although the aircraft numbers initially fell, RAFG was due to see a steady increase over the next two decades.

First, they were to inherit an increased number of Phantoms. This situation arose from the loss of bases in the Persian Gulf and Far East, such as Muharraq and Tengah, which was due to be the base for some Phantoms. There were further increases in numbers to come, which followed plan 'R', all of which suggested 'R' had shortcomings that needed to be addressed.

There was also a proposal to deploy an additional twelve Jaguars in due course; this would be at the expense of the total deployment of Jaguars in the UK. As far as the air force board and RAFG were concerned, this was acceptable. What the air chiefs liked about the plan was that it presented, as they saw it, an unassailable case for four airfields to present to the

Treasury. Therefore, it would be of much less concern to press ahead with the development of three airfields to take Phantoms, Buccaneers, and Harriers, bearing in mind that the fourth airfield, not considered for closure, would be safe from any Treasury attempts to look elsewhere. This was Gütersloh, the last remaining airfield which sat east of the Rhine and was currently home to the two interceptor squadrons with the Lightning F2 (F2A after the upgrade).

Therefore, at an AFB meeting on 26 September 1968, the proposal for a UE of thirty-six Jaguars to RAFG and twenty-four to UK commands, expected to be Air Support Command, was made.

RAF Germany Order of Battle as of August 1968

Base	Unit	Aircraft	Role	UE
Brüggen	213	Canberra B(I)6	Strike	12
Brüggen	80	Canberra PR7	Recce	10
Gütersloh	2	Hunter FR10	Fighter Recce	8
Gütersloh	4	Hunter FR10	Fighter Recce	8
Gütersloh	19	Lightning F2/2A	AD	12
Gütersloh	92	Lightning F2/2A	AD	12
Laarbruch	16	Canberra B(I)8	Strike	12
Laarbruch	31	Canberra PR7	Recce	10
Wildenrath	3	Canberra B(I)8	Strike	12
Wildenrath	14	Canberra B(I)8	Strike	12
Wildenrath	17	Canberra PR7	Recce	10
Wildenrath	Comms Sqn	Various	VIP Comms	8

Proposed Future Deployment of RAF Squadrons (Envisaged) as of August 1968

Base	Sqn	Aircraft	Role	UE
Brüggen	TBC	Phantom FGR2	AD	10
Brüggen	TBC	Phantom FGR2	AD	10
Gütersloh	TBC	Jaguar	Strike	12
Gütersloh	TBC	Jaguar	Strike	12
Laarbruch	TBC	Phantom FGR2	Strike	10
Laarbruch	TBC	Phantom FGR2	Recce	10
Laarbruch	TBC	Buccaneer S2	Strike	12

Laarbruch	TBC	Buccaneer S2	Strike	12
Wildenrath	TBC	Harrier GR1	CAS/BAI	12
Wildenrath	TBC	Harrier GR1	CAS/BAI	12
Wildenrath	TBC	Harrier GR1	CAS/BAI	12
Wildenrath	Comms Sqn	Various	VIP/Comms	8

What the table above demonstrates is that in 1968, the strike role was to be concentrated as a larger force on just two bases, instead of the hitherto deployment of placing one squadron at each of the rear bases. As for the Jaguar, at the time, it was not yet clear as to whether it could be deployed as an air superiority fighter; it showed some promise in this direction.

While the RAF were happy with the proposals, the Treasury, which had to give final approval to funding, was expected, almost certainly, to raise the relevance of the proposed strength in the long term. Furthermore, as the plan shows, the Phantom was expected to replace the Lightnings in the air defence role. Simple logic suggested developing Gütersloh for Phantoms. The move to the new generation of aircraft brought the matter of Anglo-German relations to the fore, namely that of aircraft noise. Even as the first Phantom squadron at Brüggen, 14 Sqn, began receiving the first of its new aircraft, a local newspaper, the Heinsberger Volkszeitung, was already complaining about the noise made by Lightnings that were on deployment to Wildenrath in September 1970. These aircraft had been in theatre since 1965, albeit based elsewhere, but had for a while, been based at nearby Geilenkirchen. A particularly pejorative passage read:

> The Lightnings, cause of the unbearable noise of the past few weeks, belong to a Fighter Squadron, which is at present temporarily based at Wildenrath. The extensive training flights of these aircraft, with the associated din, can be rather frightening. Their low-level sorties are certainly very disturbing for the local people. Experience shows that it is possible to adjust to a certain amount of noise, but there is a limit, an observation made by countless people living in the vicinity of the airfield.

The Wildenrath station commander, Gp Capt. D. M. Scrimgeour, accompanied by two other officers attended the council offices in Wassenberg, to discuss the noise level and suggest possible ways of alleviating the problem. The local government suggested the routing of flights over more agricultural land and not the more densely inhabited areas near the base. Eventually, the subject of jet noise, specifically referring to RAF operations, reached Air Vice-Marshal John Aiken, deputy C-in-C RAF Germany, who explained in a later interview that the jet noise of all NATO aircraft based in the Federal Republic was unfortunately unavoidable and said simply, it is the 'price of freedom'.

Aiken did further explain that all NATO aircrew were obliged to carry out the kind of training that caused the complaints; essentially, this was low-level training. Sure enough, if one feature or facet of rural life across north-west Europe in 1970 was ever prominent, it was the amount of low-flying military jets and nothing would change until after the Cold War.

Aiken emphasised the NATO rules on keeping clear of densely populated areas (as one might expect); in the case of supersonic speed, this may only be exercised under strict conditions—i.e. over selected sparsely populated areas, specially marked, and over the sea. Within NATO, RAF Germany was responsible for the defence of the airspace over North Rhine-Westphalia, Lower Saxony, and part of the North German coastal countries and shared responsibility for flight safety control of the air corridors to Berlin. AVM Aiken pointed out that there had been to his knowledge a single violation by a pilot who had 'apparently intentionally' violated the noise protection rules and that this man had been suspended from duty, repatriated to the UK, and subsequently dismissed from the RAF.

On the subject of the day, the deployment of Harriers and Phantoms to RAF bases in Germany and local rumours that they were louder, Aiken admitted that the rules, however tight, were no panacea against aircraft noise. Not only military but civilian aircraft were now prevalent in much greater numbers. Aircraft engines were only expected to get quieter in the next ten to fifteen years' time. Unfortunately, everything the RAF were going to deploy at the bases in North Rhine-Westphalia—Phantom (Brüggen & Laarbruch), Harrier (Wildenrath), Buccaneer (Laarbruch) and Lightning (Gütersloh)—were relatively powerfully engined aircraft and consequently noticeably noisier than those they would replace.

To protect the people living near the British bases during engine trial runs, bafflers (detuners) had already been built at Brüggen and Gütersloh, and the building of more at Wildenrath and Laarbruch had started. What was also explained to the German press and local communities was that the Harriers were to have about thirty 'small landing sites' identified within 30 miles of Wildenrath only, given the VSTOL nature of the Harrier. This aircraft would need to be able to operate independently of a large airfield, which in a crisis would be particularly vulnerable.

This was sold as a means of limiting the problem by spreading it more evenly around, with each site seeing a visit from exercising Harriers no more than a maximum of twice every month. The *Rheinische Post* reported in October that an army officer, Colonel Brown from BAOR, said in an interview that 'the appearance of the "Harrier" at the exercise site in Leuth could even be an attraction for children and adults'. Col. Brown was the BAOR liaison officer with the German authorities. Achim Klingenburg writing for the *Rheinische Post* added that the colonel's actual intention was to explain the role of BAOR to the authorities controlling Venlo Heath exercise area and how it contradicts the aims of the Maas-Schwalm-Nette Nature Park.

Klingenburg regarded the letter as the result of concentrated efforts to break the heath area away from the control of the military authorities. The colonel, if this is so, had a point to make; Venlo Heath had been used as a military exercise area for almost thirty years while the nature reserve was constructed only recently, in 1965. Furthermore, it should have been clear at the time that the heath would remain a military exercise area. Klingenburg poured scorn on this point, reminding his readers and Col. Brown that the area was first requisitioned by the German forces in 1943; Klingenburg wondered whether 'the British consider themselves the heirs of the Great German Luftwaffe'.

Brown went further, asserting that the necessity of military training required no further explanation. 'The efficiency of the forces must be secured'. Consideration from the military authorities had gone as far as to discontinue exercises on Venlo during weekends, that practice firing at night would take place only occasionally, and that the German authorities were always notified in advance. The German fire brigade had been called five times in five years and only once was it deployed to fight an actual fire.

The Buccaneer Mk 2 was to be the principal strike aircraft taking over from the Canberra. With the intention to base twenty-four in two squadrons in Germany, subject to treasury agreement, this paved the way for RAF Laarbruch to be retained; the UK reply (to the forthcoming NATO force planning questionnaire) would include Laarbruch as a firmly planned asset well beyond 1970. A further reassessment in April 1971 altered again the projected make-up of the RAF in Germany beyond 1975; most of the problems that concerned the RAF previously had been addressed.

The air staff had changed their minds about photo reconnaissance and air defence fighter deployments, described as likely to command approval militarily, money permitting. RAFG was essentially huddled on the Dutch border, and therefore might easily be called RAFNL. Then there was Gütersloh, nearer East Germany than Holland. As such, it was an indispensable asset. The latter was, indeed, a good distance east of the Rhine and surrounded by BAOR garrisons and barracks at Münster, Osnabruck, Krefeld, Paderborn, Bielefeld, Herford, Detmold, Lippstadt, and Minden. The city of Dortmund is located just 87 km down the A2 to the south-west.

It was noticed that the Harriers, due to their relative short range, should be deployed forward of Wildenrath. This became an argument essentially over which of the Lightning and Harrier had the shorter range and which needed to be positioned as far east as possible. The air defence fighters based at Gütersloh had a good reason to be there; it was a long-held view that this was the most suitable base for the interceptor force to meet the peacetime IAF/QRA task. They were ideally situated in the middle of their assigned area of responsibility. Even in the event of war, despite Gütersloh's obvious vulnerability, the Lightnings would still operate from here and, whatever circumstances dictated, would, if possible, return westwards to the nearest available allied airfield; to switch bases would largely be a 'relatively expensive and messy business'.

More a headache of a problem, which caused a good deal of fuss, was uprooting and swapping the simulators; this was not the only money-eating concern. The long-term plan, only six months previously, still envisaged placing the two fighter squadrons, once re-equipped with the Phantom, at Brüggen, and three Jaguar squadrons at Gütersloh, two with the tactical strike role and one reconnaissance unit. Long-term costings even suggested there would be enough funds available for an additional reconnaissance Phantom squadron, one in Germany in addition to one already planned in the UK. This would be desirable but would mean the long-term retention of the two Lightning squadrons in Germany. They also wanted four additional Jaguar squadrons, two to be based in Germany.

Revised plans, after August 1968, were approved to place forty Phantoms in the strike role at Brüggen, then replace them in turn with thirty-six Jaguars. A further revision added twenty-four more Jaguars to this figure. However, the total UE of sixty Jaguars were to be split into four squadrons of fifteen aircraft each, rather than five squadrons with twelve apiece. The rationale for this was to avoid the additional works services required to provide separate unit infrastructure. The four-squadron breakdown would also lead to fewer aircraft required for the QRA commitment and still meet with SACEUR's requirement.

An earlier 1968 plan placed three Jaguar strike squadrons and one in the reconnaissance role, all at Gütersloh; this had been arrived at due to the expected short legs of the Jaguar following early assessments of their lo-lo radius of action. 'Lo-lo' is jargon for 'low level, low level'. In sortie planning, high and low level are expressed as 'hi' and 'lo'; they are used in describing the sortie in terms of which legs are conducted at high or low level.

The findings limited them to Gütersloh as their operating base. The type's radius of action performance was clarified in early 1970, prompting the Jaguar's deployment in the strike role to be reconsidered. A further salient point here was the sleepless nights caused by the inevitable requirement to store nuclear weapons just 70 nm from the closest point of the border with East Germany. The vulnerability of Gütersloh if it had the strike role was, on second thoughts, too great a risk.

This was not all; as always, financial considerations played their part and to put Jaguars at Gütersloh would require funding to build a larger weapons store area that would need to take nuclear stores. However, there was insufficient room within the airfield confines to build on, so more land would need to be purchased. Logic dictated that the Harriers were the most suitable aircraft to operate from here for many reasons; they would be able deploy, around the immediate area, to smaller airfields, forest clearings, access roads, farms, fields, and the town square. The very nature of the Harrier and its ability to deploy made it a prime candidate for Gütersloh, given its exposed position which would in the event of hostilities see it abandoned immediately. They would also be right in amid 1st British Corps (BAOR) with whom the Harriers would work hand in glove along with a new helicopter wing, also to move to Gütersloh.

The whole concept seemed to awaken a sudden realisation that the Harriers should have gone straight to Gütersloh. Things take time, and from 1971, the Harriers were arriving at Wildenrath; they were then having to forward deploy the 85 miles to Gütersloh to use the ranges. On the other hand, using Gütersloh as a forward training base was still possible using existing manpower and equipment. Sufficient domestic accommodation existed but was judged to be of poor quality. One of the arguments still standing against deploying the Harriers to Gütersloh was the belief that the air defence fighter wing was going to remain there as well.

Gütersloh was still, geographically, the best airfield for the air defence role and shorter reaction time. This was in relation to both the Berlin corridor and the declared North Rhine-Westphalia region. In the event of war, when Gütersloh would instantly face a likely short period before being overrun, the interceptors would get airborne to meet the incoming airborne threat, and if they survived the initial encounter would recover to the clutch bases or anywhere still in friendly hands.

If Brüggen was to host a larger wing of Phantoms/Jaguars in the strike role and the Harriers and helicopters (Wessex/Puma) at Gütersloh, it would almost certainly mean the interceptors, of whatever type, would need to move somewhere else.

The provision of air defence facilities at Wildenrath was estimated to cost about £90,000. Swapping personnel between Gütersloh and Wildenrath would also create a lot of turbulence. There was also the problem of the mis-matching simulators. There was the recently installed Lightning Mk 2A simulator at Gütersloh, and £750,000 had recently been spent on a new building at Wildenrath to accommodate two Harrier simulators. New simulator buildings would be needed again, and it would take about two and a half years from a confirmed decision to the construction of a new Harrier simulator at Gütersloh. Due to the depth of specialisation of simulators, rather than being utilised to accommodate a Lightning simulator, the empty building left at Wildenrath would be better utilised housing a new Jaguar simulator.

This proposal was, for all reasons of administration and operations, most unwelcome. Therefore, the upshot on balance was to leave the Harriers at

Wildenrath and the Lightnings at Gütersloh. Taking into account the long-term view, accommodating a change in deployment, should it become indispensable to do so, would be possible as the cost set aside for building the nuclear storage infrastructure at Gütersloh came in handy. The decision for the long-term deployment of RAF winged units in West Germany was settled as of 26 April 1971. This was assuming that the Lightning would remain as the deployed interceptor. It was also taken into consideration that the money saved by not building the nuclear storage infrastructure at Gütersloh would be eroded if the Harriers and Lightnings were to swap. So, the strike role was destined to remain at Brüggen and Laarbruch. A final total of thirty Phantoms were to take up residence at the former and would, according to the 1971 planning, hand over in the late 1970s to a force of sixty Jaguars, deployed as four squadrons. Twenty-four Buccaneers would carry the bomb from Laarbruch.

The other deployment change was to form the reconnaissance F-4 Phantom squadron at Laarbruch instead of Brüggen. This single squadron, albeit with far more capable Phantoms, replaced a lot of armed and unarmed reconnaissance units—namely, two Hunter and three Canberra PR squadrons.

No. 2 Squadron's Phantoms would hand over to some of the Jaguars drawn from the proposed Brüggen wing. From 1970, the first of the three strike squadrons to re-equip with the F-4—14 Squadron—began their acquaintance with the big McDonnell Douglas fighter. The F-4 was a monster and an aircraft that brought capabilities and performance all inside the one airframe that both the RAF and the Royal Navy (also a Phantom operator) had never had before. The two squadrons that took on the Blackburn Buccaneer S Mk 2 made history as the first RAF aircraft deployed with the British bomb, outside the V-force. The structure of RAFG was now in the process of both a far-reaching upgrade and a radical re-alignment. Brüggen and Laarbruch would be home to an enlarged nuclear capable force, which would, by the leap ahead in performance of both types, be far more versatile, survivable, and adaptable. The aircraft deployed would be just as able to conduct close air support and conventional attack; the Phantom had an even wider repartee.

The close air support role largely neglected since the early 1960s was to be vastly improved, as a squadron from the Far East, 20 Sqn, was to re-deploy to Wildenrath where it would join 4 and (by 1972) 3 Squadrons to re-equip with the Harrier. Two former Canberra reconnaissance squadrons, 17 and 31, were to re-equip with Phantoms and move to Brüggen, where they would join 14 Sqn, assigned to strike duties. No. 16 Squadron would remain at Laarbruch but replace its Canberras with the Buccaneer, becoming the last to do so in 1972; it was also joined by another unit, 15 Squadron, previously disbanded with the contraction of the V-force, in 1965.

All this took until the latter end of 1972 to fully complete. There was one more change in procedures to come. On 2 May 1973, a new directive was issued to the AOC-in-C RAF Germany; this directive made clear that he was the custodian of all British nuclear weapons assigned to RAFG custody, security, and control, in accordance with SD 814 (RAF nuclear weapons duties, simply referred to by the RAF police, when so engaged, as '814 Duties') and for their handling both in peacetime and times of international tension within the terms of Ministry of Defence letter AF/ZA.71/67/456.

This letter was issued on 10 May 1971. A further letter of instruction—AF/ZA.71/67/363—issued on 22 May 1972 and in conjunction with TD 811 (RAF alert procedures—general war) applied exclusively to those nuclear weapons issued only to the Buccaneer squadrons based at Laarbruch.

This did not mean that the RAFG commander retained full operational control of the British bombs; full autonomous control of the force would transfer from SACEUR on the issue of a NATO alert message, meaning SACEUR retained oversight during peacetime, while during periods of tension, upon receipt of direction by alert message, the RAF Laarbruch station commander, in this case, would take responsibility. This would be subject to the implementation of a complimentary RAF alert measure for the transfer of operational command of the base's nuclear arsenal.

The RAFG commander was also to issue written instructions to the station commander at RAF Laarbruch, detailing the day-to-day handling, security, and custody procedures of the British weapons held at this station. While the Laarbruch weapons were assigned to the control of SACEUR, approval for their use would have to be given by the British prime minister. Should Laarbruch face an attack by ground forces placing the weapons in danger of falling into enemy hands, the station commander was to arrange for the evacuation of the weapons to a safe storage place in the UK, very similar to that practiced under Exercise Quick Train.

Due to the change in circumstances at Laarbruch, the issue of British bombs being stored on German soil arose. The Buccaneer had always carried British weapons following their initial entry into service with the Royal Navy; this was before the question of their being used by the RAF. Logic dictated that the RAF jets would be the same for all reasons of cost and time.

The German government, having had some time before the Buccaneers arrived, indicated that they welcomed the intention to deploy these aircraft and, more to the point, their attendant nuclear bombs, but said they would like to conclude a formal agreement beforehand. Clearance was obtained from the prime minister, Harold Wilson (these proceedings were concluded before the change to the Conservative government of Edward Heath, in 1970), to go ahead with a formal approach to both the US and West German governments to prepare for the changeover; this was particularly significant because it would alter the situation regarding the established control.

Initial concerns for the British were that by issuing formal notification to the West Germans, it might be taken to suggest that they were being invited to have a say over the use of the British bombs on German soil. What particularly concerned the British government was that diplomacy dictated that they would have to consider any proposals while hoping the Germans would not pursue anything awkward; if they did, then the following would need to be resolved:

> The obvious political implications of any suggestion of German control over nuclear weapons.
>
> The possibility that the interposition of any separate form of bilateral control additional to that already exercised by nations through the NATO council might weaken the effectiveness of the deterrent.
>
> The possible repercussions on the arrangements already existing in regard to American weapons.

The British were also anxious to give the American authorities a chance to comment on the matter before approaching the Germans; as of July 1969, this could not be delayed much longer as deployment of Buccaneers would not be too far away, by which time everything had to be in place to permit the Buccs to be operated as intended.

The specific device to be delivered by the Buccaneers in Germany was to be the WE177A, specially designed for low-level delivery from high performance aircraft. This was the direct successor to Red Beard, a weapon which was never deployed by the RAF in Germany but by the V-force, which also carried a version of WE177 exclusively from 1969. This followed the end of the Blue Steel role, rendered obsolete by the full deployment of the navy's Polaris submarines. The WE177 was ready for use first in 1967, the first recipients being the Navy's Buccaneers. Obsolescent nuclear weapons were to be withdrawn from service and fissile material was to be recovered for use in the WE177A programme. The defence secretary therefore informed the prime minister that, with Treasury agreement, he had issued an order for additional WE177As for the Buccaneers declared to SACEUR.

The NATO nuclear planning group met in London the same month to review the tentative guidelines for the possible initial use of tactical nuclear weapons by NATO. The attending ministers reviewed a paper jointly produced by the United Kingdom and the Federal Republic of Germany. In short, the document reaffirmed the need to maintain sufficient tactical nuclear forces as part of the spectrum of deterrents within the NATO strategic doctrine, which ran from conventional forces through to the tactical nuclear to strategic forces.

The Brüggen weapons remained the Americans' responsibility. The long-term intention was to replace the American bombs as soon as sufficient numbers of the British-built WE177s became available. Being an American aircraft made the Phantom an ideal candidate to be sent to the back of the queue as far as the WE177s were concerned.

Therefore, the Phantom wing at Brüggen continued to be governed by US regulations, just as the Canberra boys were before. The overseeing responsibility in this case was assigned to the commander of the United States 3rd Air Force. He also had control over the nuclear weapons issued to the F-104 squadrons, so assigned, within the Belgian, Netherlands, Canadian, and Federal German Air Forces. The versions of the Phantom operated by the RAF and Royal Navy differed markedly from any other in operation with any other air arms across the world. The UK Phantoms were to be powered by Rolls-Royce Spey low-bypass turbofans as opposed to the General Electric J79 turbojets, fitted to all other models. The F-4s issued to British forces fell short of the projected performance expected by the RAF. Specifically, there were some performance characteristics which met or even bettered expectations; these were rate of climb, time to height overall, and acceleration.

The disappointment was in combat ceiling, range, and endurance; the lighting and burning ceiling of the engines' afterburners fell short as well. When the Phantom was being considered for UK service back in the early 1960s, much of its performance was predicted, not proven, and extrapolated from flight test results from development versions of the Spey engine. The combat ceiling was attributed to the Spey's lack of its predicted performance at higher altitudes. The shortfalls in acceleration and maximum speed were attributable to the airframe and its accommodation of the fatter Spey engines. It was also noted that the Americans had even experienced disappointment in the performance of Phantoms that had been fitted with the more up-to-date version of the J79 engine. The shortfalls in predicted performance were something of a surprise as data derived from calculations on the Spey engine by McDonnell Douglas and Rolls-Royce had forecast a much-improved aircraft. This data was also checked by the US Navy department and the Ministry of Aviation, a British government body.

All agreed about the British engine version of the F-4. The oversights were in misreading the figures based on the hidden drag areas on the basic US aircraft design, which were predicted on the modifications on the engine nozzles on the Spey-fitted aircraft. The original data was found to be wrong therefore the Spey-based information was wrong. This was an engine/airframe interface problem, which could have been resolved if more time could have been made available before getting the aircraft into service. A similar problem was encountered when making similar calculations based on the basic F-111. The F-4M and the F-4K (the specific naval version) possessed a startling performance relative to the aircraft they would be replacing, and still better by most margins than the Jaguar (its proposed successor at that time).

The latter's entry into RAF Germany was long-predicted, well before the first of the Phantoms arrived at Brüggen. For all the obvious shortcomings, no one was keen to go down the road of proving such in order to pursue some form of compensation. This would have involved a series of complex and lengthy performance trials to establish the alleged performance limits that may well not have been proved to a satisfactory degree to determine liability. Furthermore, the RAF had 'no means in law' to compel a contractor to 'foot the bill' should such costly trials have provided a strong enough case.

Most off-putting of all was the cost balance between pursuing the manufacturer over the failure to meet specification and the cost of trying to belatedly meet specific performance markers to rectify the Phantom's performance. The Spey engine was not deemed to be a contributor to the reduced performance, such as speed at high altitude and ceiling attained; it produced the level of thrust expected but with alterations to the nozzles and boat tail drag. The British Phantoms were most closely compared with the US Navy F-4J/N, which the F-4M/K were expected to outperform in certain measures and reach parity within others. The following shows a comparison table for the F-4J and F-4K in contrast to one another:

Phantom Performance Comparison

		F-4J	F-4K
Engine		GE J79	Rolls Royce Spey
Maximum speed at 36,000 ft	Expected	2.25 Mach	2.10 Mach
	Achieved	2.09 Mach	1.96 Mach
	Shortfall	7%	7%
Combat ceiling Supersonic	Expected	57,550 ft	54,700 ft
	Achieved	55,750 ft	50,500 ft
	Shortfall	3%	8%
Combat ceiling Subsonic	Expected	49,500 ft	51,500 ft
	Achieved	51,500 ft	48,600 ft
	Shortfall	+ 4%	6%
Acceleration Vmil to Mach 1.2	Expected	0.48 min	0.54 min
	Achieved	0.56 min	0.54 min
	Shortfall	17%	*

Rate of Climb	Expected	11,350 fpm	15,000 fpm
At 35,000ft	Achieved	14,200 fpm	15,500 fpm
	Shortfall	17%	*
Time to climb	Expected	1.25 min	1.20 min
To 35,000ft	Achieved	1.10 min	1.09 min
	Shortfall	*	*
Maximum Specific	Expected	0.124 nm/lb	0.148
Range	Achieved	0.119 nm/lb	0.116
	Shortfall	4%	16%

*Within margin of error range when assessing performance, so assessed as zero shortfall.

What will come as absolutely no surprise in these cynical times are the reasons that both the RAF and the RN finished up with Spey engines powering their F-4 Phantoms at all. Both services had reviewed their respective requirements and agreed that the performance, accurately determined on the narrower J79s, was acceptable and not worth what was already forecast to be a high cost sustained by fitting the bigger, heavier Speys. However, economic, industrial, and political arguments prevailed, and the British government decision was to press ahead with the Spey-engine re-fit. This decision was taken in October 1965.

Furthermore, the cost of each engine was reduced by £15,000 by reducing the VMAX specification from Mach 2.4 to 2.1. The industrial advantage was assistance to Rolls-Royce in the development of the TF41 and later RB211 engines. RR had no other major project at the time and was about to run into the red. On reflection, the RAF understood the pragmatic nature of the government from a national point of view. Yet as events bore out, the uniformed services noticed that the Spey decision was one of the least cost-effective steps taken over the period. Amortising research and development costs, each Spey Phantom cost £2,250,000 instead of the approximate £1,000,000 for an off-the-shelf F-4J, -N, or -E for example.

Interestingly, the estimated cost of the J79 engine model was arrived at post sterling devaluation, which had led to the cancellation of the F-111. As a result, the services found it very difficult to obtain financial approval to carry out the major improvements that would have redressed the outcome.

The major improvements sought were aimed at regaining the more improved performance originally expected. As it stood, the performance of the British Phantoms was only slightly inferior to its closest US comparison, the F-4J, -N, and -E, except in acceleration below 450 knots and in take-off distance where it was in fact better.

Payload cruise performance was similar, but a big improvement was expected here. Most telling of all, given all the contemporary literature in the public domain about the British Phantoms, which never fought shy of pointing out any short comings, the aircraft failed to reach the magic Mach 2 according to the trial data; however, such specifics tend to be too rigidly applied.

The RAF Phantoms deployed at Brüggen were to carry the Mk 43 and Mk 57 US bombs; the latter was designed to be delivered by aircraft travelling at supersonic speeds but was commonly carried by maritime aircraft including the RAF's Nimrods and had a maximum yield setting of 20 kt.

The former was a 2,000-lb + device, which had a yield of 70 kt to 1 mg. No. 14 Squadron was scheduled to commence the training syllabus toward operational effectiveness from November 1970, with training to be complete by May 1971. The aim was that 14 Sqn would become operational by August while 17 Sqn should reach the same standard and qualification in November.

Despite the previous special handling operation of Canberras, new infrastructure was required among such improvements as deemed necessary. This was to ensure Brüggen would meet SHAPE requirements for the purpose intended. A widening of the doorway to the existing special armaments storage facility, this was expected to be ready by the end of May. Only minor maintenance services were required to the main gate and the perimeter fence for which the station commander at Brüggen was responsible. There was some concern that the modification states of some aircraft would be compatible with the strike role by the target date; this matter had been referred to the Phantom engineering project officer, who was investigating and would report back but did not envisage any major problems.

It was well into 1971 before clearance to carry nuclear weapons was established. In January 1971, a pre-operational nuclear safety study was conducted concerning the Phantom FGR2s (F-4Ms). The study comprised a presentation at RAF Rheindahlen by HQ RAF Germany staff officers on all aspects of the system, demonstrating loads with dummy weapons at Brüggen and a detailed review of the USAFE publication *Technical and Nuclear Safety Analysis*. The expectation of the study was that it would lead to the granting, in about three months' time, of American authority to release the US bombs for operational service with RAF Phantoms. 26 June 1971 was the date for the final capability inspection by the inspector general of munitions from HQ USAFE to ensure that all aspects of the Phantom system were ready to be declared operational. For this to be passed, copies of the 'nuclear weapons clearances', the orders under which the weapons were to be handled and deployed, would need to be in place at Brüggen by the day before, no later.

Air Vice-Marshal David Evans (ACAS) told the VCAS that there was 'no give': 'If these weapons cards were not held by the station at the time of the inspection, the operational declaration of 14 Squadron and the tactical evaluation of the base would be delayed yet again'. The pressure increased because the operational due date had slipped several months already, due to incidents involving the installation of the bombs on Phantom aircraft, specifically affecting the reversion of the potting compound used in electrical connectors installed in the aircraft. As well as the administrative and maintenance oversight, the final line of security of the armed Phantoms continued in the hands of the US Air Force Security Police, who were armed at all times and under instructions to shoot to kill anyone entering the housing of a nuclear-armed aircraft. No room for flexibility could be accommodated.

The RAF provided the outer ring of security. This arrangement existed across NATO through to the end of the Cold War, where the Americans made their own atom bombs available for others to set off. A little-known point probably is just how many air-delivered tactical nuclear weapons were stored around NATO air bases, and which units were assigned the role of carrying them in anger should we have got to that point.

In 1971, the F-104 wings of the Belgian Air Force at Kleine Brogel, the Dutch at Volkel, the Canadians at Baden Solingen, and the West German Air Force at Memmingen, Lechfeld, Buchel, and Norvenich all operated under very much the same arrangement.

The atmosphere at Brüggen retained a distinctly American flavour until 1976, when the last of the Phantoms were replaced by the Jaguars. As with the Buccaneers, the Jaguars brought the end of British reliance on the American bomb in RAF Germany. The key to the change was that Britain eventually produced enough WE177 weapons to supply demand. The WE177 from here on was the standard issue device carried by RAF aircraft, save for the anti-submarine role.

US weapons continued to be carried by the maritime patrol units. The Shackleton previously carried the American Mk 101 bomb, as did the Nimrod thereafter, until replaced by the B57. This arrangement required the basing of US Navy maintenance personnel and a US marine security detachment at RAF St Mawgan.

By October 1971, 14 and 17 Sqns at Brüggen were competing alongside the remaining Canberras of 3 and 16 Sqns. This produced an interesting result which reflected admirably on the latter.

The Phantom had not been in West Germany months before they were called upon to prove their mettle against the clunking old Canberras. One could put it down to the Phantom crews being yet to get their feet under the table, but they were humbled by the big unwieldy first-generation jet bomber. The Salmond Trophy Bombing and Navigation Competition in October 1971 produced the following results:

Unit	Type	Score		
3 Squadron	Canberra B(I)8	8,630 points	(86.3%)	1st Place
16 Squadron	Canberra B(I)8	8,577 points	(85.8%)	2nd Place
17 Squadron	Phantom FGR2	8,529 points	(85.3%)	3rd Place
14 Squadron	Phantom FGR2	7,606 points	(76.1%)	4th Place

The winners of the competition, 3 Squadron, were themselves on the eve of disbanding and re-equipping with the Harrier GR1 in the very conventional offensive air support role.

No. 31 Squadron had started their own conversion to the Phantom FGR2 during October and received their tenth F-4 on 23 October, three days after the Salmond competition.

This was quite a busy month for the command as they also took over control of the Bloodhound support unit based at RAF West Raynham in England. Three more Harriers were delivered to RAF Wildenrath this month, bringing the total delivered so far to twenty-six GR1s but just two T2s. Two of the GR1s were unavailable for use as they were to undergo the change to the new more powerful Pegasus Mk 102 engines. The new power plant provided an extra 1,000 lb of thrust changing the aircraft designation from GR1 to GR1A. By the end of the year, a total of thirty-five Harriers had been delivered to Wildenrath. Four of them had been on the Mk 102 engine retrofit programme at Wittering in Leicestershire. The first of the Buccaneer squadrons, No. 15, had received six of the Mk 2B aircraft at Laarbruch.

Even before the command fully re-equipped with the Phantom, work was already proceeding with preparations for the Phantom's replacement, the BAC Sepecat Jaguar. The Jaguar was an aircraft that truly looked the part, but with a performance that, on the face of it, was not particularly remarkable. It was half the size of the Phantom and it had a lesser range and upper ceiling, limited, according to what little profile info was released, to about 45,000 feet. However, certain aspects remained classified for many years and, as the following pages reveal, its performance and handling characteristics were not easily dismissed.

The Jaguar started life in the late 1960s intended as an advanced jet trainer. However, the potential of this aircraft was such that its deployment as a close support jet was pursued instead while the idea of a wholly advanced trainer was abandoned because the advanced trainer outgrew this role. Eventually, the Jaguar was assessed as a far more sophisticated and capable airframe. The arrival in service of the Jaguar presaged the redeployment of the Phantoms to the air defence role, in turn moving most of the Lightnings on to retirement.

The Jaguar in time proved itself but on entering service, the aircraft's performance did not impress; a common term of endearment at the time was that reheat was needed to get the aircraft to taxi.

During the 1970s, the Adour engines were uprated from 7,305 to 8,040 lb augmented. On paper, the performance figures were respectable enough. The Jaguar was supersonic at all altitudes. It also supposedly had an eye-opening rate of climb; data recently revealed in the public domain states a time to climb to 30,000 feet of 1.5 minutes, this suggests an initial rate of climb in the order of close to 40,000 feet per minute. It may seem illogical at first glance; to explain, time to climb refers to the maximum rate of climb under the aircraft's own power from take-off. Initial rate of (or zoom) climb refers to the rate of climb attained when the kinetic energy of forward flight is used to boost performance in a pull to the vertical at full power. The latter is not sustained, but the initial rate of climb upon rotating the nose is at its most robust.

Its low-level performance was second, if at all, only to the Buccaneer. The Jaguar's ability to look after itself (something which one does not make any comparison to regarding both the Buccaneer and Canberra) was such that Jaguars flown by RAF pilots for the sultan of Oman's Air Force, where possible, deemed its need for an escort of 'Hunters' as quite essential. The typical formation mix was about four Hunters to cover a flight of four to six Jaguars. A standard 'fluid 4' was the most favoured tactical formation, with a similar Hunter formation escorting from the rear about 2 miles in trail. The typical speeds, practiced with a full weapon load, were 450 kts for cruise and 540 kts (for as long as possible) during ingress, weapon delivery, and egress. These sorties were being flown normally at around 100 feet. Over flat terrain, the pilots found they could provide cross-visual cover; when the height is reduced, however, the pilot can develop forward tunnel vision, thus placing almost total reliance on passive electronic warning systems.

The Oman pilots found that these ultra-low-level escort missions provided excellent training in all terrains, including against both land and sea targets. Over the sea, they found they were quite successful at penetrating AEW-controlled fighter CAPs, where the escort successfully engaged the defending fighters, allowing the Jaguars to press on.

The most interesting finding of all was the Jaguar's attributes as an interceptor. Routine training in this role was carried out primarily to give intercept controllers practise. Given the Jaguar has no AIR system, these training sorties were of little value from the perspective of the pilots, but the benefit to controllers was beyond doubt, allowing more complex scenarios to be put together involving various attack aircraft in varying numbers with various numbers of fighters on CAP.

The exercises were regularly carried out with aircraft from a US Navy aircraft carrier. The Jaguar, flown in the role of interceptor, proved itself equal to the task, obvious limitations notwithstanding. Flown clean, it could hold CAP for a reasonable period of time and surprised at least those USN aircrew not familiar with it by its low-level energy and manoeuvrability. Described as 'like the Lightning, from the same stable, it likes to be flown hard and fast'. Not surprisingly, just the same, this glowing report also made the point that the aircraft was flown clean and near to the operating base with the majority of air combat training sorties flown overhead. The Jaguar was at times described as a 'Jekyll and Hyde' aircraft. As soon as drop tanks were fitted and ordnance, the Jaguar was radically different both in terms of performance and behaviour. Whatever the merits of the Anglo-French jet, group captain air plans submitted a request to the RAFG senior air staff officer for at least eighteen Phantoms to be retained in the dual strike/attack role beyond 1975.

The loss of eighteen Phantoms to air defence was considered as more than justified by the increased contribution to the strike/attack role. A further proposal was made that Phantoms should also retain a secondary reconnaissance role once converted to air defence. The RAF worried that the Jaguar, if relied upon entirely, would leave a void in the night/all-weather reconnaissance capability. None of this indicated immense confidence in the Jaguar.

Its pending arrival in RAF service was met with concern by the Air Force Board. Both the AMP and VCAS warned that the forecast of available pilots with ground attack experience would be insufficient to meet the introduction of the Jaguar during the period 1973 to 1976. Demand for such would be at a peacetime peak during this period. The numbers would certainly fall way short of the demand. Plans for the Jaguar's introduction had been altered to minimise the impact and a search for serving pilots on other types, with ground attack experience, was on to increase the supply to meet the demand. This was still going to leave a deficit.

At the end of 1971, forty pilots completed basic flying training and were considered suitable for the fast jet stream but were a part of the backlog for advanced training prior to reaching the relevant OCUs. On the other hand, a surplus of Hawker Hunters, with a few years of useful life left in them, were available as this type had just been withdrawn from frontline operations. A squadron of about seventeen Hunter FGA9s and a T7 could certainly be formed. This unit would then be a *de facto* operational unit (in intent, an operational training unit), allowing for an expansion of current ground-attack-experienced pilots in the early years of the Jaguar's introduction. This would also take pressure off the pre-OCU backlog.

The squadron would be assigned to 38 Group (Air Support Command), giving it operational status, but it was not to be declared to NATO. As for the extent of effective training, there was enough space within the UK low-flying system to accommodate the increased usage and room on the East Coast ranges. There was also a need for 30-mm ball ammunition, inert SNEB rocket pods with launchers, and perhaps practice bombs and carriers.

West Raynham was initially chosen as the home for the new squadron, providing the UE did not exceed fourteen aircraft. At the time, work was being carried out on the airfield at Wittering and it was proposed that the squadron should move here in October. In the meantime, FGA9 airframes with a healthy fatigue life—enough to see them through to 1976 at least—were available and just needed servicing. The Avon 207 engines were in short supply as those they had available required a lot of in-depth maintenance. This could be rectified with an increase in the overhaul rate.

Eventually, the RAF generated two such Hunter squadrons to feed the supply of sufficiently rated pilots through to the Jaguar OCU at Lossiemouth. Thus, by early 1977, 45 and 58 Squadrons at Wittering were disbanded and the fifth and final RAFG Jaguar unit, 20 Sqn, had formed at Brüggen.

Along with the Buccaneer and Phantom, the third new tactical fixed-wing type arriving in service at the end of the 1960s was the Harrier. Unlike the former two, the Harrier specifically addressed the distinct lack of a recognisable tactical support fighter. A document issued in 1967 (then revised in August 1968) detailed the deployment and operational concept of the Harrier.

A supposedly definitive document produced jointly in April 1972, by RAFG and an MOD working party, determined the 'Role of the Harrier', the main task of which was to provide close air support to the forces of NORTHAG. In addition, the Harriers in Germany would be involved with 'making a contribution' to battlefield approaches and flying a daylight tactical reconnaissance task of the NORTHAG battle area and its approaches. The Harrier's reputation precedes it, but frankly speaking, the aircraft had short legs and was supersonic only in a shallow dive. That said, its initial rate of climb was quite stupendous, about 50,000 feet per minute, achieving parity with the English Electric Lightning in this regard.

The Harrier's true appeal boiled down to a specific and unique aspect of its performance, which had made it a legend and household name; this would be its VSTOL party trick. A source of fascination at air shows for decades through the successful design of jet nozzles, which could be pivoted to face downwards to allow the aircraft to sit on a continuous thrust of hot air, it never failed to impress. I am sure this was widely understood by most, but the public marvelling at the Harrier's invisible plinth (just a constant plume of hot air) never seemed to abate at air displays. Truthfully, VTOL (as opposed to STOL) was a costly operation to get a limited range and weapon load up, but if the target was close by, it could come in handy. The Harrier could not lift vertically with a full payload.

By 1972, the RAFG squadrons were primarily committed to developing dispersed site operations but had no night capability. The aim was to provide this capability in the fullness of time. Of the three squadrons (3, 4, and 20), 4 Sqn had the specific secondary role of reconnaissance of battlefield targets in NORTHAG's area, so the recce pods were all assigned to them.

Yet all three units were primarily assigned the attack role. Nos 3 and 20 Sqns had a limited reconnaissance capability by the permanent fitting of the port facing F95 camera and a voice recorder. The MOD (air) were looking at the idea of using the Harriers assigned to the OCU at Wittering in Leicestershire as reinforcements for the RAFG squadrons. The study was not yet complete in 1972, but an interim plan to deploy twelve Harriers from 233 OCU to RAF Wildenrath at the 'simple alert' stage was authorised.

As for the fourth operational Harrier squadron in the RAF, No. 1 Sqn (based at Wittering) could deploy to Wildenrath as an independent unit, but it could not deploy into the field as an extension of the Harrier force with their equipment of the time. The period 1970–71 brought a significant change in fortune for the RAF' posture on the Continent. After the political vacillation and ineptitude of the preceding decade, the start of the 1970s promised and delivered vast improvement after all. Not only were the old and obsolete to be replaced, but the scope and versatility of the command was to be positively transformed. To boot, rather than see another round of cuts to numbers, the orbat was actually destined to expand and, in terms of the nuclear role, offer greater autonomy.

To guard against a surprise air attack, all Harriers would disperse within the perimeter fence to various individual hides. Any aircraft not so deployed at the time of an air attack would be ordered onto a survival scramble. The remainder would stay 'hidden' in dispersal. The aircraft would then remain deployed on base until tasked or further imminent attacks, particularly a land assault.

Despite the decision to base the Harriers at Wildenrath long term, it was accepted that this placed them 180 nms from the likely area where they would be engaged in the event of hostilities, too far for any effective use. Therefore, in the event of sufficient warning, all thirty-six Harriers would be deployed to forward sites; each squadron was allocated two, a primary and a sub-site. With all three squadrons deployed, three primary and three sub-sites would accommodate all the RAFG Harriers.

The field wing operations centre, located at a primary site, would oversee tasking that would be passed to each of the squadron operations centres at each of the primary sites. The whole tactical deployment required the involvement of several other units allocated from both the army and the RAF. No. 21 Field Signals Regiment were responsible for external and inter-site communications links. BRUIN battlefield communications equipment was used for communications between the deployed force and external agencies. Within the confines of a Harrier deployment zone, the internal comms would relay field telephones, PYE (UHF) radio sets, and Stornophone (VHF) radio equipment. The latter, rationed to one per site, was quite new and still subject to evaluation.

The deployment was further reliant on the army, in this case the Royal Engineers, for preparing and maintaining the deployment sites and associated logistics areas. No. 38 Field Regiment, Royal Engineers, would reinforce BAOR in times of tension but their specific task would be to support the deployed Harrier force. At such a stage where they were no longer required for the Harriers in the first instance, they would make themselves available to BAOR once again. No. 38 Field Regiment was ordinarily based at Ripon in Yorkshire. If deployed as required, they would move as an entire unit irrespective of the level of personnel and equipment required. A contingency plan, Operation Huntsman, covered the deployment of the unit—the advance party travelled by air and the main party by road and sea, assembling in a harbour area. The unit would then establish a central base in the deployment area.

Work on preparing the sites was to be completed no later than seventy-two hours past the declaration of simple alert. Once the initial work required was complete, only a reduced number of the engineers would need to stay on for further maintenance work, to ensure the continued operation of the Harriers. Among the preparations were the laying of a forward pad at each site for vertical recoveries of Harriers, along with the preparation of access tracks and hides, camouflaging of hides, logistics parks, vehicle access tracks and the construction of alternative sites as required.

What the engineers did not have, which both RAFG and BAOR considered essential, was secure communications. The engineers had C42 radio equipment, which operated on VHF but was insecure. They were not expecting to upgrade to a secure system until 1975. In the meantime, they would have to use authentication tables, codes, and codewords. This was considered acceptable enough in the interim.

When fully deployed, 38 Regiment, Royal Engineers, consisted of 864 personnel with 335 vehicles. Ironically, the responsibility for the actual ground-borne defence of the deployed areas themselves fell not to the army but to the RAF via the RAF Regiment. Indeed, this kind of role was as close to the RAF Regiment's original reason for existence as it was possible to get. Specifically, 2 RAF Regiment field squadrons and a headquarters, all based at RAF Wittering, were assigned the task of confronting the expected physical threat from small groups of saboteurs. Such groups were loosely defined as possibly operating in groups up to ten armed with automatic weapons, grenades, and plastic explosives. Added to this was the threat of a chemical attack, which could be dropped by air directly onto the sites or dispersed up wind as a non-persistent agent. Again, under Operation Huntsman, the entire RAF Regiment-assigned force based at Wittering would deploy by air and sea at the stage of military vigilance, this being the NATO military posture before simple alert (originally 'single alert').

The element traveling by sea would deploy by road to the harbour. This was the defence plan for the Harrier sites during any transition to war period.

The manner in which the regiment personnel would be deployed would be at the immediate discretion of the RAF Regiment wing commander in charge of the deployment. The principal aim, however, would be to prevent an enemy force getting within sufficient range to employ weapons against the assets, including aircraft, fuel storage, and other valuable targets—the *raison d'être* of the regiment.

With this aim, the defence around each site would ordinarily consist of two concentric circles of defence, the inner one made up of all and any available personnel, while the outer would be the responsibility of the RAF Regiment. The inner circle would be composed of set positions near vulnerable points. What was not possible was any overlap between sites to provide mutual support between them. Therefore, reinforcements may well become necessary in the event of a concerted attack. To address this matter a mobile force would be located at one of the sites as central as possible.

Routine ground defence tasks were to be divided between specialist and non-specialist tasks. The specialist tasks, helmed by the RAF Regiment, included such things as hidden daytime observation posts, night listening posts, patrols by day, and guards for convoys by both day and night. The non-specialist tasks included daytime sentries and close defence; they were dependent on the number of other personnel available. This varied depending on the requirement for operational flying balanced against the assessed threat to the sites at the time; the priority could be either. The bulk of the ammunition assigned to the RAF Regiment was held at Bracht and would be moved forward on the same ammunition trains carrying the Harriers' weapons.

The deployment from Wittering would carry 100 rounds of ammunition per man for immediate use. The deployment sites naturally relied on concealment. Air attack was the first consideration in this regard, and the compromise of the sites was expected through 'systematic enemy reconnaissance or by random overflights'. While an observed recce flight by enemy forces would not necessarily be followed up with a subsequent air attack, the deployed unit and affiliates had to be ready to redeploy to an alternate. A random discovery from the air was not, in fact, expected to be followed by an air attack for at least two hours. Therefore, redeployment of all had to be managed inside this period.

At least one, preferably two, alternative sites had to be available to each primary. C-in-C RAF Germany would retain control over the RAFG Harrier force until the NATO simple alert stage. At this level and providing MOD London also accepted that simple alert had been reached, the Harriers would fall under the control of commander 2nd Allied Tactical Air Force. The RAF Regiment deployment from the UK would be placed under the operational control of the Harrier force commander on arrival at Wildenrath—or as would later be the case, Gütersloh, the same for the army's 38 Field Regiment. The station commander of the Harrier base in Germany would automatically become the force commander.

The concept and nature of the Harriers and the helicopters very much placed them at the service of the BAOR directly, not just in terms of operational support, but how they would be positioned—to move out into the open environment and leave the infrastructure of the home base behind. Some might think this meant the rest of the RAF in Germany could have a soft existence staying on base, which during peacetime is hard to argue against. The tactical deployable nature of the Harriers and helicopters meant this element of RAFG, like much of the army, spent time living under canvas and coping with the privations of life 'in the field'. Like any air force or military arm, each element adapts to exploit the best of the prevailing circumstances. As such, most high-performance aircraft need to have the required airfield infrastructure to operate from; they cannot operate from anywhere else. The inevitable positive flow from this, in the long term, is permanent facilities. This has always presented a bone of contention with the other services generally. The army, by their nature, are destined to deploy into open terrain and adapt as best they can. The navy's lot is to live in the typically cramp conditions at sea, whether serving on a frigate or an aircraft carrier and worse still for submariners.

Aircraft carriers bring another dimension to air power, but no panacea answer; they have their own shortcomings, attendant bugbears, and problems. When the Harrier wing eventually repositioned to Gütersloh in 1977, the process of upgrading to the Harrier GR3 had just been completed. Equipped with Lazer Tracking and the Mk 103 Pegasus engine, it produced 21,500 lb of static thrust.

September 1978 brought the opportunity for the units of RAFG to exercise their principal roles further afield. Exercise Northern Wedding was a NATO maritime exercise. It involved most of the Germany-based RAF units. No. 2 Squadron (AC) carried out sixteen anti-ship reconnaissance missions.

Of the pilots selected for this, three had previous maritime reconnaissance ops training during 'best focus' training exercises. Their targets included a heavily escorted convoy and an amphibious task force. This came as a refreshing change from photographing static land targets. On 15 September, they gained some very good images of the amphibious assault force running from a lee shore in 'storm 10' conditions. No. 15 Squadron, while flying a purpose-built maritime aircraft, the Buccaneer, were, ironically, miscast in the role of maritime anti-ship operations. This became evident as the crews struggled in a very demanding environment.

The Bucc crews still got some valuable cross-training as they flew their charges in the role for which it was originally intended, even though harsh weather conditions curtailed many sorties. Another exercise was conducted to test the response to a Warsaw Pact attempt to shut off the corridors; Exercise Peddle included the deployment of three pilots, nineteen engineers, and two Jaguars from 2 Sqn to the Luftwaffe base at Faßberg. From here, they flew twenty-one recce sorties for Tripartite forces against 'live targets' in the field. Close air support was provided on this occasion by Jaguars of 31 Sqn, also operating from Faßberg, alongside American and French units, 480 TFS/52 TFW (USAFE), F-4Ds and EC 1/11, Jaguars (FAF). The squadron generated a lot of praise for the extent of good quality reconnaissance photos for the CAS squadrons. Exercise Cold Fire, another NATO exercise, involved 2, 15, and 16 Squadrons.

Buccaneer tasking involved interdiction sorties into Belgium and France. As such, they did not carry out any sorties in support of forces in Germany, which was thought unfortunate 'as the opportunity to practice interdiction in the "field" is invaluable'.

Nos 15 and 16 Sqns Buccaneers were also tasked against targets in the UK, the ORB does not state plainly, but clearly, they were flying in the role of 'orange air' (playing the role of enemy air forces in a NATO exercise; Allied elements identified as 'blue air'). The UK sorties entailed high-level approaches and returns, hi-lo-hi. The FRG low-flying areas usually set at 250 feet were deactivated for unexplained reasons for the duration of the exercise. This forced all aircraft to a minimum height of 500 feet and, in some areas, 1,000 feet, meaning it was quite unrealistic.

No. 2 Squadron's recce targets were like 15 and 16's—largely outside the main theatre of operations and were described as neither realistic nor useful. Only a few of 2 Sqn's pilots were tasked with operating over various army units while manoeuvring, but because of the lack of field targets, their capabilities were not fully utilised. Coltishall-based 41 Squadron were deployed to Laarbruch to participate.

The purpose of deploying 41 Sqn's Jaguars was to exercise the squadron personnel's nuclear, biological, and chemical procedures; they were assigned to operate from 2 Sqn's standby facilities. The further purpose was to try out the 'integrated guard plan' for the dispersal area. All RAF Buccaneer units were equipped with a flight of two-seater Hawker Hunters for check flights and maintaining currency. Nos 15 and 16's Hunters were involved as well, although they flew less than thirty-six hours between them. To put this in perspective, this compared with almost 600 hours for the Buccaneers.

As Cold Fire took place at the same time as Peddle, resources on 2 Sqn were rather stretched. No. 15 Squadron began training for Red Flag '78 during September as well; this meant practicing ultra-low-level flying at 100 feet as would be expected in a hostile environment such as would be encountered in Eastern Europe.

Public Displays by RAF Germany

RAF Germany as an RAF Command was not troubled to quite the same degree as the home-based commands to participate in public flying displays, but they still received a substantial number of requests each year to participate at air shows and other similar events on the continent. A process was in place to ensure that all requests for RAFG equipment to participate in flying or static displays were placed before the appropriate authority. This was HQ RAFG (ops 4). Not surprisingly, however, authorisation had to be further obtained from the MOD (air) in London. Some requests were received directly at the air bases whose station commanders were then obliged to forward them on to Rheindahlen also, when applicable, in consultation with the British air attaché in Bonn.

In 1973, displays by RAFG aircraft were subject to restrictions. Flypasts were limited to 250 feet above ground level. Other displays that did not amount to a full aerobatics display went under the description of a 'performance demonstration', which entailed flying by a single aircraft involving high speed runs, steep climbs at maximum power, minimum radius turns, and LABS manoeuvres but not involving actual aerobatics. The performance demo had been utilised over the preceding years in order to place a large number of individual aircraft displays before the public during the widespread Battle of Britain displays. This made it possible to provide a degree of impressive display flying without the need for time and resource consuming full aerobatics practices. All display sorties were to be flown no lower than 300 feet above the highest obstacle in the display area, except take-offs and landings.

Interestingly, 'ground attack demonstrations' were cleared down to the minimum height for the weapons technique being demonstrated. 'Formation drills' (the performance demo sequence relied on in place of formation aerobatics) entailed teams of aircraft performing various formation patterns/ changes at varying speeds and configurations and various manoeuvres, but again avoiding defined aerobatics. The minimum height for these displays was 500 feet above the highest obstacle in the display area. Solo aerobatics were available to be authorised for operational aircraft and pilots approved by SASO HQ RAFG could practice down to 500 feet above the highest obstacle in the display area. Those aeros pilots—already approved by HQ RAFG but not yet seen by the SASO—were cleared no lower than 1,500 feet.

Further ground attack profiles were to be performed in public, at the time, only by Harrier and Phantom aircraft. Formation aerobatics, dog-fighting displays, and crazy flying were all prohibited by RAFG aircraft without exception. Formation aerobatics teams were, up to the end of the Hunter era, very much allowed.

More aerobatics limitations were applied; continuous and hesitation rolls were permitted to be performed only by Lightning and Harrier aircraft. This was curiously at odds with the rules in place for Strike Command who allowed Phantom and Buccaneer to fly these manoeuvres.

Further select restrictions were applied to any displays by Lightnings. Ordinarily, speeds used in aerobatics were at the pilots' discretion. In the case of the Lightning, the following limits were applied (minimum speeds): entering a loop, 400 knots (if reheat used, this is to be selected before entering loop and must be de-selected when completing the loop); rolling, 350 knots; inverted flying, 350 knots; and minimum radius turns, 250 knots.

9

The Tornado Arrives

Following the saga of TSR-2 and subsequently both the F-111 and AFVG, work was underway from 1968 to salvage something from the debacle. An immediate and interim solution was to accept two aircraft, which were already comfortably established in front line service with other air arms.

Looking beyond the Buccaneer and Phantom, the Jaguar was already in the pipeline, even if the prototype was yet to fly at the time of the F-111 cancellation. With the AFVG cancelled as well, the Jaguar was already being planned to replace the Phantom, so the latter could be redeployed to replace the Lightning. The Lightning's superlative airframe and engine performance, as impressive as it was, contrasted with its limited fuel capacity and limited avionics and weapons suite.

The versatility of the Phantom comfortably addressed these shortfalls, with only a relative light trade-off in performance. At the other end of the transfer, the consensus was that the Jaguar was an inadequate replacement for the Phantom; despite being smaller and lighter, its general performance shortcomings were well known.

Little has been said about the true virtue of the Jaguar's survivable attributes in the event of flying an interdictor mission, particularly at night in the least hospitable weather conditions over Eastern Europe's hilly terrain. It possessed inertial auto navigation, was armed with 30-mm cannons, and typically flew operational sorties with two wing tanks fitted. Its small size and sustained low-level high speed had clearly been assessed as suitable for low strike. However, the Jaguar was not necessarily the aircraft that the new embryo design was expected to replace.

Harking back to the AFVG and only a short few months after its cancellation, a new design was on the drawing board, another international partnership project. The government signed a memorandum of understanding with the governments of Belgium, Canada, Italy, the Netherlands, and West Germany, with a view to developing an aircraft that would replace the Canberra, Vulcan, and Victor in the RAF. As for everyone else, it would replace the F-104. It would incorporate a variety of tactical roles. The ensuing period descended into a clash of interests as all moved to harmonise and agree a design and development.

On 20 January 1969, Denis Healey, defence secretary, was asked about what appeared to be a government attempt to rescue the Anglo-French AFVG, with the Anglo-German variable geometry aircraft feasibility study.

An international company was established with BAC, Messerschmitt-Bölkow-Blohm, and Fiat. The result of the new venture went by the title 'Panavia', officially recognised on 29 March 1969, at which stage Belgium and Canada had left to pursue alternatives.

The project working title said it all—multi-role combat aircraft. The agreed design incorporated a feature gaining popularity on both sides of the Iron Curtain at the time, and one originally pursued by Barnes Wallis—the variable geometry wing. The swing wing appears to have fallen from favour among high-performance military aircraft designers since.

Many jets from the same era—F-111, F-14, and while never to enter service, the AFVG (advanced fighter variable geometry)—all shared this feature. On the other side of the Iron Curtain, the SU-17 and 22 were already operational. The MiG-23, TU-22, and the SU-24 (a contemporary of the multi-role combat aircraft (MRCA)) were produced over the coming decades. In the strategic high-performance role, the US Rockwell International B-1B Lancer and the Russian Tupolev TU-160 Blackjack remain in service today.

Otherwise, VG wings have not proved to be quite the revolutionary concept they might have been. The initial conclusions were due at the end of the month. A few months later, Healey was being questioned by Tam Dalyell on the issue of what advantages the new MRCA offered over the Harrier in a multi-combat role. Healey explained to his fellow MP that the Harrier was a battlefield support aircraft for ground forces, not a multi-role aircraft. The question rather than the answer said a lot about the grasp of some MPs over issues upon which they choose to raise questions, sometimes rhetorically.

By May 1969, just the UK, Italy, and West Germany were left, the others having concluded that the project aimed to produce an aircraft that went beyond the scope of capabilities and tactical range they were looking for. There were other differing objectives that were difficult to reconcile.

Some months on from the establishment of Panavia, a change of government had taken place, but the project was to continue. Lord Balniel, the minister of state, announced to parliament on 20 July 1970 that the governments of the United Kingdom, the Federal Republic of Germany, and Italy had agreed the previous year to enter upon the project definition phase; the results had led to agreement on the feasibility of developing a twin-seat multi-role variable geometry aircraft that would meet the requirements of all three countries. The incoming government had reviewed the project since and concluded that it was the most economic means of meeting the requirements of the RAF and replacing aircraft in the strike, reconnaissance, and air defence roles in the late 1970s and 1980s. There was also the advantage of realising a collaborative European project of technical and industrial importance. There was some misinformation that the MRCA was a German-led project, even though they had no experience in the field as such. This was incorrect.

Before the first MRCA prototype flew, work was afoot to ensure it could deliver the latest American nuclear device—the US Mk 61, as well as the WE177. The wiring for the latter, Specification 342, could be adapted to be used with any new weapons offered by the US to other NATO air arms. The US Mk 61 bomb weighed 695 lb. The Germans in the meantime were looking to operate a larger device of some 2,100 lb. Cooperation with nuclear weapons within NATO was more mixed than the straightforward one to one arrangement between one country and the US.

The Royal Netherlands Navy had use of a storage facility at RAF St Mawgan for their Lockheed P2 Neptune maritime ASW aircraft, under that air arm's commitment to SACLANT. The MRCA was easily the largest single NATO project outside of those of the USA.

For the RAF alone, an order for 385 aircraft was initially placed. What is so unusual is that all were delivered; this may have had something to do with the political climate yet again. The order stood without being pruned even once through the gestation period of the 1970s. This meant it survived three general elections and four prime ministers from July 1970 toward the latter half of the decade, not that there were no attempts to not just reduce the number or the specifications, but to cancel the entire British contribution and requirement for any production airframes.

A group of MPs on the government backbenches in 1977 sought to alter the government's defence policy radically. From the retirement of the Canberra through to the retirement of the Buccaneer and Jaguar in the early 1980s, all could be regarded as an interim period. The MRCA, named the Tornado in 1976, was the definitive alternative to all the preceding cancellations. As was customary, the first Tornados went to form squadrons in Strike Command at Honington and Marham. No. 15 Squadron was the first RAFG unit, receiving its first Tornado GR1s in 1983. Eventually, a peak of no fewer than eight squadrons would become operational in Germany.

Seven of these would carry the WE177C bomb with the eighth assigned to the reconnaissance role. Laarbruch was selected as the sole base for RAFG Tornados. The rest would be based in the UK along with two conversion units and an evaluation unit. This did not take account of the Tornado air defence force (which represented a further seven squadrons), an OCU, and an evaluation unit, all home-based. The Tornado altogether became the most sophisticated high-performance combat aircraft to be deployed in numbers which had not been seen since the build-up of the Hunter and Javelin force.

Before we got there though, there was the usual road to negotiate, fraught with the media's desire to find anyone connected to the programme willing to condemn it. Then there were the parliamentarians, doing their bit to bring about cancellation. Ill-informed negative comments could be found easily. The acronym MRCA provided a couple of unflattering nicknames. Ask anyone in a light blue uniform what they thought of the MRCA at any time during the 1970s, and you would usually get one of a handful of stock replies, in the form of either 'Mother Riley's Cardboard Aeroplane or Must Refurbish Canberra Again' or more resignedly, but no less cynically 'it's the TSR-2 all over again.' The way things were going, that was not an unlikely prospect, so used to promising projects being cancelled as all had become.

The decision to issue a requirement for the MRCA was as clear an indication as any that the Buccaneer was not quite the substitute for TSR-2/F-111/AFVG. The new aircraft was ambitious, given its international representation, even though three of the original partner nations had pulled out. MRCA survived this first set back. The developing nature of international companies, even within the defence industry, meant the MRCA was to be designed and built by three contributory aerospace groups from three different countries.

Between 1968, when the first memorandum of understanding was signed by the six partner nations, the Canadians were the first to step away from the project concluding that it was a weapon system being designed very much so with the European theatre in mind. What perhaps the Canadian government were not happy about was that for the home defence, the MRCA would be very much the sledgehammer with likely nothing but walnuts to crack.

Canadian home-based air defence and tactical air power was in the hands of two combat types; the job of air defence was entrusted to the McDonnell Douglas F-101 Voodoo while F-5A Freedom Fighters filled the remote concern that a tactical attack fighter might be needed. The RCAFs F-104s were concentrated in West Germany and replacing all three squadrons with MRCA on a like for like basis could not be justified. The F-18 Hornet became the all-round choice for the Canadians. They began retiring the F-104s of the RCAF Baden Söllingen tactical air wing from 1986. The Belgian and Dutch governments withdrew from the project later in 1969, having concluded that the way the design was shaping up it would be too complex, too close to being a strategic type, and too expensive.

To be fair, they were each looking for a higher agility jet, which was clearly noted in their alternative choice of the F-16 to replace both the Mirage V (Belgium), NF-5 (Netherlands), and the F-104 in both arms. The respective requirements of the remaining three partners differed somewhat as regards what aircraft they were looking to build in terms of specifications, such as would it need to be single or two-seat, single or twin-engine. All three were in broad agreement that the aircraft would principally meet the requirements of ground attack, for the RAF this was now to be the true definitive replacement for the Buccaneer, Phantom, and remaining Vulcans. Ultimately, the air defence variant, on the cards from an early stage, would finally allow the last of the Lightnings to receive their pension.

The Jaguar, one might have thought, was the most urgent in need of replacement, in Germany, even though it was the most recent arrival. As adept as it was as a low-level strike fighter, it did not possess the ability to survive the hostile environment of Warsaw Pact airspace to anything like what was expected of the MRCA. Yet the Jaguar was not on the chop list, not yet anyway. The new design was settled as a variable-geometry winged twin-engine platform with a crew of two.

The prototype flew for the first time on 14 August 1974, from Manching in West Germany. The Germans had secured preference for hosting the Panavia headquarters and a good deal of influence over the development and design of the aircraft. This decision was due, certainly in part, to the huge order for 600 airframes initially put forward, later reduced to 324 following a review. The Italian government ordered 112 aircraft.

Aside from the loss of three international project partners, the MRCA then had to weather attempts by parties within, who either had little faith or a separate agenda. One Luftwaffe officer at the project HQ in Germany actively tried to brief against it. There was a suggestion that the Germans simply wanted to benefit from the technology derived from the input of others to assist in a separate project of their own. Ultimately, if either of these reports had any real legs then supposedly the MRCA/Tornado would not have survived. The cynics of the day were predicting that to take any such elaborate and promising military aircraft with so many clashing interests involved through from inspiration to operational declaration was as likely as training chimpanzees to fly it.

The MRCA had already flown in prototype form, both in Germany and the UK, and was well on the way to becoming what would be the backbone of Anglo-German-Italian offensive air power. The project was quite some way advanced and on track when in 1977, a defence study group led by Ian Mikardo, MP, might have succeeded in scuppering the project at least as far as British interests were concerned. Acting as an unofficial think tank, the study group pooled their efforts into a softback book entitled *Sense about Defence*; the title was worded to convey the impression that the contributing authors knew their apples when it came to the subject of defence interests.

The angle was to urge the government to commence drastic cuts in defence spending, largely affecting conventional arms, the justification for which was to counter the growing strategic nuclear capabilities of the USA and USSR. The proposed measures, even if suggested, as varying alternatives were drastic to say the least. The impact on the country's defence structure and assets was, not surprisingly, couched in language to convince all that the intention was to be nothing but pragmatic while placing Britain and NATO's security and defence interests at heart.

The authors were clearly sensitive to any likely charges of recklessness or ulterior motive, suggesting their position was merely counter-intuitive but sound. Cost savings in defence and finding extra funding for schemes such as extending the state school leaving age were more the driving point of the book. That such a low-priority policy proposal was freely felt to be of such a national imperative that savage cuts to the defence budget on the scale recommended by Mikardo and Co. could be fully justified really beggar's belief.

Mikardo believed that comparisons between the military strength of NATO in relation to the Warsaw Pact was flawed anyway and the usual selection of facts to make the case were listed, including comparisons of GDP percentage spent on defence. All were presented as unfavourable because the British defence budget was at the time 5.24 per cent compared to West Germany's 3.58 per cent without considering Britain's wider range of commitments, Northern Ireland emergency, Cyprus, Hong Kong, and Gibraltar. Then there was Germany; here, the bulk of the army's front line was based and, similarly, more than half of the RAF's tactical assets, all in accordance with the various post-war treaties and agreed NATO defence plans. It is likely these were not fully considered, but this amounted to a cost which countries on the continent were not troubled by.

The *Bundeswehr* were essentially entirely home-based with no internal strife/armed insurrection (such as Northern Ireland and the potential of other overseas flashpoints, such as Belize or Cyprus) to deal with, save perhaps the nuisance of the Baader-Meinhof Gang (a terrorist organisation). This was a problem for all NATO forces based in Germany. However, the Baader-Meinhof Gang lost its entire leadership in 1972 due to the Bonn government's counter terrorist operations.

There was also Britain's remaining commitment to the South East Asia Treaty Organisation. Further, there was of course the strategic nuclear deterrent, gifted to the country by Clement Attlee's government. Just why West Germany did not have an independent nuclear deterrent, but France and Britain did is certainly steeped in the complexity and sensitivity surrounding Germany's post-war rehabilitation. West Germany's unique post-war history needs to be considered before making comparison with Britain, regarding foreign and defence policy.

In any case, the Mikardo book proposed several defence economies, all for the greater good. One of the range of options was to reduce the BAOR from its 1975 level of 55,000 personnel to a strength of 30,000. Quite how this was expected to reduce the likelihood of a nuclear confrontation between the USSR and USA is inexplicable. It was more likely to press NATO to decide sooner on the release of battlefield/tactical nuclear weapons because of a quicker collapse of conventional resistance. The consensus was that NATO's conventional forces were already too weak to provide any kind of worthwhile resistance to a Soviet-led Warsaw Pact incursion across the inner German border. The overarching worry was that NATO would be the first to deploy a tactical nuclear retaliation in a desperate attempt to cripple the advance. In such a case, the bombs would be dropped as far east as possible to protect the home real estate as best as possible. Any thinning of the level of NATO conventional forces brought that nightmare scenario closer; it certainly did not push it further away.

The MRCA at this stage was well along the road of development, yet Mikardo's think tank proposed axing the project entirely. After the time and money wasted on TSR-2, Britain's reputation for seeing through large defence projects would be severely damaged, and far less likely to secure international involvement or commercial interest in the future.

The study group recommended running on the existing Jaguar and Harrier as they were good enough at the time; the Jaguar, whatever its shortcomings, was expected to continue to deliver tactical nuclear bombs some miles east of Potsdam, with no forecast long-term replacement. The Buccaneer was, for all it represented, a step ahead of its predecessor, but to rely on them any longer than absolutely necessary was not a good idea.

Similarly, as the Jaguar was originally intended as an advanced trainer, to place it in the strike role indicated a certain level of faith in the aircraft. Yet ultimately, it was a stop gap until a more realistic aircraft became available; this was the MRCA/Tornado. The idea that the RAF would accept without protest the continued reliance on the Jaguar in Germany would place a great deal of faith in their ability to make do and mend. The study group were also fully aware that the MRCA programme included 165 air defence interceptor variants. Logically, air defence assets were much easier to accept, or more difficult to argue against. For those who found maintaining any kind of military readiness objectionable, on the grounds of concern that the country took an unduly aggressive stance, a pure defence weapon logically is more palatable.

The study group accepted that being able and ready to deliver a nuclear strike was an integral component of the national defence posture. Yet even here, the authors of *Sense about Defence* were prepared to see the Tornado ADV disappear. *Sense about Defence* proposed upgrading the then new Skyflash missile and extending the life of the F-4 Phantom. This level of forward planning was necessary in any case, but with no interceptor in the pipeline to replace the Phantom and the still residual Lightnings, it would be a lengthy run on with rising costs and safety risks. If the Tornado was discontinued, it would still be necessary to identify an immediate replacement, even if the old jets were to continue onwards into the 1980s, which they did anyway. The study presented no suggestions in this case.

Ideally, two new fighter designs were required to meet the future (but separate) air defence requirements of the UK and West Germany. The former needed a long-range interceptor with emphasis on the ability to address the demands of UK airspace, given range and climate and the type of adversary expected (long-range Soviet reconnaissance bombers). Continental Europe required an agile fighter. There were two respective American candidates available in the shortest term to meet this requirement—the F-14 Tomcat would be ideal for the UK, with the F-15 Eagle able to meet the requirements of the central European theatre. It would be unlikely in the extreme to imagine any British government accepting such a costly upending of defence policy, much less such an alternative being suggested by Ian Mikardo and his *Sense about Defence* co-authors, especially given the fact that both alternatives would come from huge US defence industry giants.

Whichever proposal *Sense about Defence* put forward was accepted, had it been so, the result would mean a very serious degrading of the UK defence doctrine as accepted by our NATO partners, perhaps the end of the MRCA programme for West Germany and Italy as well. The study group's proposal suggested that there are some politicians who simply cannot see the logic. If any kind of standing conventional force is to be maintained, seeking to do it in little more than a token fashion accrues no benefit. It could unintentionally lead to an attempt by one side to snatch at a window of opportunity, through military means, the very scenario which gave many sleepless nights through the Cold War.

It was always an argumentative point through the Cold War whether NATO's degree of readiness to meet Soviet-led aggression, however that might have come to pass, was justified. Was it unduly provocative or was it lacklustre? It was what it was—a balance maintained to avoid the outbreak of war. Beyond that, one can never be certain that the military posture on each side of the Cold War rested on an endless guarantee.

Far-left sentiment was widespread across not just north-west Europe; it was quite abundant in the USA, particularly during and immediately following the Vietnam War. On the other hand, the overall mood was tempered by rational thinking. Both pacifism and belligerence were quite unappealing to all the democracies. The balance, one way or the other, always endured. Alas the proposals posited in *Sense about Defence* were not accepted by Mikardo's own party executive. The government of Jim Callaghan continued the MRCA programme and the Tornado lived to ripe old age. This might be seen as further evidence that the British people overall favour placing only mild to moderate governments, from either Labour or Conservatives, in office.

All British governments have steadfastly dismissed any attempts, wherever from, to introduce radical policy proposals that look like going overboard in either direction. At the same time the government was looking to reduce the nuclear QRA role, professional advice was that within the framework of NATO, any initiative to change the commitment should come from SACEUR. QRA tasking in peacetime was based on the number of aircraft per squadron. Such tasking was less severe by 1976 than it had been. One aircraft per eleven was the previous rate; it was spread to one in every squadron of eighteen or less. A UE of nineteen to twenty-four aircraft required two aircraft to be on QRA; twenty-five or more aircraft per squadron brought a demand for three primed ready to go.

The new ratio allowed one Buccaneer from each of the two squadrons at Laarbruch to be so assigned. For the new Jaguar squadrons at Brüggen, planning was still to be based on a UE of fifteen aircraft each. This meant the number of Jags on QRA could now be reduced from two to a single aircraft per squadron. The overall basing, eventually at Brüggen, was expected to reach sixty aircraft overall; this number meant that a supplementary additional two aircraft would be called for. The figures of squadron numbers and overall basing were later revised to twelve and forty-eight respectively as twelve Jaguars were required to replace the Phantom in the tactical reconnaissance role at Laarbruch.

Air Vice-Marshal David Craig (a future CAS and, in 1977, ACAS (ops)) welcomed the change saying he believed they were hitherto over-providing on what was presumably our reaction to a surprise nuclear attack; AVM Craig was referring to the previous MAD doctrine, enforcing a higher degree of readiness. By 1977, the operational profile and planned deployment of the Panavia Tornado was known, it would be able to carry either WE177A, B, or C nuclear devices and a comprehensive range of conventional weapons:

Nuclear

1. WE177A 600 lb
2. WE177B 950 lb
3. WE177C 950 lb

Conventional

1. 1,000-lb unguided (retarded or ballistic)
2. 1,000-lb laser guided (AST 1229)
3. BL755 or replacement cluster bombs

4. ASR 1217 airfield cratering and area denial weapon
5. AST 1226 ASGW to replace Martel
6. AST 1227 short-range air to surface missile, advanced Battlefield for late acquisition off bore sight attacks against hard targets and tanks
7. AST 1228 future defence suppression weapon
8. two 27-mm Mauser gun

The TFR was optimised so that the aircraft could be flown at 600 kts at 200 feet, hands free, continuously through the entire route. Any loss of the TFR would result in an automatic pull-up. At the time, a total of 220 Tornado GR1s (just for the RAF) had been agreed; this would sustain a front-line squadron strength of 144 aircraft with an inventory of twenty-five jets for the OCU/TWCU.

The plan as of 1977 was to use the GR1s to phase out all the remaining Canberras, Buccaneers and Vulcans. As history has revealed, in the case of all three, complete withdrawal from service did not happen quite as planned. By the time the first Tornados were delivered to RAF Cottesmore, to start the build-up of the Tri-National Training Establishment, no Canberras flew in either strike or attack. However, Canberras soldiered on in various other unarmed roles, such as ECM, high-altitude reconnaissance, and radar calibration. The Buccaneer kept its job as the primary anti-ship strike platform back in the UK while the Vulcan continued for a short while as a tanker.

Of the 144 front-line assigned Tornado GR1s, eighty-four would be assigned to SACEUR in the overland strike/attack role, but not less than half based in Germany. A further thirty-six were to be allocated to the overall control of SACLANT, specifically in the maritime strike/attack role, and twenty-four jets would be assigned to SACEUR for reconnaissance duties. On completion of the force build-up, the twenty-five jets of the OCU/TWCU would be declared to NATO generally. The transfer of these aircraft to NATO would take place when the transition to war state reached 'simple alert'.

The overland aircraft would be operating in the European Central Region and on the northern flank. The maritime Tornados would operate in the Eastern Atlantic and Channel areas. The Tornados would also be included in any purely national contingency requirements, but there were no specific plans to assign aircraft to any non-NATO roles. As for how they would be deployed, a wing of thirty-six aircraft divided into two strike/attack squadrons to be based at RAF Laarbruch. A further thirty-two would form two more squadrons, which were to be based at RAF Marham, in Norfolk. A further sixteen aircraft would form another squadron to be based at RAF Honington. There were to be two reconnaissance units of twelve aircraft a piece, one assigned to Laarbruch.

The base for the second squadron was, as of 1977, yet to be determined. Lossiemouth was to be the home of the maritime wing, also formed of two squadrons, with an establishment of eighteen aircraft each. While Lossiemouth would be the home/northern base, a southern base—St Mawgan—would be made available as a forward operating base for eighteen aircraft. Any enthusiast visiting St Mawgan/Newquay airport at any time since 1989 may have wondered why the HAS complex was built here when the base last operated Nimrod.

The St Mawgan Tornados would naturally cover the south-west approaches. The OCU for the Tornado would be split in two—the TTTE at Cottesmore, for initial flying training, while the TWCU would concentrate on weapons and tactical training. The latter formed with the remaining eleven jets at Honington. Of all the planned Tornado basing plans, no mention was made at this stage of Brüggen, where four squadrons of Jaguars formed the bulk of the RAF strike force in Germany.

The basic GR1 Tornado variant had seven principal roles to cater for—dual capability, strike operations, overland attack, counter air, close air support, maritime attack operations, and reconnaissance. Close air support was a priority role of the RAFG squadrons. Given the NATO primary aim, in the face of Warsaw Pact aggression, the first concern would be to prevent an overwhelming advance by the WP land forces during the early stages of hostilities. In conventional terms, the Tornado GR1 came into its element just as it would in the more emphasised interdiction strike task, attacking the enemy's forward armoured formations in poor weather and or at night.

This was expected to be the initial sortie tasking of the Laarbruch-based squadrons. The UK-based GR1s, unless forward deployed, would likely be precluded from this role. The reconnaissance squadron at Laarbruch would be expected to gather timely intelligence of enemy movements between the forward edge of the battle area and a position 15 degrees east. This presumed recce flights no further east than Poland but to be able to operate even that far under the circumstances would be optimistic. The recce GR1s would operate primarily at night and probably in daytime, only if weather prevented other reconnaissance aircraft from operating effectively.

The aircraft's navigation and weapon delivery system were considered second to none. Penetration of hostile airspace at very low level and withdrawal in the same manner were what this machine was all about; medium-level operations were not ruled out just the same. When operating at very low level, transit speed typically was expected to be at about 480 kts with an attack speed of 540 kts.

These speeds were arrived at as a compromise between reduced vulnerability and maintaining a worthwhile radius of action. All GR1 aircrew, regardless, would train for both the nuclear strike and the conventional attack roles. Operating from Germany in the former, the Tornado would seek to deliver a WE177 bomb to targets situated east of 21 degrees longitude, then hopefully return home. The approach to the target was to be conducted from take-off as a lo-lo-lo-hi profile. UK-based squadrons assigned this would be set targets east of 18 degrees east of the prime meridian.

If a low-level attack was out of the question, then the Tornado crew would deliver the weapon in a dive or loft manoeuvre. The Tornado could carry two nuclear weapons for two possible targets. Again, specifically relating to the RAFG squadrons, counter air operations would form part of their primary role against airfields and the command, control, and logistics apparatus of East Germany and Western Poland. The success of Warsaw Pact air operations against the West would be dependent upon this. This is where the airfield denial weapon used against runways in Iraq would be to the fore again alongside the 27-mm cannons.

In the maritime role, the Tornado would be able to reach targets north-west of Iceland from Lossiemouth and south-west of Spain from St Mawgan. It was 1979 before the first production line Tornado GR1s were delivered to the RAF for acceptance. In 1980, the TTTE began training the first of many Tornado air and ground crews, while the Jaguar and Buccaneer continued to hold the line at Brüggen and Laarbruch.

That same year, shortly after the Conservative government of Margaret Thatcher took the reins, the new defence secretary, Francis Pym, was looking for further economies; RAFG was in the crosshairs again. A brief was prepared for the secretary of state, himself a veteran of the Second World War, but now with a job to do. The brief referred to the Brussels treaty of 1955, under which the UK was committed to maintaining a tactical air force in the central region under the auspices of NATO. Royal Air Force Germany met this requirement at the time with two strike/attack/reconnaissance wings (Buccaneers and Jaguars), one tactical attack wing (Harriers), and one air defence wing (Phantoms). All RAFG bases were defended, specifically, by medium and short-range SAMs (Bloodhound and Rapier), RAF Regiment field squadrons, and one battlefield helicopter support squadron with Pumas. From August 1983, in addition, 18 Squadron would be available to support the BAOR, with Chinooks.

At the time, RAFG strength equated to the operational deployment of the Belgian and Dutch air forces, both committed in full to the Central Region defences. The standards achieved by the RAF had repeatedly shown in TACEVALs and other exercises to be the highest sustained of allied countries. The nightmare scenario of Armageddon, defined during the Cuban Missile Crisis, was different to the likely development in 1980. Nuclear weapons notwithstanding, the first instance for NATO air forces was to reduce the weight of enemy air attack through both defensive and offensive air operations, including close air support and battlefield air interdiction for the army.

Forty-eight hours was believed to be the possible warning time which both the joint intelligence committee and NATO's own intelligence division believed possible. Upon this hinged the whole reason in pragmatic terms for basing a forward sizeable air force on West German soil. Nothing the entire other in-theatre allied air arms were expected to do could win the war by teatime, or Christmas. The air forces were to hold off the enemy advance long enough to allow for reinforcements arriving from the UK and North America.

In 1980 during Exercise Crusader, the Americans rehearsed, for the first time in history, flying an airborne infantry assault force direct from bases in the United States non-stop to the drop zones on the European mainland. The drop was dramatised in a moment of unintentional light-hearted absurdity when a reporter from AFN stood in a field, microphone in hand, watching while paratroopers, who last stood on American soil, floated toward this German field with full combat kit. As one paratrooper landed and began disengaging himself from his chute, our eager reporter caught up with and ran alongside him, waving the mic under his nose for a response to the question, 'excuse me sir, could you explain your mission here in Europe?'

The soldier, clearly harassed, looked at his interrogator with an incredulous expression before having the presence of mind to politely point out that he was too busy to give a press interview, not even to AFN or *Stars and Stripes* for that matter. The exercise also involved the movement of an additional 30,000 troops, including 10,000 territorials from the UK, many of which were crammed into accommodation across the Low Countries as well as the FRG, as your author can testify.

The idea of going to such extraordinary lengths was to avoid as best as possible the resort to nuclear retaliation. Crucially, Hansard records that all the reinforcement troops from the UK were in place within forty-eight hours of leaving their bases. The brief for the defence secretary could be regarded as quite timely. Should an enemy force break through the allied lines, it would very much fall to the air forces to blunt that advance. Therefore, RAFG was a core integral part of the Central Region defence structure.

What was also reflected upon for the Defence Secretary to consider was that not a single defence review had amounted to anything but a further cut in resources, capabilities, and (as a result) flexibility and the ability to endure. RAFG was now a 'lean' organisation. In 1980, the command had a strength of 11,477 men and women—8,407 were based on the four frontline airfields while 3,070 were deployed in admin and operational support tasks elsewhere on the continent. Not counting equipment costs, the running of RAFG came to 15 per cent of this area of expenditure from the RAF's budget and represented rather less than 2 per cent of the defence budget overall. If, as was being looked at by the government, RAFG was loaded up and transferred back to the UK to stand ready to meet a sudden Soviet attack on West Germany from there (an event which could very well be precipitated, even by such a move alone), then savings would amount probably to £50 million at 1980 costs.

The rest of the costs—a further £141 million—would be offset by finding basing for the squadrons, compensation payments for the personnel for whom a posting could not be found (though this would be the least of incurred costs) and works services at the repatriation bases. There most certainly would not be any old bases resurrected or new ones built and the cost that would entail. Further, dual basing would become necessary leading to cramped conditions and perhaps reduced effectiveness. There would also be a need to construct new weapons stores and maintenance facilities. A report from the Defence Working party on the status of RAFG, in particular the strike element, in 1980, set out the requirements looking forward to the period 1984 to 1987, essentially when the RAF in Germany was to replace all Buccaneers and Jaguars with the Tornado.

The ASM programme for Laarbruch envisaged two Tornado GR1 squadrons with an establishment of eighteen jets each alongside two reconnaissance squadrons, one with twelve Tornados initially (a second to follow) and one with twelve Jaguars. The wartime concentration of Tornados at Laarbruch was expected to expand to sixty aircraft. This was too large a concentration on a single airfield; it looked far more realistic to use two, but what stood in the way was the high cost of support for the Tornado. Financial considerations meant Laarbruch remained the only airfield considered suitable to house the entire Tornado force in Germany.

The RAF considered disbanding or moving the recce Jaguar squadron to allow the second Tornado recce squadron to be housed here. Anyone with any knowledge of how the Tornados were deployed in Germany might be puzzled as to why Brüggen did not figure in the Tornado equation up to this point.

Quite simply, Brüggen was to remain as a base officially for all the Jaguars, at this stage, and it is likely they would have retained the strike role alongside the Laarbruch Tornados. The Brüggen Jaguars were to be replaced in time by AST 403, an air staff combat design that would become the Eurofighter Typhoon. The DWP in 1980 had concluded that the Jaguar could not be run on in service in the high-threat Central Region without an expensive improvement programme. Thus, the RAF had to consider replacing them with the Tornado GR1 in the mid-1980s.

To add to this, by the end of 1980, as the first Tornados began delivery to RAF Cottesmore, it was revealed that the aircraft's range fell 20 per cent short of expectations. Another unforeseen limitation was that the JP233 airfield denial weapon further degraded its radius of action. To compound this, the number of tanker aircraft available was insufficient. So, extending the range of Tornados operating from the UK would not be routinely possible. Therefore, the decision was to base a larger proportion of the Tornado force forward in Germany, naturally to gain the maximum operational response.

The revised conclusion was now that the Tornado GR1, for all the misgivings about another suitable airfield in addition to Laarbruch, was to be expanded. The decided operational number of Tornados remained unchanged, but these would be dual based; while twelve of the eighty-four would be assigned the reconnaissance role, the remaining seventy-two were now to be split thirty-six at Laarbruch and forty-eight at Brüggen. The existing wings of twenty F-4M Phantoms and thirty-six Harrier GR3s were to remain unchanged in the short term, but the Bloodhound SAMs of 25 Squadron would all be removed by the end of 1983. By this time, all the RAF Regiment Rapier units would be upgraded with the DN-181 blind fire radar.

The Harriers would be replaced by the AV-8B or Harrier GR5/7 in due course. Early in 1981, the government appointed a new defence secretary, John Nott. The new man started his own review. Again, another Defence Working party set about looking for substantial defence savings and would need to have the RAF element in Germany explained again. Of particular interest and something the RAF were keen to explain in detail was the role of the Harrier force in Germany, including its use of off-base forward sites for operations in support of 1st British Corps (BAOR) specifically CAS (close air support) and BAI (battlefield air interdiction). Such operations allowed close cooperation with the army and would involve high sortie rates.

The Harriers needed to be deployed in theatre to be at all effective. The reason for this is none of the forward operating sites could be activated within the minimum warning time of forty-eight hours otherwise. Therefore, the in-theatre basing of Harriers was essential. This may all seem obvious to those in any way sympathetic to the NATO posture, but the political realities were that such points had to be spelt out to the political establishment, and more than just once.

Another crucial benefit of basing Harriers in theatre was the routine experience gained by all involved in attaining the optimum standard of performance and familiarity. Should the force be UK-based, they would be virtually ineffective and too slow to respond to a surprise Soviet military intervention, which was always a likelihood. The in-theatre helicopter support, as of 1981, rest with 230 Squadron (the RAF's other Tiger squadron) equipped with thirteen Puma HC1s; this single squadron was inadequate as far as meeting the demands of the BAOR and RAF Regiment squadrons was concerned.

That point made, the support helicopter force was still a vital asset for moving stores quickly during any transition to a war footing and the movement of special forces teams. To shift this one chopper squadron back to some place like Benson or Odiham would certainly reduce the *Deutsche Mark* expenditure, which successive British governments regarded as a thorn in the foot. Again though, these units needed to be somewhere in Germany, if they were to hold any military value and stand a chance of playing their part to the full of either thwarting or slowing down a Warsaw Pact intervention on any scale.

Regular training, with the army in-theatre, was invaluable. The RAF Regiment were in theatre because with all the other RAF elements present and with such vital and sensitive components as the tactical nuclear force, their contribution was indispensable. In the 1980s, each of the four remaining bases were assigned their own regiment rapier low-level air defence squadron. As the brief for the secretary of state pointed out bluntly, 'These units are essential for the defence of our air bases and could only be withdrawn if we closed the airfields they protect'. To spell it out, if they go, everything else must go as the vulnerability of the airfields would be unacceptable.

As well as the Rapier squadrons, the regiment had two field squadrons deployed, one each at Brüggen and Laarbruch. This level of protection was a requirement of SACEUR. The same was true for the short-range air defence units; if the ground defence elements were withdrawn, NATO could claim that the UK government had claimed infrastructure hardening expenses (such as hardened aircraft shelters) under false pretences. The implication was that we had no intention of standing-to at all. NATO would quite likely seek compensation. A review of the future basing plan for Tornado considered the idea of dual basing—in this case, retaining the jets in the UK during peacetime, but deploying them to RAFG during conflict. All studies had shown that such an arrangement was, as with the Harriers, operationally less effective and more costly than having the aircraft stationed in Germany.

That this was looked at as an option indicated how much the government was desperate to find financial savings. It is understandable that the political will to go on paying for such a large military force on the continent was not very strong, but militarily speaking, there were few options to do otherwise. Should the Tornado squadrons be housed routinely at UK bases but deployed to Germany when tensions rose, this would deprive the units of valuable regular in-theatre training. It would require additional operational and domestic accommodation and incur delays in the arrangement for spares and engineering support. When the time came to deploy for real or even during exercises, air transport would be hampered by the need to move all out to the continent; this would be at a time when such aircraft could also count on being very busy.

More military transport aircraft would be needed and reliance on civilian aircraft would not be advisable, at best negligible. Otherwise, arbitrary withdrawals would infringe the Brussels Treaty and likely the Quadripartite Agreement. Such a move would be opposed by the other NATO members and the US (so CINCENT thought) may start their own withdrawal. With a whiff of recent political developments on a wider scale concerning Brexit, if the British position in the 1980s was to hole up on the British mainland, this could be seen as adopting a 'fortress UK' approach.

This could be detrimental to European unity. Pursuing a policy of UK basing of the entire fleet of Tornados was not recommended. Even if the operational arguments were dismissed, there would be no actual financial savings for several years other than the foreign currency exchange savings. To base all the RAFG assets in the UK would put immense pressure on bases at home; there was simply no room. The most likely area to be looked at would be the east of England, but this alone would prove very difficult as the amount of infrastructure work involved would amount to £40 million per wing, assuming locations would be found. The premium for maintaining the same wing in Germany would take several years to recoup.

In conclusion, the DWP reported that RAFG was the leanest and most combat-ready operational command in the RAF:

> We are committed to provide it by treaty and there is not a segment that can be withdrawn for cost saving reasons without damaging operational capability and incurring political risk and difficulty.

The start of 1980 did not augur well. During the Red Flag Exercise in the Nevada Desert on 7 February, Buccaneers deployed from Laarbruch were demonstrating their customary ultra-low-level twisting and turning. During one particular sortie, observers were stunned to see one of the Buccaneers—XV345, from 15 Sqn—simply disintegrate with no apparent cause. Both the pilot, Flt Lt Ken Tait, and the navigator, Flt Lt Charles Ruston, were killed. The cause was established as the structural failure of a wing. This resulted in the grounding of all Buccaneers. Subsequent checks found that many of the Buccs were suffering from metal fatigue almost certainly due to their time spent at such low level coupled with high-speed manoeuvring.

The checks found several aircraft were beyond economic repair and were subsequently scrapped. Only the previous year, Strike Command formed an additional squadron, 216, following the transfer of RN Buccaneer operations, which now due to a lack of sufficient airframes would have to disband. After some weeks further into the year, the VCAS was confident enough to report that BAE, the procurement executive, and the delegated engineering authority looked likely to agree that the Buccaneer could return to operations in July. A lot of work had been carried out on the fatigued test specimen, and the preliminary warning instruments indicated no further evidence of cracking. The AAIB had recovered more pieces from the crash site in Nevada, which showed no signs of catastrophic failure in the rear spar area.

The AAIB and RAE were coming to the conclusion that the cause of the accident in Nevada was either an up- or a downdraught on the wing, which brought a heavy strain to bear on an already weakened wing structure. A consensus of opinion was hopefully going to be reached on the airworthiness of the Buccaneer. More importantly, the evidence for allowing the aircraft back aloft had to be sufficient to inspire sufficient confidence in the crews to climb back on board. So subject to agreement being reached on the resumption of flying, it was hoped that a public announcement could be made before parliament rose on 8 August.

A consensus was reached early enough for an announcement to be made on 28 July. RAFG had almost doubled the number of aircraft in its strike force since 1970, but the grounding of the Buccaneers meant a seriously degraded orbat. Over the years since the creation of NATO, successive British governments, while seeking to ameliorate the expense of the military posture in Germany, had had to accept the circumstances and fulfil the NATO commitment. While the conservatives in 1980 were looking again at 'defence requirements', the Labour party conference welcomed its new leader, Michael Foot.

Under Foot's leadership, the opposition were about to slide further toward an even less agreeable position. In 1981, before the Falklands invasion, the government were struggling to maintain public support in an atmosphere of deep public spending cuts. The Labour party naturally took to attacking such cuts vociferously. On the other hand, the opposition adopted a position on NATO and defence that possibly signalled a leftward lurch.

An early defining symptom of how radical the party had become was demonstrated by a breakaway element that formed the centrist Socialist Democratic party, but the main opposition to the government remained the Labour party. In 1982, the government had its own rethink on defence cuts, following the Falklands campaign. The opposition under Foot had reassessed the UK's defence and security arrangement and reached a different conclusion.

The Labour party now pursued such a change in defence policy that it would significantly alter not just the UK military disposition but also leave a hole in the orbat of NATO forces in the central region. Before the UK went to the polls in 1983, Michael Foot accused the government of smearing the Labour party's policy on defence the day following its publication, 17 May. The party's manifesto contained a twelve-point emergency plan that did include the scrapping of the proposed Trident missile system, a refusal to deploy Cruise missiles, and the start of negotiations for the removal of all nuclear bases from Britain, all within the lifetime of a Labour government.

The proposed defence policy relied on an agreed pursuit of a non-nuclear NATO. This would mean Polaris would be de-commissioned, and all other means of launching nuclear warheads would be removed subject to there being no conventional use for them. Specifically, the BAOR's Lance surface-to-surface missile could be retained as a conventional heavy weapon, but its primary reason for being was to deliver a nuclear warhead; therefore it could be deemed surplus to requirements. For the RAF, this meant the removal of those weapons carried by a variety of aircraft, but not necessarily the aircraft themselves. Those aircraft involved were the Nimrod, Jaguar, Buccaneer, and the new Tornado GR1. The manifesto aimed to reduce defence expenditure 'in line with other major European NATO countries'.

Proposed policy, as always in party policy manifesto, was far from specific. Yet what size and shape the RAF in Germany would be in remained a matter of conjecture. What was far more unrealistic was the expectation of a non-nuclear NATO, in the face of a very nuclear Warsaw Pact. The plan to remove all US nuclear weapons from the UK, would place an unacceptable strain on Anglo-American relations without a doubt. The US operated a nuclear submarine base on Holy Loch in the west of Scotland and the F-111 squadrons based at Lakenheath in Suffolk and Upper Heyford on Oxfordshire. To use a modern term, the F-111s could be re-purposed for the conventional role, but it is more likely Washington, DC, would seek to move them somewhere else.

Such an imposition by one country on the rest of NATO, to such a drastic degree, could not have elicited a more dramatic response from the White House. With relations between the directness of the US government and the seemingly fair-weather approach of the European NATO countries, such a reckless proposal could well prove to be the last straw.

The Americans, if they were to show willing, could always accommodate a hostile British administration by seeking to rebase the F-111s elsewhere on the continent, but the availability of space would prove to be an obstacle. The notion that the US would simply accept Foot's radical limitations impacting NATO's entire operational structure was most unlikely.

That the USSR would have been encouraged to exploit such a growing crack in relations could not be determined, even in retrospect, but certainly would not come as a surprise, certainly in the long term if not the short.

The party also vowed to end arms sales to a list of countries that it described as 'oppressive regimes', none of which could be described as communist. To be fair, the UK did not have any arms trade links with any communist countries and were not likely to. However, the Labour party manifesto included one fully paid-up NATO member as one of the proscribed oppressive regimes—Turkey. On top of everything else, this would seriously question the UK's position within the alliance.

It was also the case that with the heavy offensive air armada of the Warsaw Pact parked just the other side of the inner German border, the air defence fighters available to CINCENT was fewer than the number the RAF had available to defend UK airspace.

About two years or so before the first RAF Tornado GR1 touched down in Germany, other smaller NATO air arms were starting to re-equip with their own chosen replacement combat types. Essentially, this was the F-16. By 1982, the air forces of the Low Countries, Denmark, and Norway were well along the road of replacing the previous multi-role fighter that was largely in common use—the F-104 Starfighter.

The same year, the MOD were contacted by someone within the Dutch government who had an unusual request—to enquire whether the RAF's bases in West Germany could possibly accommodate a squadron of KLU F-16s. The purpose advanced was due to a lack of space on Dutch air bases. Mr Abraham Stermerdink, a former Dutch defence secretary, contacted the 2nd Lord Trenchard, then minister of state for defence procurement, with this proposal. The same proposal had evidently been made by the Dutch while Stermerdink was defence secretary at the Hague, back in 1976.

Then the request was to move F-104s from Volkel, again to an RAF base in Germany. The British suspicion was that Stermerdink was trying to get them to shoulder the Dutch tactical nuclear strike burden. At the time, anti-nuclear, anti-military, and anti-establishment sentiments were quite prevalent across the western democracies. The Netherlands was certainly blessed with its fair share of such sentiment, hence the belief that Stermerdink was trying to quell political sensitivities over their own nation's agreement to shoulder a part of the shared nuclear response burden.

The original attempt to persuade the British to host a Dutch F-104 squadron was also explained as due to a lack of basing space. Again, it was the sensitive role of the squadron in question that seemed to be the real concern. The British suspected then that the whole object really was to remove this role from Dutch soil. The British understood that this 'would play well with the Dutch political audience'.

A further approach to Lord Trenchard was a proposal to remove the other Dutch nuclear role—the Nike Hercules missiles operated by the Dutch but based in the FRG. In place of the withdrawal of these missiles, the Dutch would forward base a nuclear-armed F-16 squadron in the FRG. The British could only imagine that they were going to have to house the pilots and ground crew as well, otherwise there were questions regarding how they would fly them. This was again seen as an attempt by the Dutch to rid themselves of their troublesome nuclear task, in this case using the Nike Hercules to manoeuvre an F-16 Sqn, with nukes, onto an RAF base.

The Americans were aware of the Dutch shenanigans and had similar concerns to the British. The British assured the Americans that they would contact the Dutch at ministerial level to remind them of the importance that it attached to all in the alliance, fulfilling the current range of responsibilities, even the nuclear ones. Also, there should be collective agreement on any reduction or abandonment of any part or all of the NATO nuclear task as a whole. The concern of the Dutch that there was insufficient airfield space did not explain why there was not enough room on their bases at Gilze Rijen and Eindhoven, which each housed a single squadron of NF-5s. All the same, Lord Trenchard's letter made the British position clear:

> When we met in November of last year, you raised with me the question of whether there was any possibility of the Royal Netherlands Air Force being allowed to use RAF airfields in the Federal Republic of Germany. You explained that your air force was finding it difficult to find sufficient airfield space in your own country, and that there might be mutual advantages in an arrangement that allowed for sharing. I have looked at this idea very carefully indeed. But I am sorry to say that I have had to draw the conclusion that the RAF airfields in the Federal Republic are already fully utilized in peacetime. During war, when all our peacetime arrangements and plans would be put to the severest test, there would simply be no room at all for any further aircraft on our airfields. I am afraid, therefore, that I can see no prospect of making part of an RAF station available for use by the Royal Netherlands Air Force. May I also mention a report I have seen of an interview you gave to De Volkskrant on 30 December? In this you are quoted as saying that you suggested to me that in return for your abandoning the nuclear Nike-Hercules role in the Federal Republic, you would add an extra Squadron of F-16s to your Air Force, and that this might be based at an RAF airfield. I must confess I do not recall this part of your proposal; perhaps you have not been reported correctly. But I am bound to say that we would view such a proposal with serious misgivings, as we would any proposal by a NATO nation that it should abandon a nuclear task in advance of collective agreement within the alliance on adjustment to NATO's Theatre Nuclear Force deployment policy.
>
> I expect that this reaction comes as no surprise to you but I thought it only right that, in replying to your question about the use of RAF airfields, I should let you know how we view the principle of change in the pattern of nuclear tasks in the Alliance.

Unease about the strength of RAFG continued to place the command under the spotlight. BAOR had their own continuous review looking for any scraps at all to count toward savings. Whenever the defence budget is having its subject to review, there was is always something which is found to fall short of being indispensable. A kind of analogy would be the game of musical chairs—every time the music stops, another chair is removed and someone or something gets left out. However, this time, the outlook was perhaps a little more reassuring. It had been planned to expand the strength of BAOR beyond the 55,000 level; this would instead be held at the current level.

The introduction of the Chinook—for BAOR as much as for RAFG—would go ahead, and the introduction of the Tornado would continue as planned, including the revised increased establishment.

As a result, this time, RAFG was actually going to increase in strength while BAOR avoided contraction. This increase in strength alone could be attributed to the two new aircraft that brought a significant advance in capability and provided a leap ahead in the RAF's ability to support the army, especially when one looks back to the 1960s when the RAF lacked the ability to provide any realistic heavy rotary wing support and tactical air support. The Wessex, Puma, and Harrier had addressed these matters more than adequately in the 1970s.

The arrival of the Chinook brought a significant improvement to battlefield transport while the Tornado more directly addressed and expanded the longer-range interdiction task. It also easily managed to supplement the Harriers in closer range attack if required, which the Canberra had previously done, despite its vulnerabilities. Compared with the Tornado, the three other ground attack jets in the theatre—the Buccaneer, Jaguar, and Harrier—were restricted by a limited all-weather capability.

Operational training sorties were impossible for an average of fifteen hours per day throughout the year, which went up to 18.5 hours per day during winter. The Tornado would certainly remedy this in the case of comparison with the Buccaneer and Jaguar. The introduction of the Chinook would increase the daily lift weight from 30 to 150 tons—an increase of 400 per cent. The fixed-wing combat force would, with the introduction of the 'Tonka', see aircraft numbers increase from 132 to 144.

Given the improved capability of the new airframe this represented, no one could argue that a significant leap forward and upwards was not afoot. These two new fine aircraft would also bring a 10 per cent increase in personnel. There was an element of army support, which was very much in demand by the RAF; this was the ADR (airfield damage repair) squadrons.

Moving into the 1980s, the RAF in Germany were pressing for an RE (Royal Engineers) ADR squadron to be based in theatre for immediate deployment to the airfields. The specialist materials and plant machinery were already held on the bases, but the personnel were not.

If a short transition to war occurred, RAFG was concerned that the designated Sapper squadrons would not pitch up in time. RAFG was the only central region air force not to have an ADR unit in place. There was one RE ADR squadron based at Laarbruch, 10 Field Squadron, but their wartime role was to deploy with the Harrier force. The more logical arrangement of placing this unit at RAF Gütersloh or the nearby Mansergh barracks was being looked at together with BAOR.

An existing contingency plan was to reinforce 10 Squadron RE with two UK-based squadrons, but again this was to prepare the Harrier forward war sites. Four more Sapper squadrons were earmarked to deploy to provide the ADR function in question, but it was the timely arrival of these units that particularly worried RAFG. At the heart of all this were the limitation factors, and this is where politics re-entered the equation. The BAOR manpower ceiling would be breached if any additional RE squadrons were assigned in theatre with additional costs of accommodating a resident ADR squadron. What may help was the planned re-deployment, from RAFG, of 25 Squadron. No. 25 Sqn and the UK-based 85 Sqn were the last two such units in the RAF to operate the Bloodhound surface-to-air missile, which was now considered surplus to requirements in Germany given the presence of the RAF Regiment rapier squadrons.

There was also some expectation that 10 Squadron would move forward to Gütersloh, which would make a lot more sense. It would provide room at Laarbruch, but the BAOR personnel ceiling remained a permanent obstacle. Even while C-in-C BAOR and the army board recognised the importance of the ADR, they had not allocated a higher priority to increasing the manpower requirement. It seemed that ADR was not considered sufficiently crucial. The Warsaw Pact had increased its capability to attack airfields; this in turn led to some concern that all SACEUR-assigned Tornado GR1 squadrons would eventually be based in Germany, but crucially, the provision of a substantial ADR force was of the utmost priority.

However much a critical factor, it still needed to be successfully impressed upon the minds of ministers that an in theatre-based ADR squadron was needed and that it should not form part of the BAOR orbat. The RAF had a further argument to deploy—the reason they did not have an ADR capability themselves was due to the disbandment of the old airfield construction branch back in the early 1960s as a rationalisation move.

Air-Vice Marshal Paddy Hine (ACAS/Policy) believed in impressing upon the army the need to allow for an ADR squadron to be included in their 55,000 personnel ceiling. If not then they should take the case to ministerial level, with this approach being the most likely development. The latter course was still seen as a last resort and that approaching the DUS(Air) first would be best, bearing in mind that the Treasury was scrutinising the MOD and its application of the 55,000 level to ensure it was not breached.

The early 1980s were beset with problems. At the start of 1981, RAFG was experiencing problems with a pilot shortage. A detailed description of the Brüggen QRA commitment was prepared in a letter for C-in-C RAFG. In questions raised about RAF Brüggen, the station was described as having been built to house a total of sixty aircraft, envisaged to be Canberras at the time and composed of four squadrons with a UE of fifteen aircraft each and ninety pilots. Working on the basis of one QRA line per squadron and one for every thirty aircraft, this would provide six QRA lines to cover.

Due to pilot shortages the number of aircraft never exceeded forty-eight and thus utilised just five QRA lines. This had allowed commitments on QRA to continue to be met with a minimum establishment of seventy-two pilots, but this was proving difficult to maintain and occasionally fell short. Indeed, for some time, they had been running below the established seventy-two. The problem of maintaining the requisite number of pilots was expected to get worse. Of the reduced number, only the more experienced were qualified to hold QRA duties. They were also relied upon to provide supervision and guidance for the junior pilots. Conflict between maintaining QRA and continuity of training and experience was inevitable, and the pool of experienced pilots was also decreasing.

Other problems compounded the predicament, diminishing engineering skills and fuel restrictions. All this gravitated toward contemplating reducing the QRA lines further, from five to four. The solution being favoured was to amalgamate the four existing squadrons into three of adequate size.

This was not as pointless as it may sound. Fewer but larger squadrons would, with less management and administrative interference, allow for greater flexibility and larger formations to be flown with greater aircraft availability. Also, with three squadrons, room would then be available for No. 2 Squadron to move from Laarbruch, meaning all RAFG Jaguars would be concentrated at Brüggen. This was before the assessment concluded the Jaguar's unsuitability to continue in theatre.

This was also an advantage for when Tornados start arriving at Laarbruch. New nuclear handling procedures were issued in 1980. All handling procedures were to be brought into line with the NATO standard. The new procedures were to be incorporated in the UK NRP (nuclear release procedures) manual. In the meantime, however, separate detailed interim national release procedures had been issued to the RAF prior to the definitive NRP being issued. When the appropriate NATO alert measure was issued, this would be subject to the declaration of the complementary RAF alert measure being implemented.

Control of British nuclear weapons at RAF Brüggen and RAF Laarbruch would then transfer to SACEUR. This would give SACEUR the authority to use the weapons on air operations subject to receipt of the prime minister's specific national release authority for each specified use. This would be achieved by including a United Kingdom national authenticator with SACEUR's release message.

The British prime minister would send a national approval message to SACEUR containing the UKNA, also to be copied to C-in-C RAFG, his standby headquarters, and the British delivery unit commanders, which were the Brüggen and Laarbruch station commanders. British nuclear weapons were to remain in national custody throughout and were not to be released until both messages containing the UKNA had been received. These would need to be authenticated by the respective British unit delivery commander.

Under RAF alert procedures, general war would see the following signal communicated 'TSD 811'. When TSD 811 measure 400 was issued, the two station commanders became the custodians in place of the RAFG commander. Then operational command of the Buccaneer and Jaguar forces would transfer to SACEUR. The nuclear weapons stored at Brüggen and Laarbruch would then be released; the Buccaneers and Jaguars would be armed and ready in response to SACEUR's 'BLUE DOT FIVE', a coded message for selective release, and a 'RED HOTEL ONE' coded message, for general release. In each case, however, the prime minister's national approval message was required. The message from the prime minister, whatever it contained, would override SACEUR's authority for release.

Further TSD 811 measures dealt with the response to a security threat to the nuclear stores. Should there be a serious risk of the weapons falling into enemy or subversive hands, they were to be evacuated or, if necessary, destroyed.

These actions would be in accordance with TSD 811 measures 316, 317, and 318. Measure 316 specifically covered the authority to issue the order to destroy stocks; this remained with HMG through the CAS. Yet if for any reason this was not possible, procedures would be followed under measure 400, meaning the authority would have passed to C-in-C RAFG but in case of communications failure (i.e., RAFG commander and deputy no longer contactable for whatever reason) then the power to order the destruction of the weapons would be passed to the station commanders of Brüggen and Laarbruch. The station commanders were therefore empowered, *in extremis*, to order the evacuation of all personnel using all available means or the destruction of the weapons as deemed necessary.

This was the further revised procedure rehearsed in Exercise Quick Train back in 1961, when the weapons were US-owned and maintained with key American personnel among dependents and others who had to be evacuated with the upmost haste.

With the eventual arrival of the Panavia Tornado, the promised quantum leap in capability and versatility certainly brought the greatest jump forward since the introduction of the Phantom.

The eager anticipation was tempered by shortages of personnel. C-in-C RAF Germany, Sir Jock Kennedy, sought to reduce RAF activity within West Germany to avoid overstretch caused by the pilot shortage. Comparisons made with two–three years earlier, about 1978, had revealed that pilot numbers (experienced ones in particular) had indeed fallen progressively, especially within the Jaguar force. This was compounded by the equally worrying, corresponding fall in the level of engineering personnel.

The reason for this was not a simple matter of poor recruitment or of engineering personnel putting in their PVR to head off to Saudi Arabia or Oman. The numbers were supposed to have risen to accommodate the need for an increase in technical tradesmen forced by the AMS/HAS programme on all four airfields. Tasking otherwise had remained constant while the additional need for the HAS pattern of operations had remained undermanned. With the emphasis on obtaining excellent results during TACEVALs, the workload may well have increased, particularly where flying tasking was concerned.

The thinning out of first tourist aircrew was the problem which needed to be addressed, by reducing the burden. However, the caution here was to avoid reductions reaching too far, which could lead to a reduced establishment. The RAF wanted to avoid taking out the elements of squadron service for aircrew that made it even more interesting, such as exchange tours with other allied air arms and other off-piste activities. Sir Jock reported, 'we do not want our crews to feel that there is no room for enjoyment within their profession'. The C-in-C also drew attention to the strains endured by the Harrier force in particular due to the nature of the Harriers' very specific battlefield role. The Gütersloh wing was away on deployments and field deployments throughout much of the year. Problems with personnel morale existed, despite the Gütersloh establishment being increased by 400 additional posts over the preceding five years.

These posts had been added to meet the high tempo of field deployments that left morale extremely low. Taceval was regarded as one cause of misery, and anyone who had contended with this NATO by-product of the Cold War, was concerned, would likely understand what is meant by when I describe it as a cause of misery. Taceval was perhaps feared by all concerned, even more than a Warsaw Pact invasion, with all it demanded and always when everyone was at their very worst.

RAFG had developed a pathological pursuit of excellence in Tacevals. On their own, these surprise tests of an air base's competence were very exacting and caught personnel on the hop too often. The idea was to test the alertness and procedural proficiency of base personnel, not to try and catch people out, which is more how they were viewed. This near obsession had become too narrow a focus; there needed to be a more realistic way of preparing all personnel, not just to pass a Taceval but to reassure NATO that everyone was ready to go to war at the drop of a hat, at any hour on a rain- and wind-battered winter morning. Therefore, to improve levels of readiness, experience, and training, as well as maintain a sufficient degree of currency with operational procedures, a Mineval would need to be held every six weeks. The turnover of RAFG personnel was quite high—about 10 per cent every three to four months.

These exercises provided excellent training and ensured every aspect of the station was tested, ensuring a good showing during the more definitive

Taceval. The Minevals had to be maintained at a minimum number to ensure that a full war posture could be attained within the magic forty-eight hours.

The air staff came to regard Minevals as a more crucial exercise than the Taceval. This would be difficult to convince the station and squadron commanders who placed all on the outcome of the Taceval. These transition to full-scale war exercises were competitive and pitted RAFG stations against others through NATO. The morale of an RAF station would soar each time they did well before the examiners.

No. 15 Squadron at Laarbruch became the first to convert to the Tornado GR1, and the fourth GR1 unit overall. They began replacing their stalwart and venerable Buccaneers with the new jets, officially forming on 1 September 1983.

The RAF News played on the old adage 'The Bucc stops here' as a headline for a short article covering 15 Sqn's transition. Approval was also sought to fly a pair of Buccaneers around the world on a globe-trotting tour, showing off the older aircraft's unrefuelled range between stops. Permission was denied. It would seem that such a demonstration of endurance might just highlight a shortcoming in this yardstick with its replacement.

The rate of conversion to the Tornado from both the Jaguar and Buccaneer in Germany took place in relatively short order. The conversion of the Laarbruch wing continued at quite a rate compared with the leaden movement just over twenty years later with the delayed conversion of RAF squadrons to the Eurofighter Typhoon. The Tornado GR1 introduction to RAFG, in particular, was full speed ahead.

On 29 February 1984, 16 Squadron Buccaneers officially disbanded. Two months earlier, the new 16 Tornado Squadron began to work up and by the beginning of March were able to formally declare themselves operational. The last Buccaneer aircraft departed Laarbruch on 15 March 1984. However, the Buccaneer was not quite done with RAFG as three aircraft belonging to 237 OCU had been declared to SACEUR in the Pave Spike laser designator role. This was likely because the number of aircraft and crews of the Lossiemouth OCU was to increase to six aircraft and eight crews by December. The unit would deploy to Laarbruch during exercises.

Meanwhile, the Laarbruch Tornado wing was to build to three squadrons—15, 16, and 20—by August 1985. The unit establishment of each would be twelve aircraft plus one IUR (in-use reserve). The optimum crew establishment was to be eighteen, but in the interim would stand at sixteen in order to ease the output from TTTE (Tri-National Tornado Establishment) and to match the reduced level of flying hours caused by a lack of spares and a surfeit of inexperienced ground crew. By early 1984, 15 Squadron had all its compliment of thirteen jets and fifteen trained crews. No. 16 Squadron had ten aircraft but expected to reach its full complement by 30 April. In the meantime, they had ten navigators and six pilots.

The Laarbruch wing so far had received a stock of 'special weapons', BL755 cluster bombs, and 1,000-lb high-explosive bombs. Weapons yet to be delivered included 27-mm Mauser cannon ammunition. The guns were already installed, but what was described as the instability of the ammunition in storage delayed training and operational clearance. AIM 9L Sidewinders and LGBs (laser-guided bombs) were expected by mid-year, while the JP233 munition dispensers were expected by the end of the year. ALARM (air-launched anti-radar missile) were expected in 1987. In addition, BOZ 107 chaff and flare dispensers and Sky Shadow ECM pods had been delivered and were already routinely carried.

No. 15 Squadron was expecting to be fully operational in both nuclear and conventional roles by the end of the year. Through 1984 to the end of August 1985, 16 Squadron had completed a programme of intense operational training. The schedule included a squadron exchange with one of the F-111 units at Upper Heyford in August 1984 followed by a Lone Ranger exercise to Cyprus on 28 September and a deployment to Decimomannu, Italy, from 31 October to 21 November. The Lone Ranger exercises involved a single aircraft, unsupported, deploying to an overseas location. In 1985, sixteen were expecting to be conducted between Germany and Goose Bay.

Laarbruch was also expecting the first Tornado flight simulator in RAFG to be in use by April, during Air Chief Marshal Sir Keith Williamson's visit.

In April, the system was undergoing acceptance trials. Among problems to be resolved were the lack of TFR (terrain-following radar) training areas in the FRG and Low Countries. Another problem not necessarily connected to the build-up of the Tornado force arose during squadron generation exercises. The squadrons were often unable to meet the additional ancillary commitments such as guard and sentry duties; this matter was being addressed through the allocation of extra station personnel.

Laarbruch had also recently lost a Tornado (ZA451) following a Lightning strike, which was under investigation. The fourth operational flying unit at Laarbruch was 2 Squadron, still equipped with the Jaguar GR1/T2. No. 2 Sqn's role as a tactical reconnaissance unit was assigned to SACEUR as a daytime recce squadron with a limited day attack capability. Their establishment stood at twelve GR1s and a T2 with an establishment for sixteen pilots; at the time, they had seventeen. In the attack role, the Jaguars would carry 20-mm Aden cannons and BL755 cluster bombs. For reconnaissance, a recce pod with optical cameras and infrared line scan was fitted. The aircraft were expected to carry AIM 9L Sidewinders in due course. This then was the state of affairs at RAF Laarbruch as of March 1984. Conversion of the Jaguar strike wing at Brüggen to the Tornado GR1 was due to commence shortly.

By April 1985, the conversion of the third Brüggen squadron, 14, got under way. On the first of the month, however, one of the squadron's Jaguars crashed in open country near Celle. The pilot, Flying Officer G. Brough, ejected safely and the incident was subject to a board of inquiry. The other two squadrons, 17 and 31, continued with their build-up on the Tornado GR1. Meanwhile, two holes were deliberately blown in the southern taxiway; this was for the benefit of 52 Field Engineer Squadron, so they could practice filling them in again.

By the end of the month, 31 Squadron had notched up 330.35 hours; 17 Sqn, 202.4 hours; and 14 Sqn, 3.45 hours on their new charges. A rather unsettled period ensued with several aircrew officers being posted in from a variety of locations and units to each of the three. As 14 Squadron were still in the early stages of conversion, they were still effective with the Jaguar, and on 15 May, they commenced the final Jaguar armament practice camp to Decimomannu.

The Jaguars achieved some excellent air-to-ground results and demonstrated their worth in air-to-air combat manoeuvring. On 1 July, 16:00Z, 31 Squadron were declared to SACEUR and assumed the QRA commitment. No. 31 Sqn also mounted the first Brüggen Tornado exchange as five aircraft with ground crew flew to Cervia in Italy, while four Fiat G91s with their attendant personnel deployed to Brüggen. The Brüggen ORB recorded that the QRA status of 31 Squadron was a first for both Brüggen and, perhaps, the RAF—that two types of aircraft had mounted nuclear QRA duty simultaneously at the same airfield.

By November, all three squadrons had completed conversion and, together with Laarbruch, RAFG now fielded the most potent strike force since the start of the Cold War. By early 1988, seven units at Brüggen and Laarbruch were now operational with the Tornado with one more squadron redeployed from 1 Group, Strike Command. No. 9 Squadron, the first in the RAF to be declared operational with the Tornado, was sent to Brüggen at the end of 1986. This completed the order of battle—eight Tornado squadrons with the two enlarged Harrier units, the two Phantom air defence squadrons and the two helicopter sqns, 230 with Pumas and 18 with Chinooks.

RAF Germany was now at its strongest point on record and operating more aircraft than at any time since the early 1960s, making it far more capable and formidable. The next step was a further upgrade for the Harrier wing at Gütersloh—namely, the introduction of an entirely new jet. The GR5 would be delivered to 3 Squadron, very much as an interim version; the more definitive GR7 was to go straight to 4 Squadron following which 3 Sqn would get GR7s. This brought a true all-weather night capability for the battlefield support Harriers and a wider array of ordnance. The most neglected element was the air superiority fighter wing at Wildenrath.

The plan for the Phantoms was that they would soldier on until about 2003, with various upgrades. By the time 2003 arrived, the expectation was that the

EFA (European fighter aircraft) would be ready to replace the old American naval fighter. It was also announced by the government in early 1989 that forty more Tornados—both GR1s and the definitive air defence model, the F3—would be ordered, though mostly GR1s. This would allow additional squadrons to either form or convert on top of the standing plan for seven F3 squadrons and eleven GR1 units.

Through the summer of that year, the RAF struggled with personnel retention as many sought to leave early. The world was never going to change and an attempt to stand up to the totalitarian authorities in Peking met with the kind of sledgehammer on a butterfly response that brought no surprises. The strategic balance still had to be deftly maintained, despite the internal security concerns of the Chinese Communist Party. Since the previous summer, there had been snippets of information that seemed to suggest there had been breaches of the usually watertight border controls behind the Iron Curtain. People were successfully risking life and limb to cross over into the West.

Publicly, a spirit of goodwill had been demonstrated in one of the most demonstrative ways possible. The Soviet Union sent over a pair of MiG-29 Fulcrums to take centre stage at the 1988 Farnborough SBAC Air Show. Your author was tasked (unofficially) with collecting a video sample of the aircraft being put through its paces, close up, for subsequent analysis—an opportunity it was thought may yield something worthwhile. So along I went and inadvertently chose the day that both aircraft went unserviceable, so I returned to Gatow empty handed. The likelihood of any interruption to the *status quo* was seen as so fanciful that when I brought the possibility up with an RAF officer at Gatow that same year, I drew an incredulous look. I was convinced that the unique circumstances of the continuing arrangements over West and East Berlin would, sooner or later, prove temporary, if long term.

The city was a single entity. It was a nation's capital and yet it was still suspended in time since the end of the war. Berlin remained a city of occupation, with the military police of each of the three western powers patrolling their respective sectors at all hours. One could be stood at a bar in the Europa Centre on a Saturday night and at any time, the Royal Military Police (known colloquially as 'Redcaps') would appear in their 'Home Dress' khaki uniforms with white belts and sidearms, just passing through on patrol. Allied servicemen could not be arrested by the Berlin police; they could be detained until their national MPs had been alerted, who would then make any arrests deemed necessary.

There were the more familiar signs of Harry Palmer's Berlin—the Europa Centre, the Zoo Bahnhof, the calcified remains of the Kaiser Wilhelm Memorial Church. There was the Soviet War Memorial, built from masonry taken from the ruins of the Reich Chancellery. Through the Cold War years, the memorial was guarded round the clock by a ceremonial guard drawn from Red Army units based in East Berlin, as if outside the main gates of Buckingham Palace.

Checkpoint Charlie, the much-publicised point of access between the two sides of the city manned by US military police on the western side, was a real Cold War landmark. However, this was not the only point of access.

Some members of the Allied Forces were, for security reasons, forbidden to cross into the east, such as those with access to sensitive information.

The *U-Bahn* (underground train) moved freely between both sides of the city. Once arriving at a stop on the other side, East Berlin police would enter the train to check passes. If at this juncture, someone with access to sensitive information happened to still be on board, they would be in a pickle, having realised all too late that they had ended up in East Berlin. Regardless of whether they made an error through absent-mindedness, confusion, or having over imbibed before heading back to the billet, they would be in serious trouble.

The East Berlin police would take them into custody for traveling in the Eastern sector without authorised travel documents. Instructions, in such circumstances, were to say nothing but to request to speak to a Russian officer. This could be quite a trial but would eventually mean the handing back of the hapless airman/soldier to his own side. From there, a debrief would follow with the individual invariably sent home and security clearance withdrawn. The possible consequences of allowing such an individual to remain in a sensitive post in West Berlin, or anywhere for that matter, after any contact with the communist authorities, no matter how fleeting, was too great to risk. This was all part of the tapestry of Berlin in the Cold War, the city divided into two halves by opposed ideologies. An island of Western liberalism and democracy sat in the middle of a Marxist authoritarian state, bordering more communist states to the east toward the USSR.

I often tried to imagine a similar fate befalling the United Kingdom, with a guarded wall or patrolled fence running from Bristol to Hull, the north side hosting the armed forces of several nations, formally as occupation troops now to guard against the forces of a totalitarian power on the south side, while London is split in two—west and east, or north and south, with armed checkpoints and foreign military powers present as the ultimate authority on their respective sides, opposing each other as they follow a routine farrago of rituals all in the name of protocol, to ensure no diplomatic incident arises threatening to upset the delicate balance. There would be restricted and non-deviating roads, rail and air lanes being the only route for people of the democracies to get in and out of north or west London, and only from the border to the north. Yet worst of all, families would be forever divided with one side not permitted to travel to the homes of those on the other. There would be opposing sets of British armed forces, facing one another, each committed to an opposed political ideology. Many worried this version of Berlin would be a settled and permanent outcome.

10

Down with the Wall

Since 1982, Christian Fuhrer, a Protestant pastor in Leipzig, against threats and intimidation, managed to lead a church congregation at St Nicholas Church. They were not necessarily Sunday gatherings for worship; what irked the authorities were the gatherings under the banner of 'Peace Protests' every Monday since 20 September 1982. The authorities had responded with attempts to block access to the church and intimidating those flocking to the pastor's calls on all to gather and pray for peace.

This left the authorities, intolerant at the best of times, feeling most uncomfortable about the direction events were moving in. Economic difficulties were becoming a growing source of discontent across the Eastern Block, even in the GDR, which held the same reputation for economic competency as its Western counterpart, and prudence in relation to the rest of the Warsaw Pact, the USSR included.

Strangely, the pastor was never arrested. His followers grew despite threats and attacks, lethal threats at times, by the *Volkspolizei* (People's Police), the East German police force. Seven years on, the church gatherings were still taking place and with a growing congregation. On 9 October, amid growing unrest, the police and army were authorised to use force on such protest gatherings. However, this did not happen. There were growing protests expanding to 70,000. Toward the end of 'peace prayers', a political manifesto was read out. This manifesto was not a list of policies but a simple call for non-violence. A chanted slogan quickly spread—'*Keine Gewalt*', simply and directly translated as 'No Violence'.

There had been similar demonstrations two days earlier to mark the fortieth anniversary of the GDR. This had been responded to in more predictable style by the authorities. There were no attributable deaths, but 3,500 arrests were made and some people were injured.

This time, the police and army were unsure how to react. If they had been on duty along the wall and were confronted with a desperate situation, a man or woman or a couple of desperados making a forlorn bid for freedom, that would be one thing. These were isolated incidents, and the rules were clearly understood—clear orders to open fire were acted upon in such circumstances, and a long-established precedent for this had been established.

Yet faced with a situation where no one offered any resistance with no attempt to breach any walls or perimeter was another matter altogether. The crowd may have annoyed the guards' sense of compliance with authority, but they offered no resistance; they merely got under the skin, and the police and troops were not about to open fire and start emptying their magazines into a large crowd of their fellow countrymen, who offered no discernible physical threat. Others started gathering at all six of the Berlin Wall crossing points. More locals turned up in greater numbers.

The guards had no idea how to react and were facing demands from the protesters to open the gates; their counterparts on the western side were watching events unfold. Both sides would have been wary of how this might transpire. If someone in authority on the East German side gave the order to open fire on the crowd, perhaps this would have been all that was needed—someone to take responsibility, so they would simply be following orders, then this point at which the eve of the end of the Cold War was reached could very much have gone the other way. Indeed, a very ugly, messy and deafening scene could have literally been the opening shots of a third world war. Yet nothing happened at this stage and all melted away again, but the authorities were already compelled to confront the growing unrest. More protests in Leipzig, and elsewhere, took place, attracting greater numbers.

On 18 October 1989, Erich Honecker, the man who had ruled East Germany as its president since 29 October 1976, resigned.

Pressure had been mounting certainly since local elections in May, which appeared to be held, relatively, in an atmosphere free of intimidation. The official results were exposed as fabricated nonsense. Claims that the ruling SED (*Sozialistische Einheitspartei Deutschlands*, the Socialist Unity party of Germany, known in the West as the East German communist party) had enjoyed a massive landslide, causing further agitation among the people. Elsewhere, other Warsaw Pact states (including Poland and Hungary) had taken relaxed measures; Hungary had started dismantling its own electrified fence along the border with Austria. Through this, thousands of East Germans on holiday in Hungary escaped with comparative ease into Austria. Rumours going back to 1988 had been circulating about crossings, albeit made covertly, but made with relative ease. Honecker was a former political prisoner of the Nazi regime and had been liberated by the Russians in 1945. He had been a member of the German communist party and resumed his political career after the war.

A hardliner, Erich Honecker had attempted to resist reforms brought about by Mikhail Gorbachev. Anti-communist sentiment and the May elections were factors that increased tension. Unease had been growing over the preceding months, despite requests from Honecker for Soviet military assistance to crush dissent. This had been the case in Hungary in 1956 and Czechoslovakia in 1968.

Honecker found himself alone. He was primarily responsible as the state security secretary back in 1961 for the construction of the Berlin Wall. He was also instrumental in the policy of shooting anyone who tried to escape to the other side. He was replaced by Egon Krenz, described only as a marginally less hard-line communist party member. However, when Krenz appeared in front of the TV cameras, something seldom seen from behind the Iron Curtain, he was smiling magnanimously. The porous border between the GDR and Czechoslovakia had been sealed on the orders of Honecker. Krenz ordered the border open again on 1 November. From here as in Hungary, East Germans could cross from Czechoslovakia into Austria and freedom.

On 9 November 1989, a press announcement was accidentally broadcast from the Berlin Wall. The announcement simply said that people from East Germany could cross freely into West Germany. This was the result of a misinformed press conference presided over by the leader of the communist party chapter for Berlin, Gunter Schabowski; he was aware at short notice that East German citizens could apply for permission to travel into the west without the previous restrictive conditions imposed. He had just been handed a piece of paper, by Egon Krenz, with some details about the 'proposed' changes.

This was an update to a more restrictive easing of travel laws released on 6 November. They were more relaxed but intended to be temporary and not officially to be released until the next day. Why Krenz chose to hand Schabowski this text without any further briefing remains a mystery. Schabowski had no knowledge of these changes. He had not been present at the committee meeting where they were placed before the central committee plenum earlier that day.

At the press briefing chaired by Schabowski, he told the gathered reporters that a new law was being introduced that would allow permanent immigration between east and west. A German reporter asked when this would take effect and Schabowski said, as far as he was aware, with immediate effect. The minister for foreign trade, Gerhard Beil, who was present, attempted to explain that the new travel laws were yet to be placed before the council of ministers. What was more to the point is they were only intended to relax immigration and migration laws; they were not intended to lift restrictions on movement comprehensively or completely.

However, Schabowski confirmed that the new law took immediate effect. Each time he was asked a question about the new travel laws, he had to refer quickly, but with a degree of uncertainty, to the piece of paper Krenz had handed him moments before the press briefing. He also confirmed that the new law included West Berlin. Another reporter, Daniel Johnson of *The Daily Telegraph*, asked what this meant for the Berlin Wall.

Schabowski seemed to be caught off guard, as if something had just dawned on him, then tried to explain that the wall was subject to the larger disarmament question. The conventional Armed Forces in Europe Treaty (CFE) had been initiated back in January 1989 and he was possibly referring to this. Afterwards, in a separate interview with Tom Brokaw of NBC, Schabowski confirmed again that East Germans could emigrate with immediate effect.

The press conference finished at 7 p.m.; four minutes later, German citizens on both sides were picking up on this and took it at face value. Then significant groups of people started to gather on the east side. The East German Guards were unaware of what was in fact a premature, and incorrect, announcement regarding the proposed free movement of German citizens from both sides.

The Stasi appeared short on instructions and reacted initially with token and forlorn attempts to control the situation but to no effect. The press conference had been broadcast everywhere by now, and widely interpreted as a comprehensive removal of travel restrictions, meaning anyone could legally cross back and forth across the now very redundant wall with impunity.

Used to direct orders with no room for compromise, just as in the Nazi era, the Stasi structure was unable to find someone who knew how to respond without a directive from further up the ladder of authority. They seemed to find themselves further detached from proceedings. People started to follow one another back and forth while others brought tools including sledgehammers and pickaxes to hack away at this hated symbol of ideological and cruel division.

Soon, entire families and larger groups moved in and out through broken sections and checkpoints. The movement remained continuous and a party atmosphere developed. The American, British, and French military guards did not react; they could only look on. There came a point where any kind of armed response from either side under any circumstances would have resulted in a massacre. The Cold War was over.

For their part, the East German Guards' response, such as it was, appeared to dissipate. A sudden flow of people just wandering back and forth was not scripted for. The news spread in West German media outlets that freedom of movement across the IGB and the Berlin Wall was now legal. The East German authorities were led by the broadcasts from the West and accepted the chain of events.

The guards initially tried to intervene by attempting to repair sections of wall that had been damaged, but in due course, they gave this up and resigned themselves to looking on, some disapprovingly, others with a more resigned or even partisan mood. Yet all were puzzled, waiting for orders to do something, while watching the growing back and forth ebb and flow of human beings including young families with small children. This was the end of the *status quo* as it had stood, effectively since 1945, which many people, myself included, had been born into and grown to adulthood with. The backdrop to the 'Boomer' generation's formative years saw the curtains finally close on it.

At the time the wall came down, the disposition of the RAF in Germany and the other air forces of NATO's central region had never been better equipped and ready to meet the expected adversary. There was one more nail to be hammered into the coffin of communist East Europe—in December, a popular uprising against an even less sympathetic ruler than Honecker, took place in Romania. On 16 December, the Hungarian community in Romania went on public protest at the government's attempts to deport their equivalent to Christian Fuhrer, Pastor Laszlo Tokes. Tokes' crime was to say in public what everyone knew—that Romanians had no idea of their human rights.

Riots followed in the city of Timisoara. Nicholae Ceausescu, the president, left for Iran two days later, leaving his subordinates to crush what was by then widespread civil disobedience. When he returned on 20 December, matters had developed. The country was now consumed with a nationwide uprising.

On the morning of 21 December, Ceausescu gave a speech from the balcony of the central committee building in Bucharest. It was entirely predictable— the people involved in the protests in Timisoara were fascists; socialism had achieved so much in Romania. About two minutes into the speech, the 100,000 or so people foregathered in the palace square started jeering and booing. The president continued to extol the virtues of socialism and the October Revolution while trying to defuse this uprising. While Ceausescu continued to get round the crowd by promising pay rises 'for the workers', the sound of explosions and either fireworks or gunfire or both came from the periphery. As the situation got worse, Ceausescu was seen trying to gesture with his palms for all to settle down. It was a futile gesture, as if trying to command the sea not to roll to shore.

Between then and the early hours of the next morning, Ceausescu lost any grip he had on the situation. Civil war now ensued with the army firing on the revolutionaries. By 9.30 a.m. on the morning of 22 December, the defence minister, Vasile Milea, was dead, circumstances unknown. However, the revolutionaries believed he had been murdered on the orders of Ceausescu because of his perceived limp response in the early stages of mere protests. He is said to have despatched troops to Timisoara without ammunition. Many soldiers believed he was murdered as well. This began a shift in loyalty in the army.

Victor Stanculescu, the new defence minister, had accepted the post but had seemed reluctant; he certainly did not do his boss's bidding. Victor immediately ordered the remaining loyal troops back to barracks and demonstrated his loyalty, and pragmatism, by advising the president and his wife to accept being evacuated by helicopter. The plan was for the Dauphin helicopter to land in the palace square; this was out of the question as the square was seething with anti-Ceausescu demonstrators. The back-up plan was to land on the terrace roof of the central committee building; an aid attempted to guide the helicopter in with a white tablecloth or curtain.

The pilot, Lt Col. Vasile Malutan, tried to land on the terrace roof. He successfully put down. As the Ceausescus were on their way with their escort to the terrace roof, the co-pilot turned and told the skipper that demonstrators were climbing onto the roof. The Ceausescus were at this moment brought through the terrace stairwell entrance and the chopper crew thought they looked like they were being propped up by their aids and two vice presidents, Manea Manescu and Emil Bobu. They were ashen-faced as Ceausescu was pulled in by the crew and two other Securitate officers scrambled on board. The demonstrators were running toward the aircraft. The Dauphin helicopter was designed to carry a maximum of four passengers; once they had managed to pull in Mrs Ceausescu and squeezed her in with the two pilots, there were six people on board.

The small helicopter got airborne and Lt Col. Malutan flew to Snagov. On arrival, Ceausescu, as with all dictators, believed he had an iron grip on command. He ordered his saviour, Lt Col. Malutan, to contact his HQ and order three more Dauphins, two loaded with armed troops. This Malutan did; when he spoke to his own CO, he was told that there had been a revolution and that he was on his own—the final words were 'good luck'.

Next, Ceausescu ordered Malutan to fly the entourage with him to Titu. Malutan said he would, but could only carry four, not six passengers, so the two vice-presidents waited behind. The Dauphin flew off, and near Titu, Malutan started to manoeuvre the aircraft, dropping height then gaining again rapidly; he told the president this was to avoid anti-aircraft fire. The president panicked and ordered the pilot to land; he did, in a field near a road leading into the town of Pitesti.

Malutan had made his mind up—the situation was desperate, and he did not want to be on the wrong side. He told his four passengers they were on their own. The two security men flagged down two cars. One was driven by a doctor, just as reluctant as anyone else to get involved; he was made to drive the entire party to Titu.

The doctor faked engine trouble. The party were left to flag someone else down, this time a bicycle repairman who said he would take them to Targoviste. On arrival there, he dropped them off at the Agricultural Technical

Institute and handed them to the safe custody of the institute director. He led them to a room and locked them in. They were subsequently arrested by the local police; the revolution was complete.

Ceausescu and his wife were held at the local barracks for several days until their 'day in court'. This was on Christmas Day, 1989. Ceausescu seemed to be living in another world; he denounced those former members of his inner circle and government ministers as traitors. His trial lasted two hours before the death sentence was passed; he still had a right to appeal against his sentence, though this was ignored. In a matter of minutes following sentence, Nicolae Ceausescu and his wife, Elena, were taken out the back of the makeshift courtroom and shot by a firing squad of just three paratroopers.

Both the West and what was still the USSR colluded in the uprising. On New Year's Eve, USAF transport aircraft were flying in supplies, but the people's revolution, against communist socialism, was over.

11

Options for Change

The collapse of the Berlin Wall is one of the most seismic moments in history. The path that history has taken since has been determined by this one event, just as the Cold War itself had its die cast not first and foremost by the Second World War, but by the initial event which set it in train. Every event to 9 November 1989 could be traced back to 28 June 1914—the day when Archduke Franz Ferdinand was assassinated by Gavrilo Princip, a nineteen-year-old idealist, nationalist, and member of the Black Hand Gang. This in turn led directly to the First World War, the one which was to 'end all wars'. The outcome precipitated the rise of Hitler, which could most likely have been avoided, were it not for the spiteful and unrealistic demands for war reparations and humiliating limits imposed by the victorious Allies. It is incredible to think that victors' justice over 100 years ago brought the world to this situation, and since then to our present circumstances in 2022. From the First World War, a chain of events has been linked through the Second World War, the Cold War, and now the war in Ukraine.

As 1990 dawned, the chances of conflict between NATO and the Warsaw Pact looked most unlikely, and the change in the military outlook developed quickly. Western and Eastern Block countries' defence and security policy since the end of the Second World War had been very much justified and shaped by the fear (or more specifically, mistrust) of one another. Whether one side or the other, or both, were justified in their worst fears, we will thankfully never know for sure, but speaking from the point of view of a citizen of a key Western power, I think we did the minimum to ensure that each viewed the outcome of conflict as something that would profit neither side.

The next step was to determine what the world was going to look like. The Soviet Union loosened its political grip on its satellites, and all sides agreed that conventional as well as nuclear arms had to be reviewed and reduced.

It was only a month or two before the next round of monthly periodical aviation magazines carried editorials speculating on the long-term future of the armed forces, on both sides. Essentially, magazines in the UK started pondering over how the RAF would be restructured and whether, beyond the need to maintain a minimum level of force capability, it could be justified. Were there other hidden threats that were very real, but not necessarily prominent?

It was not too long before irony played its part and Saddam Hussein invaded Kuwait. From the point of view of the RAF, there seemed at first glance an obvious proposal. The defence review noticed a couple of front-line roles that were being fulfilled by more than one type. Each of the two roles had an old and a new aircraft type assigned to it. Conveniently, the older aircraft were in the minority. The choice appeared logical, and this was the chosen path. With such a prominent number of Tornados, essentially forming the backbone in both offensive and defensive operations, the older, less relied-upon aircraft provided an easy answer to the question of which squadrons and how many aircraft should go. This simple choice eased some of the headache caused by options for change.

The two old types in the frame shared a naval origin, and it has been long said that both owe their existence to a flippant competition between American and British designers to build the ugliest aircraft. The result was the Phantom and the Buccaneer. Both aircraft were soldiering on because they both continued to meet certain performance parameters that bettered that of the corresponding Tornado variants. As the standing numbers were no longer required, it was easy to see both types as surplus to requirements.

The last of the Buccaneers were withdrawn from Germany in 1985; the last continued to operate from Lossiemouth with 12 and 208 Squadrons, together with the OCU. The Phantom, on the other hand, remained the AD fighter of choice for RAFG and was expected to remain so, had circumstances not changed. Two more squadrons, 56 and 74, were also soldiering on with the Phantom at Wattisham in Suffolk; all were to go. Both these third-generation aircraft were expected to keep at it until about 2003–4.

The conclusions of the review were first made public in the summer of 1990 and confirmed both the Buccaneer and Phantom were going. In addition, half the Germany-based Tornado squadrons were to be removed. This was handled by MOD with some sugar on the pill—the Laarbruch wing was to disband. However, three of the squadrons were to live on as the reserve identities of the Jaguar, Harrier, and Tornado GR OCUs, while one (2 Squadron) returned to the UK.

The existing Tornado GR1 wing, already at Marham, would be re-assigned to replace the Buccaneer wing at Lossiemouth; the rest of the changes largely revolved around the re-assignment of squadron numbers. This was to ensure the survival of the earliest and most illustrious units. It has long been the

RAF tradition to preserve and strengthen historical lineage among the most venerable and notable squadrons. No. 617 (The Dambusters) Squadron lives on today because of its celebrated past, despite being likely the youngest surviving squadron in 1990.

The reduction in the British forces orbat had already reached its conclusions by July 1990 when the invasion of Kuwait took place. The 'Options for Change' defence review was expected to see some cuts for sure; frankly, while far-reaching in any normal set of circumstances, the cuts were surprisingly light.

The changes were announced just as Saddam Hussein ordered his armed forces to invade Kuwait. The consequent reaction of the United States, United Kingdom, United Nations, and most of the Arabic world culminated in more than just words of condemnation this time.

Operation Desert Shield—another coded reference from the Americans which could not be clearer as to the nature of the operation it referred to—was commenced within hours. The age of constant news bulletins ensured the whole world was certainly aware of the outline as well as some details of military preparations to defend Kuwait. The physical response from the UK began with Jaguars and Tornado F3s deploying from the UK and Tornado GR1s deploying form both the UK and Germany. Any expectation that this dramatic turn of events would force a rethink about 'Options for Change' was for the birds.

Besides, Western politicians were determined that this was a minor reversal of the new world order that would soon be put to rights; it was a temporary inconvenience. The world was in for something of a surprise as the future unfolded in the years ahead, but the view of the European democracies, the UK not least among them, was that quantity when it came to defence budgets was now dispensable, even following the present cuts. More would follow under the banner of 'more means less'.

As the build-up in the Gulf continued, the concern that Saddam was giving no serious indication that there might be room for manoeuvre became more apparent. There was clear concern that where the world was heading was global conflict after all. Various preparations to be ready for a considerable level of escalation included some lesser-known deployments in preparation for any military engagements spilling outside the theatre of countries involved.

One response from the RAF was to send Phantoms from 19 Squadron to Akrotiri in Cyprus. The rationale for this was to be ready to defend Cypriot airspace in the possible event that the conflict expanded beyond the confines of the Gulf states, should there be a collapse in the most unlikely of coalitions put together under American leadership. There was anticipation that the Iraqi armed forces showed greater resolve and ended up pushing toward the Mediterranean. The Iraqi Air Force could have made a more determined stance and lashed out at coalition Allies to the West, such as Syria?

Prior to the stage where we were several days deep into the Operation Desert Storm or to use the slightly less dramatic and telling British choice of reference for operations in the Gulf, Operation Granby, the contribution of RAFG squadrons was quite substantial—Brüggen and Laarbruch each supplied a large deployment of Tornados. The celebrated Tornado crew, John Peters and John Nichol, were serving on 15 Squadron, commanded by Wg Cdr 'Pablo' Mason when they were deployed. The two variants of the Tornado stood out during the Gulf War for quite different reasons. The air defence variant, the F3, was deployed in force early on essentially aircraft from Leuchars-based 43 Sqn and 29 Sqn at Coningsby, there being no Germany-based F3s.

The Tornado F3 initially deployed to Dharan in Saudi Arabia to conduct both defence patrols over Saudi and Bahraini airspace and to conduct air superiority missions over Iraqi airspace. Due to problems with the aircraft's SIF/IFF equipment, they were excluded from the latter task and used to defend allied controlled airspace only; this problem was later resolved. The GR1s from early on flew very low-level interdiction missions against Iraqi airfields. This led to a high casualty rate.

Altogether, six Tornado GR1s were shot down during Operation Granby, one from 27 Sqn, Marham; two from 15 Sqn, Laarbruch; one from 31 Sqn; and two from 17 Sqn all based at Brüggen. Five of the crew were killed—Wg Cdr TNC Elsdon, Flt Lt RM Collier, and Flt Lt SM Hicks all from 17 Sqn, and Sqn Ldr GKS Lennox and Sqn Ldr KP Weeks, both of 31 Sqn.

A unique weapon employed by Tornado GR1 crews was the JP233 munitions dispenser—a large pod, with the appearance of a Norwegian Jarlsberg cheese, with the rows of large holes underneath, was carried under the aircraft fuselage which then flew down or across the target airfield's runway depending on what was to be achieved. Batteries of small bombs were released, which exploded on impact, blasting craters. Following on would be parachute-delayed munitions, first dropping the SG-257 cratering bombs then the HB-876 anti-personnel mines. The latter were pre-set to explode after a period of time or if disturbed. This would make any attempt to remove, defuse, or fill in the previously blown crater virtually impossible.

However, to correctly dispense the JP233's contents, a relatively slow but steady, very low path was to be flown by the aircraft and its crew. This presented the attacking aircraft as a particularly prominent target to ground-based air defence systems. To survive such a mission would require a great deal of luck.

Peters and Nichol, however, were carrying out a very low and 'fast' pass over Ruma airfield to drop 1,000-lb high-explosive bombs. They encountered heavy anti-aircraft fire on their attempt to fly clear. Wg Cdr Nelson and Flt

Lt Collier, also of 15 Sqn, were the only ones of the six losses that employed the JP233; the rest used either the 1,000-lb air-tossed or LGB (laser-guided bombs). The latter could be dropped with a considerable degree of accuracy from higher altitudes and indeed was when Flt Lts Clark and Hicks took part in a precision attack against an airfield in Central Iraq at the time, relying on Buccaneer aircraft from Lossiemouth to mark the target. It was the Buccaneer crew who reported detecting a SAM launch against the formation. It is ironic that the first time units from RAFG should fly in anger since the creation of NATO would be against a former Middle East ally, and just as the Cold War ended, rather than targets inside Eastern Europe and the USSR.

Following the destruction of the Berlin Wall, much attributable to 'People Power', the idea of Western NATO governments using the Gulf crisis as justification for reversing the process, which was progressing while the Soviet Union itself was reaching the point of dissolution, was out of the question. The thaw of East/West relations, kicked off by negotiations between Mikhail Gorbachev and Ronald Reagan (the Trump of his day), had been accelerated by the proletariat; Stalin would have been proud.

It was still possible for events to be thrown into sharp reverse, and this very nearly happened; more than once over the next few years, internal instability in Russia brought about attempts at armed insurrection. Within two years, the first such incident occurred in 1991, an attempt to do something along such lines was made by a 'hard line' coup in Moscow. However, the coup's plotters failed to secure the support of the armed forces and quickly collapsed. The rest, as they say, is history.

End of an Era

The year 1991 is officially seen as the year the Cold War finally came to a close. It was not without incident as the RAF in Germany was about to start drawing down, against a backdrop of deployments in anger for the first time in the command's history and forty-two years since the foundation of NATO. The contract to stand sentinel against the possibility of a Soviet-led military incursion across the inner German border was fulfilled and without a return to hostilities in Europe. After all these years, RAF Germany deployed in anger for the very first time while in the process of shutting up the shop.

The RAF moved out quite quickly, certainly by comparison with the army. By the end of 1992, Wildenrath and Gütersloh were gone. The army had bagged Gütersloh in that time-honoured fashion whereby the army inherit the real estate the RAF abandons as the latter contracts. Wildenrath, the first of the purpose-built 'Clutch' bases, was handed over to the local German authorities in April 1992. Today, it is largely occupied by Siemens' transport and automotive division. Much of the base's infrastructure has now gone.

Brüggen and Laarbruch remained operational for the remainder of the decade. The Brüggen strike wing remained unchanged, until the government's strategic defence review of 1998 determined that 17 Squadron should disband along with other units across HM forces.

1995 was a significant year for anniversaries, including the fiftieth anniversary of VE/VJ Day. Following on from the 1991 Gulf War, no fly zone enforcements over Southern Iraq and the Balkans further involved units of RAFG. Essentially, the Brüggen wing were involved in direct bombing missions against Serb positions in the Kosovan conflict in 1999. GR1s of 9, 14, and 31 Squadrons took part in these operations flying direct from and returning to Brüggen.

No. 17 Squadron's disbandment took effect on 31 March 1999—rather ironic under the circumstances. The last RAF units to leave Germany did so in 2001. Nos 9 and 31 Squadrons returned to Marham in Norfolk while 14 re-deployed to Lossiemouth in Moray. The two Harrier squadrons took up station at Cottesmore following the disbandment of the TTTE while 230's Pumas moved to Benson in Oxfordshire and the Chinooks of 18 Sqn to Odiham, Hampshire.

Since then, HM forces have been deployed in overseas conflicts almost continuously with particular emphasis on the invasion of Iraq in 2003, operations in Afghanistan, the Libyan uprising, and air operations mounted from Akrotiri in Cyprus over Syria and Northern Iraq against ISIS. The certainty in all this is that HM forces must get on with these campaigns with ever shrinking resources. So much has come to pass. In 2019, the seventieth anniversary year of NATO, the RAF has been compelled to retire the one aircraft that proved best suited to the counter-operations against ISIS—the Tornado GR4.

The Tonka was to have served on (originally) until 2024. The out of service date was brought forward to save money and with the replacement aircraft, the F-35, far from ready to take over. The tempo of the campaign has not shown much sign of lessening, but it has been reported that ISIS, if not defeated outright, are now very much on the back foot. Many have questioned why some kind of settlement has not been pursued, but just what would the Islamic state bring to the negotiating table, and in return for what? Given their track record, there does not appear to be any room for compromise.

In the meantime, the Tornado has been retired and the Typhoon, a thoroughbred interceptor, has had to be modified for the ground attack role, again, to help fill the gap left by the former, leaving the new jet with a sizeable reputation to live up to.

When the government announced the conclusions of the 'Options for Change' review, RAFG had a battle order of twelve operational combat squadrons, two rotary squadrons, a communications squadron, and six squadrons of the RAF Regiment, which included four SHORAD squadrons with Rapier. This alone overshadows the entire RAF front line in 2019 and typifies the insistent attitude of successive governments that the Cold War mentality (translation, robust defence posture mentality) was at an end and no longer relevant.

On 27 January 2019, *The Daily Telegraph* reported that the member states of NATO agreed to increase defence spending, collectively, by $100,000,000,000. This amounts to honouring the commitment to the already pledged 2 per cent expenditure of GDP on defence, by each member state. Hitherto, only four member states have been meeting this target. The report attributed the reverse in the overall trend of the last thirty years to European concerns about President Trump's questioning of the very point of NATO and the commitment of the European nations to the alliance, following the Russian annexation of the Crimea and invasion of East Ukraine.

Concerns about the likelihood of the United States withdrawing from the alliance were only one thing to worry about; in February 2019, the United States withdrew from the INF Nuclear Treaty signed with Russia. This was followed by an announcement that Russia was going to follow suit. Then on 6 February 2019, it was announced that Macedonia would become the thirtieth member state of NATO. Since 1991, defence budgets across the member states of NATO have, for the most part, fallen significantly, but the world was not supposed to have reached the situation it has. With a resurgent Russian hegemony led by Vladimir Putin, a newly drawn Iron Curtain now seems to divide the Baltic states and Poland from Russia.

The latter have a small NATO military presence and due to the lack of adequate air defences in these countries, save Poland, a rotation of NATO Allied Air Force fighter units has, since March 2004, maintained a continuous interceptor fighter quick reaction alert service, usually based at Armani in Estonia or Zokniai in Lithuania. A further dimension to contend with is the attempts by the European Union to establish a separate military force and to have the French seat on the UN Security Council relinquished in order that it can be replaced by one representing the EU as a single entity. As NATO celebrates its seventieth birthday, the world seems to be moving to become ever more dangerous and unstable.

Centred on Europe, war had returned, this time shrouded by other attendant problems—a viral pandemic and fuel shortages, compounded by the fact that many NATO/EU countries have rendered themselves dependent on Russia for oil. Conflict with a resurgent Russia has been a growing likelihood for many years, ruled by an ambitious expansionist, Vladimir Putin; in many ways, he is more dangerous than the Soviet-era presidents, who, for all their totalitarianism and mistrusting view of the West, acted with sanity. In a rather less clear fashion, the EU is seemingly attempting to solidify itself as a nation state; this is strenuously denied by those who see Brussels as the head of a family of nations simply seeking cooperation rather than forming one significantly large federal state.

For many years and long after the drastic cuts to defence spending forced, by the austerity cuts of 2010, the British government has long defended against continuous reports of losses in capability and even the credibility of HM forces by repeating the stock reply, 'we have the fourth largest defence budget in the world'. Twelve years on, in 2022, that can no longer be claimed as the British defence budget slipped to seventh place behind France and India.

We wait to see what the future holds, but there is one inescapable concern—that the resolve of Britain's—nay, NATO's—defence posture after 1991 was replaced by a refusal to accept that the post-Cold War promised peace dividend was anything but fleeting.

12

Memories

This last chapter is given to those who served or were detached on occasion to Germany. The stories remembered here essentially reflect the fond memories from a lighter point of view, and I hope they provide an insight into the mindset and lives of those who stood watch over the Iron Curtain through the Cold War era. Most of those who have been happy to let me print their recollections are identified just by their name—no rank or unit necessarily provided—but their respective contributions will give the reader some idea of what they were up to. So with tales from both air and ground crews, here is a most welcome trip down memory lane.

Inter-NATO relations

RAF Gütersloh, early 1970s. One of the barmen in the Officers' Mess was a German: Willi.

Detachment of 6 × Italian F104s to Gut, so cue 19 Sqn pilot, who spoke the lingo, to be appointed O i/c Italians.

Five days into the detachment, said 19 Sqn pilot rushes into OM bar one evening and says to assembled throng, 'Has anyone seen the Italian officers?'

Willi's droll response was, 'Yes, sir ve had the same problem during ze var!'

Brought the house down!

Gareth Cunningham

Unauthorised Flying

In the 1950s a very senior Officer had been alerted to claims that RAF Canberras were flying under Bridges in Germany, a Cafe owner had posted a sign outside telling all comers to pop in and watch the crazy Tommies. The Senior officer found what he was looking for. But this kind of behaviour was widespread.

Not only Canberras-they were at it in Meteors and Vampires too.

The specific story I heard was from the OC of an FR squadron and it involved two very curt 'hats on, no coffee' interviews for himself at HQ and even back at the Air Ministry in London-with two severe bollockings for his trouble.

Apparently, C in C RAFG sent his aide to said bridge to orbit around and find out what was going on. Whilst orbiting a number of assets were seen under flying the bridge!

A signal went out to all stations the next day!

Chris Liddle

Inter-Service Photo Interpreter Cooperation

In the early 1970s when 2 (AC) Squadron were on Phantoms, I was detached from the Army Photographic Interpretation unit at Rheindahlen to the Laarbruch RIC (Reconnaissance Interpretation Cell) for war role training. Besides myself there was the RIC's permanent Army SNCO photo interpreter (SSGT X) who was a bit of a character and had been on the Guards all Arms Drill course at Pirbright at some point, which he could turn on and off at will. He took great delight in confirming the RAF's worst fears about the Army. Two incidents involving both him and myself come to mind:

1. The scene is the PI cabin where SSGT X is waiting to debrief a crew. Enter stage right a steely-eyed Phantom crew, with Nav looking at his aircrew watch. Steely-eyed nav to SSGT X; 'Staff (at least he didn't say Flight) have you got the time?' SSGT X (assuming Guards Drill Instructor Persona), 'Time Sir! Glad you asked that, shows a keen enquiring mind. Time Sir is always the same; One, Two-Three, One. Moving on one and standing perfectly still on the Regimental pause of Two-Three between drill movements.'

Exit steely-eyed nav muttering about army lunatics.

2. The other was during the end of day debrief that included a short equipment recognition test using 35-mm slides. A slide of an Armoured Vehicle Launched Bridge (AVLB) is flashed up and the Squadron recognition King points to a victim and asks, 'What is it?' Victim: 'An MT-55' (this was a Soviet AVLB).

Myself: 'Oh no its not, it's an East German BLG-60 (Similar to MT-55, but with significant differences.)' I then pointed out the differences amid much joshing from assembled aircrew.

Squadron recognition King: 'How do you know that?'

Myself: 'Because, I took that photograph whilst covering an East German Army Day parade in East Berlin'. Briefing dissolves into laughter but subsequently the Squadron recognition King checks identifications with the RIC before he shows them to the Squadron.

So Much for the Fairer Sex

I took some TA reinforcements for the RIC, including three girls, and this led to a whole raft of incidents because OC RIC at the time was the original Male Chauvinist Pig, who could not understand that as the army was concerned, they were three Junior NCOs, sex was immaterial. I must point out that they were all armed with 9-mm Brownings, complete with blank ammunition. Towards the end of the exercise, I had to send one of the girls across to RIC alternate. On the way she passed a HAS in which was a Tornado with stagings and people around the cockpit. On asking why, our Heroine was told that the crew had gone LMF (Lack of Moral Fibre) and were not going to bomb innocent civilians. Her response was to go you the ladder, past various senior officers, on arrival at the cockpit the following exchange took place; JNCO: 'Are you going to fly the mission?' Pilot: 'No'. JNCO draws pistol cycling round into breech, fires at pilot then turns and looks at assembled company; 'well dig him out and put a new one in', then disappeared on original mission. Needless to say, before she returned to the original location, I had had an interesting conversation with the Staish [RAF shorthand for station commander] about her actions. The only quick excuse that came to mind was that she was a Geordie!

Peter Jefferies

Initiative RAF Style

In the early 80s at Wittering, I was locking up the APU engine test bed after civvy contractors had been doing some alterations. I spotted what turned out to be blue asbestos coming out of the walls and the test bed was out of action for a couple of months. We then had to take our APU's to Gütersloh to use their test bed. We would take across 6 engines at a time and spend a week there.

The airman's transit accommodation was dire but luckily in short supply, so the drill was to phone the guardroom and ask if they had any transit beds. You did this several times until the guardroom staff said there were no transit beds. You then presented to the OO who gave you a chit for a hotel in Gütersloh town. You checked out the next morning and repeated the same performance the next day. If you were lucky, you could spend the whole detachment in a hotel but once you were in transit, you stayed there

We used to get 6 Harrier GTS/APUs into a Sherpa for the drive over. Once we got the engines serviceable, we crammed a carton of duty-free cigs into each intake, boxed them up and sent them back to Wittering through the stores system.

(1) We then loaded up the empty Sherpa with crates of Wobbly/DAB/Bitburger etc. for the trip home. Happy days indeed.

(2) The engines always travelled back to wittering under a u/s F731 so there was no danger of them getting fitted to an aircraft with 200 cigs in the intake, not that you could miss the carton of cigs once the intake blank was removed.

Paul Giverin

A Special Request

As OC Supply at Wildenrath I had a large contingent of locally employed Germans working in the Barrack Stores. They were a bright, cheerful, hardworking bunch and I can recall on one occasion when visiting the stores, to check up on how things were running, being asked by one of the storemen if he could have the day off. On enquiring why, he wanted this, he declared with a broad smile that as a youngster they always took this day off as it was Hitler's birthday! Suffice to say that I declined his request.

Patrick Rowney

If You Can't Take the Joke, You Shouldn't Have Joined

230 Sqn, days after my theatre qualification check (where the late Chris Fynes thoroughly debriefed me with, 'You'll do!'), and I'm summoned to the Adj's office. Fynes and the Adj looking stern.

Right young Colin, we have an important job for you ... The Squadron is running out of fuel chits, so you and the pilot are flying down to the clutch to pick some up. Now these things are untraceable, so a thief's wet dream for black market sales. The pilot is planning, so get off to the armoury and draw a pistol and 10 rounds. Let me be clear, you may use the weapon if compromised- do not lose those coupons.

So, off I go, bricking it, legging it down the stairs to grab my hat and off to the armoury. The penny only dropped when the man in the hatch asked, 'Do you want a righthanded pistol, or a lefthanded one?'

Welcome to 230!

Colin Greenwood (ex-230 Sqn crew member)

Multi-Skilled

My wife had 3 small jobs around Gütersloh: dinner lady at the school at Manser Support barracks; clerk typist in one of the brown job offices; and finally, the internal mail delivery driver on camp. This was a great job, whizzing around, outside and around the base all day long. She knew the place better than I did! (I was on 230) She drove the mail about in one of the two Tannoy-equipped minivans (remember minivans?) that were used by MT to call out the troops on the married patches during wars or exercises.

On the day she found out she was pregnant with our daughter, she was, er, not quite herself- fair enough, you'd agree. End of shift, she backed her van into its strictly allocated spot when she heard and felt a loud bang! The tinkling of glass followed in slow motion. She got out, in shock, only to see that she had crashed her minivan into the only other Tannoy-van on base! The MT FS wanted so much to go ape, but she (very, very uncharacteristically) started sobbing uncontrollably. He took his ire out on the sniggering airmen, who soon realised they were going to be staying on until both broken vans were roadworthy again.

All he could pour on Mrs Greenwood was, 'You, don't wear those silly (high heeled) shoes tomorrow!'

So, at least one night in 1984 being Taceval-free is down to my unborn daughter!

Colin Greenwood (ex-230 Sqn crewman)

Always Remember the Head Count

TLP detachment, most drive to Jever in their own cars, but four or five of us use MT transport, The station MT Section were sent a request for a Sherpa minibus, the smallest they can rustle up is a 56-seat coach and driver. Now it's a long old drive in one of the RAF's finest to the top of Germany from Brüggen, so part way up the autobahn, following a discussion between the driver and the five of us, we pulled off into a 'Ratty' [*Rasthaus*, German for service station] for a food break and to use the toilets. Suitably refreshed we join the on ramp and set off again when someone says where is Ivor? Looking back, we see him in uniform standing in the car park with his bag of goodies from the shop. It took another 15–20 miles before we could turn around and as we passed the ratty, heading south, we could see him still standing there. We had to travel a fair few miles before we could pull off, turn around and then head back to pick him up. Just as well the bus wasn't full, or he would still be standing there! Ooh he, wasn't amused …

Tony Taylor

For the Purposes of this Exercise

During the early 1970s at RAF Laarbruch in common with all the other RAFG bases, preparation for exercises, particularly the dreaded Taceval, were evident throughout the station at all times. One of the most widespread signs of these preparations were notices stuck on windows announcing that they had been sandbagged although there was not a sandbag to be seen anywhere. The exception to this were the RAF Regiments Bofors gun emplacements scattered around the airfield which were fully sandbagged. On visiting one of these I was therefore amused to see that someone had stuck a notice on one wall of the emplacement announcing that 'these sandbags are a window'.

Patrick Rowney

A HAS Story—2 Sqn Laarbruch, about 1981

The Mk 1 HAS was equipped with clamshell doors. The door motors frequently failed but they could be pushed open or closed by a couple of blokes. On the inside of each door there was a 4-inch diameter steel pin which dropped into a hole in the floor in the closed position. One night shift, the lineys pushed both doors shut from the outside, only to discover the wicket door was also bolted closed from the inside.

It appeared that there was no way to get inside the HAS (which had two Jags in it) There was a circular hatch in the side of the HAS, about 12-inch diameter, for passing through a Houchin cable but it was too small for anyone to get through. Then someone remembered that some ATC cadets were at Laarbruch for their summer camp. Someone was dispatched to their barrack block. They turned out all the cadets (at about one in the morning) and took the smallest one back to the squadron and shoved him through the Houchin hole. The cadet unbolted the wicket door and the HAS was liberated. The cadet was returned to bed but the next day he was given the VIP tour of the sqn with lots of cockpit time.

Paul Giverin

Gütersloh *c.* 1970

Met. Office night duty staff [one forecaster, one observer] were accustomed to snatching 90 minutes' charp [sleep] each in the rest room/coffee bar. Each covered for the other.

One of the forecasters would retire, yawning, and within minutes exit through the ground floor window into his car, out of the gates, down to the nearest layby, and then pleasure his Innamorato for a while before returning, back through the window, back into the camp bed, just in time to be 'awakened' by the observer with a mug of coffee.

Everyone but everyone [including the snowdrops on the gate] knew exactly what was going on, but the conspiracy of silence was maintained in the hope that he would one night snag his testimonials on the window catch.

David Edward Langley

Wildenrath, Early '80s

Finished Phantom phixing around midnight, too late for the station bars. Crawl under crash gate step across road into the Pony Hof and enjoy an audience with the 'ladies' until breakfast was served in the mess.

Night flying again, strap crew in for sortie and explain that you will be enjoying supper when they return and would they give advance notice of the exact time?

'No problem we'll buzz the rugby club bar once we're in the circuit.'

[Author's note: phixing means 'fixing' but has been converted to phixing as an in-house light-hearted tribute to the F-4 Phantom, converting anything beginning with 'f' to 'ph'. There are other instances in some of the other anecdotes.]

Gütersloh, Late '80s

My role in the Harrier repair team convoy was that of beer carrier with Bedford 4-tonner and ¼-ton trailer fully loaded and tarped up. That one caused SOXMIS a few sleepless nights.

And as for my online moniker, well, I can explain everything, as I tried to at the time in the Penn Club.

RAFG memories? a bit hazy really!

Chris Phelan (ex-92 Sqn and Gütersloh Harrier Force)

Tact Required When Visiting

Well, in 1983 I was on 'EX BOLD GAUNTLET' at Gütersloh, on detachment from Suphpholk's phinest AD station. On precisely the 40th anniversary of the Dams Raid, I was flying one of HM's mighty Phantoms (not very well) and, for once, happened to be in the right place at the right time!

So, we flew past the castle by the Eder, down to 250 ft, across the dam, then climbed out. Seemed like fun, so did it again. Then another jet joined us, so we did a pairs flypast... I recall that there were people waving (I think) from the castle. Then home for tea at Gütersloh.

Mentioned it to the S Nav O when we were chatting later, he went rather white. He dug out something called 'Manuel de vol a basse altitude' (not something we air defenders had bothered with before) and pointed out that we weren't supposed to use the dams as a turning point or overfly them at low level. *Strengsten Verboten*, we were told!

'Good job we didn't tell him about saying hello to the Möhne Dam on the way home, then!' I remarked to my nav after the S Nav O had left.

But no-one ever complained!

Nick Wilcock

Another Detachment to Gütersloh

This was a French fighter [type?] *c.* 1970.

They stayed a week and were hugely successful with several wives in the Mess, such that several turned out to wave goodbye as the squadron taxied out.

Behind the scenes there was frantic activity by SWO and his minions, erasing the zaps that had been stencilled during the night.

These were very artistic representations of what I might call the flying cocks ... a rampant winged penis with bulging gonads a-dangle.

The Met. Office shutters, being ground floor, received one such. Hearing that the jankers-wallahs were erasing them, we either removed the shutter or closed it [memory fails me as to this detail].

Either way, it survived, to be displayed to selected visitors along with the back of the old Luftwaffe stationery cupboard, complete with wartime swastika.

David Edward Langley

Doing the Rounds

Wildenrath 1961. New boy on first day as Orderly Officer (No. 1 Uniform all day). Issued with a VW (proper OLD Beetle). Evening tasks included going to the other side of the airfield to 'inspect' RAF police on outer perimeter of (nuclear) bomb dump. Left the bar around 2130 to drive around LONG dark peri track; arrived. 'Halt, who goes there?'. 'Orderly Officer'. 'Put your ID on the ground and retire 10 metres'. Did so and was eventually admitted to police hut. Sergeant says, 'Would you like to continue your inspection Sir?'. Stupidly I said, 'Yes'. (Can YOU see what is coming??) 'Follow me'. Did so through pitch blackness stumbling over roots and grass. From the dark—'Halt, who goes there?' The password for the challenge was given. 'Put your ID on the ground and retire 10 metres' Did so and fell over into long grass. Highly amused policeman (with snarling dog) helps me up and points me onward. Took nearly half an hour and about ten challenges before I was shown the way back to the hut. Sergeant is waiting with a welcome tea - and a request 'Sir, please do not tell the next new boy!' Drove back to mess bar covered in mud and grass to be welcomed with howls of mirth. Happy days—and TACEVAL had not been invented.

Mike Turner (17 Sqn PR Canberras)

Weather Forecast

Nobody has mentioned the weather, so the Duty Met, man had better deal with it. The weather was indeed different, much more text-book Continental, especially so the further East one was based.

Every year, Met. RAF Brüggen ran a sweepstake for the first date with snow at a British observing site. The sweep was always won in November … try that in the UK these days.

Gütersloh and Detmold [pongos] had genuine freezing rain most winters, real evil stuff that coated all surfaces with mirror-smooth ice within minutes. Such it was that cars had an external set of windows, made of ice, and steering was a lottery.

Summers regularly reached the mid-30s C for a week or so, and the heat was quite distressing as air-con was a rarity.

And forecasting was just as difficult. Woe betide a missed snowfall, with airfields black and WingCo Ops looking even blacker.

David Edward Langley

Getting There Is Half the Fun

In 1955, posted to RAF Wahn, travelled from Harwich to Hook of Holland on a troopship, which was very overcrowded. At about 5 a.m. I went up on deck for some fresh air, the ship was at a standstill but there were lights twinkling in the distance, Holland, I thought and went scurrying down numerous steps to tell my mates. The five of us stood on deck feeling excited at the prospect of being in a foreign country when the ship's Tannoy crackled into life to inform us that the ship had broken down, we were just outside Harwich and would be returning that morning! We eventually went over the following night.

Which after living in freezing wooden huts in the UK, Goch, where we went to first, was a paradise.

Peter Goude

Gap Period

When I had a short holding session between Gnat and Hunter courses, I was at Wildenrath. Having arrived by AAC Beaver, which confused the admin folk who couldn't understand how I'd reached the General Office with no record of travel, I learned that I needed a BFG driving licence.

So, I was given the book to read before taking the tick test. I noticed that the chap who was marking it simply used a sheet of paper with holes in it, which was placed over the answer sheet—if all the holes showed ticks, you passed. But he hadn't realised that if you weren't sure and ticked 2 boxes, provided that one was correct you still passed....

Having passed the tick test first time, much to the surprise of my boss, I was permitted to drive off-camp in HM's Landrovers as my FMT 600 still showed 'Landrover'. Which was quite useful.

The BFG licence was valid for 3 years. So, when I came over in a Vulcan for a weekend, we were able to book a hire car from NAAFI or some such for the weekend as my BFG was still *just* valid. Only trouble was that it took them ages to do the paperwork and the Captain was train-critical - he needed a lift to Mönchengladbach station. So, I dropped the crew at the OM then sought out the route on the tatty map I'd been given whilst the Captain did a quick change, then off we went. Having dropped him at the station with about 10 min to spare, I had the joys of driving back in the rush hour...still in my immersion suit. On arriving back at Wildenrath I went to get my room key from reception but was 'encouraged' into the bar for a few Charlies.

Ever tried getting out of an immersion suit whilst the room is spinning after too many Charlies? I have—and it's not to be recommended!

Nick Wilcock

A Case of Mistaken Identity

Never stationed there, but visited frequently with 360, initially in WD935, the 6th Canberra B2, which was still in old black and grey. Also had bomb shackles so could winch up panniers containing lamb joints to keep the RAFG masses happy. I recall same aircraft flown into a clutch airfield with an all-RN crew, which foxed the plods, so they arrested all three for stealing the aircraft. Later on, with the T17s we were allowed to fight back when exercising with Lightnings. The Canberra could turn well at altitude and I briefly got on the tail of a Lightning at night, pressed the Tx button and called 'murder, murder'. Pity it was OC 92, not my ex-Cranwell mate, B.C., who I thought it was. Got a severe talking to.

Ian Gawn (retired wing commander)

Anglo-German Cooperation

Late 70's and 17 Sqn decide to have a week on a jolly to Memmingen, 2 × Jaguars and six troops who are also to be cross trained on the F-104.

Enter the ever resourceful he of the ('if we run a Jag outside the HAS in -20C the efflux will melt all the snow and ice', which it did, before freezing solid, along the Jag, again fame) Jengo (junior engineering officer) who decides the troops can travel in the Commer van, used for generally carrying bodies and bits and which the programme *Scrapheap Challenge* was possibly based on.

Just outside Cologne, on comes the pretty orange light, for the first time. ADAC comes to our rescue and, unknown to us, do some pre-planning. It's about 550 km to Memmingen, every 100 km, roughly, there was an ADAC [German equivalent of RAC/AA] patrol … waiting.

Arrive, eventually, at destination and go to MT. The Germans, ever diplomatic, once they had stopped laughing having seen this relic, say we can't repair it. At which point, we produce the international currency, contained in a bottle with a red label, and explain that's fine, all we want is the paperwork to say it should be scrapped.

The Germans, now very happy, duly oblige with chapter and verse as to why the heap is a death trap. However, we still have to return and, to add to the fun, they are having a 'Minival' … had this been the RAF, as we know, the admin world would have said, 'We're closed, there's a war on!' and that would have been that.

Thankfully, the Germans were considerably more realistic and thus we were booked, tickets provided c/o the Luftwaffe, on the Munich-Amsterdam express from Ulm to Cologne. Very scenic, very hospitable and free!

It was only once the heap had been returned to Brüggen, on a low loader, that the allegations of our clearly lamentable driving skills suddenly ceased.

Howard Lucas

Pride Comes Before a Fall, or a Trip?

The multi-national EX BOLD GAUNTLET ('Don't mention the word "corridor" chaps!') was held at Gütersloh one year. Spams who took everything very seriously were there with their F-15s evolving clever tactics, we were there with our F-4s and a C-130 and the French were there with their Mirage III and a C-160—to have a good time.

One evening we were having a few wets in the OM bar talking to the FAF *pilotes de chasse*. All of a sudden, some wanton PMRAFNS trollop came over and put her arms around the waist of one FAF mate. With admirable sangfroid, he carefully put down his beer and cigarette, then led her off to the Keller Bar to satisfy her rather obvious needs.

About 10 min later he reappeared, relit his cigarette, took a swig from his beer, then shrugged his shoulders and said '*Eh bien—pas mal!*' before resuming his previous conversation as if nothing had happened …

The Spams invited the FAF colonel to go for a trip in an F-15 T-bird, which he gladly accepted. At pre-flight he was being fitted with American flight kit, but when he was sized for a G-suit, he pompously announced, 'I am a fighter pilot—I do not need a G-suit'. Whereupon the US det cdr [detachment commander] sought out the meanest, most raw meat-eating rip shit of his pilots and asked him to take Le Colonel for his trip, explaining with a wink that 'He says he doesn't need a G-suit—perhaps he might be mistaken?'

A few minutes later, the F-15 was seen to take off in full A/B, accelerate to warp lots then snapping into a max rate climbing spiral to flight level nosebleed, before rolling over to spiral back down in a max rate descending spiral to initials … 'How did he like his trip?' asked the det cdr—to be told that Le Colonel had been slumped in a heap in his seat from the start of the climb until back at initials. Later he said that it had been 'Very interesting' and was then presented with his Eagle flight certificate—but not until he'd been given the traditional raw egg to eat, shell and all!

Nick Wilcock (former pilot, Phantom/VC-10)

Oops, Accidents Will Happen

431MU engine bay, posted for a month or so until tourex [end of tour of duty in post; sometimes, before leaving an overseas tour, movement elsewhere within theatre can count towards the tour, as in Tony's case] due date from RAFG, I was trying to sort out manning on 14 Sqn up until disbandment. Stuck for weeks, initially in the module store and shuffling modules about. I attempted to lift one, but it wouldn't budge, forks straining then an almighty bang and up comes the box... WTF. I looked behind and saw the late remains of the cast central heating pipe that was luckily turned off due to the time of year and drained. Box replaced and another sourced, departed RAFG before heating turned on.

Tony Taylor

The Night the Balloon Almost Went Up

'On August 20, 1968, the Soviet Union led Warsaw Pact troops in an invasion of Czechoslovakia to crack down on reformist trends in Prague'.

As Max Boyce used to say, 'I was there!'

I relate this in the full knowledge that memory is less than perfect, but I insist that the essentials are correct.

At Gütersloh we had 19 Sqn Lightnings on QRA/ Battle Flight [I don't think 92 had arrived from Wildenrath or Geilenkirchen at that time], plus 2 and 4 Sqns with Hunters, and a chopper unit. On the night of 19–20 August I was the night duty forecaster, with one assistant, in the ground floor Met Office under the tower and beside Ops. There was no flying, no weather, and I assume that the few duty personnel around were in their sacks or at least thinking about it. This probably included my observer, because we could snatch 40 winks in turn between about 2300 and 0100.

In burst an American.

'The bastards have invaded Czecho!'

In burst another American: 'why aren't you guys flying!'

Calm down dear and tell me about it.

'The Pact has invaded … our SOPs are to land at the nearest NATO base, get cracking!'

There was indeed a large US chopper parked outside the window.

Now Gütersloh is really rather near to Czecho, so that was quite exciting.

So, I did something I had never done before [or since], and rang the Staish, put the US Captain on the phone to him, woke the observer, ran off umpteen copies of the forecast for the Pact countries and awaited the hooter. Within minutes we were a tad busy, as the shit hit the fan.

When I got home my wife mentioned something about 'yet another Taceval'. Little did she know she was nearly put on a coach to Calais.

David Edward Langley

The Old Ones Are the Best

The first job we did on arriving in Sylt was to remove the wing tanks of our NFIIs ready for air-to-air gunnery. Several of us would support the empty tank ready for the chap in the cockpit to operate the tank jettison switch. We were supporting the port tank when there was a loud bang from the st'board side... We beat Del Boy and Grandad to it.

Peter Goude

Oi Yew

Landed at Wildenrath to refuel and wandering down the main drag after nipping to the NAAFI gets pulled over, for wearing my combat jacket, by the SWO. We had a one-sided conversation about how combat jackets were only to be worn on detachments or exercise blah blah. 'But I am' is my reply, that threw him, so next came an invite to get a haircut and visit him at xyz time.... 'Righto,' says I, as I wander back up to the apron, climb aboard and depart for the UK.

Tony Taylor

Round Trip

In the mess at Brüggen, Sunday lunchtime just starting my second pint of Heini, mate says 'could you do me a favour'?

The favour was to drive him to Rotterdam Europort in his VW and drop him off (his wife was in the UK with the other car) and drive the VW back to Brüggen. No problem.

We got to Europort as night was falling, filled it up from the jerry can and I then experienced my first drive in a beetle. There was a strong crosswind and this ancient beetle had a six-volt electrical system. I drove on lights like sidelights in this strong wind (it was a bit like steering a boat) and my technique was to get behind a truck and stay line astern! Two hours later I got back to base.

Never again!

Ian Booth

Season's Greetings

Food has been mentioned so, as it is almost Christmas, a reminiscence of Portadown Way, JHQ Rheindahelen.

We were privileged to do two separate tours totalling 9 years.

The Way was a close with a central small wood, with grass and shrubs.

A brake parachute provided summer shade in the middle if needed. There was a row of our garages very near.

In addition to Maypole antics on the due date, and al fresco communal BBQs in season, the annual mass BBQ was held on Christmas Eve, cooked in front of [or in], the garages, decorated with baubles and with drink to suit.

Father Christmas arrived on a garrison fire engine, with a sack of presents [not sure if they were secret Santa or targeted]. Santa had a bevvy or two and got the children [and my wife] to sit on his knee. She seemed to be there a long time.

The aftermath was for the hardy; after clearing up, many of us were regulars at St Boniface church: choir, sidesman and the rest. Attending the Midnight Mass was a bit of a duty after a heavy afternoon and evening, but we did manage it on bikes one year.

Not much prospect of such goings-on round these parts nowadays, I regret.

David Edward Langley

Local Culture

An abiding memory of service in Germany was *Fasching* or *Karneval* (Carnival) that made for a refreshing change of mood for what we Brits perceived as the sometimes very serious disposition of many Germans in the towns and cities in the Rhineland and the ones we worked alongside at JHQ.

So, the start of Lent is the time when towns in the Rhineland hold their carnival processions. In the big towns or cities such as Cologne or Dusseldorf *Rosenmontag* (Rose Monday) is the highlight of the German '*Karneval*' (carnival) season and is on the Monday before Ash Wednesday. Celebrations become quieter the next day, known as *Veilchendienstag* ('Violet Tuesday' or Shrove Tuesday), and end on '*Aschermittwoch*' (Ash Wednesday). Mönchengladbach's carnival procession was titled *Veilchendienstagszug* (Violet Tuesday Train) and traditionally takes place on the Tuesday. JHQ some other units in the area treated the day as a holiday so we all had the day off, which was ideal as BFES schools in the area were closed too so the kids had the day off as well and were keen to participate in the celebrations.

Traditionally, as I recorded alongside the photos in my photo album, the 1973 carnival procession consisted of 80 floats, 30 marching bands, and 24 dance troupes. I took my kids and a couple of neighbours kids from our MG married quarter patch to enjoy the procession—forewarned that kids should have bags to catch the sweets (*Kamelle*) thrown from the carnival floats into the crowds lining the streets among cries of '*Helau*' or '*Alaaf*'. The kids were not disappointed and came back well laden. Mum was also rewarded because flowers (tulips) were thrown into the crowd too. As seen the kids were dressed and made up to blend in with the German crowd.

Many girls in the parade '*Tanzmariechen*' or '*Funkenmariechen*' (marching girls) wear a very fetching uniform styled outfit. This consists of a very short skirt copied from eighteenth century designs. Originally worn as jacket and trousers the trousers evolved into a short dress with a pleated skirt, and very frilly knickers (to maintain their modesty as they 'high-kicked' their way through town). A wig with braided pigtails was worn and on top of that a Tricorner hat. White boots finished off the outfit.

Many of the dancers ('fools') perform energetic dances emulating St Vitus, whose name is given to the Monastery after which Mönchengladbach is named. The Monastery of St. Vitus is a large Roman Catholic Church / Abbey set high on a hill overlooking the town. The *Karneval* traditionally has floats of 'fools' or troops of dancers who emulate St Vitus in their mad dancing. According to legend, if suffering from various ailments one would say a prayer to the early Christian martyr St Vitus, and your prayer would be answered. St Vitus is reputed to have miraculous healing powers especially for those suffering from seizures, epilepsy, rabies, Sydenham's chorea (St Vitus Dance), bedwetting, and snakebite, he is also said to protect against lightning strikes, animal attacks and oversleeping! To add to his attributes, he is the patron saint of pharmacists, innkeepers, brewers, wine makers, coppersmiths, dancers and actors.

As for military participation in the procession JHQ Rheindahlen was represented by a float as was 79 Sqn Royal Corps of Transport based at Ayrshire barracks in Mönchengladbach. 79 Sqn RCT was responsible for administering the various military ambulance trains positioned in sidings at RAF. Wildenrath and in Mönchengladbach. In addition, 79 Sqn RCT was also responsible for overall control of the British Military Train 'The Berliner' that ran through the Soviet Zone to Berlin. The RCT 'float' was appropriately in the form of a locomotive sporting a Union Jack.

Carnival preparations traditionally begin in November with the election of officials etc. to run the carnival. The carnival celebrations proper kick off just before Lent with the 'Women's Carnival' on the Thursday of the week before Ash Wednesday. This is a special day for women called '*Altweiber*' (Old Women) or '*Weiberfastnacht*' (Women's Day). On this day women are allowed to kiss any man they like as long as they cut off his tie beforehand (Tip: Beware any mad-looking women wielding a pair of scissors!) unless of course you fancy the lady in question in which case wear a very old tie!

German friends tell me that nowadays *Weiberfastnacht* has morphed into a more modern form as an excuse for the women to go out by themselves for a girl's only night out, leaving the kids at home with their men.

Enjoy these memories as recorded by me in 1973.

Tony Hawes

Punctuality

The Pigs bar must have been in existence when I was at EDUO each side of 1970 but alas I missed its delights. I took my Wobbly elsewhere.

Gütersloh seems to be very well represented in these anecdotes, over-represented in comparison with the clutch stations.

In my last incarnation in Germany, I had to visit Gütersloh from JHQ several times a year: always a pleasure to arrive, but it became increasingly difficult to plan the drive to arrive at a scheduled time. How do you deal with a journey that [from memory] was not much over 2 hours, and last time took 5 hours, meaning all sorts of appointments were missed in playing catchup?

'Fly,' I hear, but that involved going 'the wrong way' to Brüggen.

David Edward Langley

Damned Dog

I was on a flying visit to Gut from Odiham and was in the NAAFI, it would have been in the late '70s and they were playing the finals of a snooker tournament when a bomb warning was called in, we all evacuated to outside the NAAFI pints in hand as the plods searched the place … We all watched as the plods Sniffer dog hopped up on the finals table knocking the balls far and wide. That went down like a lead balloon amongst the gathered crowd and coming out the NAAFI after giving the 'all clear' the said plod found his dog van lying on its side.

Tony Taylor

A New Broom Sweeps Clean

Author's note: The following story has an eerie similarity to a fictitious RAF station, Zeedorf, which featured in the novel *The Camp*, written by former national serviceman Gordon Williams.

Gütersloh had a fearsome reputation in the late fifties. At Wahn we heard tales of the 'Rocks' [service slang for RAF Regiment personnel, the RAF's infantry and ground combat arm] running riot in the local town and that discipline had broken down, in general. A replacement Staish was posted in who 'specialised in bringing ill- disciplined Stations to order. One of his measures was to put corporals in charge of sections of roads and if, on inspection, as much as a cigarette butt was found they were for the high jump!

Peter Goude

What the Orderly Officer Saw

Orderly Officer again. One of the last duties for the day was to check the kitchen for security and fire. So, in I go. Dark, except for a light in a back room. —to find one of the waitresses draped across the 'Table, Meat preparation' (a butcher's block). On top of her one of the chefs. I coughed, reminded them to turn the light out and left. Nothing more was ever said - but thereafter I only had to sit down to a meal to get instant service and the biggest steak. My mates could never understand it, and I never enlightened them! Hope books go well.

Mike Turner

Getting the Bird

25 Sqn effectively re-deployed from Leuchars to Geilenkirchen, West Germany, to re-equip No. 11 (F) Squadron. Whilst there the squadron went to RNLAF Leeuwarden for air-air firing over the Wadden islands, & during a free afternoon I went with Jack Broughton & his second Nav, one Robby Tayler, to Snaekemeer as I was a qualified RAF helmsman, & Jack & Robby didn't know one end of a boat from the other! I placed Jack & Robby one on each side of the boat in the bows & we tacked upwind by the simple expedient of when I called out a name, the other would release his sheet (jib rope) whilst the named chap would pull on his like hell! We had a great afternoon for a couple of hours until their arms ached!

Moving on Jack, by now a Flt Lt was sent to Vaerlose in Denmark, along with Yours Truly to do a flying demo at this airbase for the Danish Armed Forces Day. As we finished this & were about to land, we suffered a Bird strike! Jack told me this so, realising that if we declared it we may have to stay at Vaerlose for some considerable time until it was remedied, I told him to keep Mum, which he, bowing to my greater experience, not to say vastly inferior rank, did!! We taxied back to our hard pad in the bush & surveyed the damage; a chunk of starboard wing was quite dented but did not mean we could not fly it safely, so I briefed Jack to call 'Bird strike' when we got airborne next to return to Geilenkirchen.

We duly got airborne next day, Jack called in the Bird strike, & the Tower controller replied, 'By the way mission Rafair 03 we found it on the runway yesterday afternoon, it was a swan!' Sheepishly Jack said that we didn't notice anything then, and could we now say goodbye & change to a Transit frequency!? In September 1965 I left the RAF for good, & 8 years later when I was now an ATC Radar controller at Euro control UAC Maastricht, I caught up with Jack, Mrs. Jack & 4 sons (he was very prolific as well as handsome) at RAF Wildenrath where Jack was now a wing commander, a fully-fledged Harrier pilot & Wingco Flying to boot! There I told you he was a memorable chap, didn't I?

Roy Evans (navigator, 11 Sqn, Geilenkirchen)

Always Make a Good Impression on Arrival

I was on my first flying tour on 19 Squadron at RAF Leconfield flying the Lightning F2 when I heard that the Squadron was to be the first to deploy to RAF Germany to take over the QRA task from the Javelins at RAF Gelienkirchen. This was during the summer of 1964 when I was enjoying a spell in Cyprus also on QRA duty.

The day dawned on 4 September 1964 when the entire squadron was lined up and ready to fly to Gütersloh. I am in the nearest Lightning! I will not forget the arrival. There were 12 aircraft, in three groups of 4, lined up in echelon starboard and running in for a break left into the circuit … when we were told the circuit was right hand! It did not please the Station Commander as we broke the wrong way.

In those days, RAF Gütersloh had numbers 2 and 4 Squadrons with Hunter FR10s and 18 Squadron with Wessex helicopters. The runway was a little shorter than we had been used to and there were frequent emergency calls by ATC in the early days due to brake parachute failures. They gradually got used to such things and soon adopted a more relaxed attitude. Our role at the time was high level intercept due to the relatively poor performance of the AI 23 radar overland. We quite often flew as targets at up to 60,000 feet at Mach 1.1. Competitions?

We very rarely fired the 30mm cannon in the upper fuselage, but I do recall a trial when we flew what we called air into air gunnery just to see how the cannon worked. On one occasion, I flew with the 4-gun pack fitted (with the missile fit removed from the lower fuselage). On pulling the trigger all hell let loose as violent vibration set off about 6 or 8 emergency captions! Most of the lights, fortunately, subsequently went out.

Towards the end of my tour, we started low level operations, shutting down one engine to conserve fuel a bit, but this did not really pick up until we were equipped with the more capable F2A version of the Lightning ... in my view perhaps the best of them all as it had a much greater fuel capacity like the F6 but retained the cannon capability lacking in the F6 (at least at the start).

Ian McFayden (pilot, 19 Sqn, Gütersloh)

A Royal Flush

Back in December 1964, HRH Prince Phillip visited RAF Geilenkirchen.

Here is the gist of it from Roy Evans who was serving as a Navigator on 11 Squadron at the time.

First port of call was 5 Sqn, the other Javelin outfit, known as the East End Kids, as they were on the east end of RAF Geilenkirchen. 3 Sqn were the bomber boys (Canberras) then us on 11 Sqn at the west end. The CO of No. 3 Sqn said he wasn't going to clean ALL his hangar, so cleaned just half & put up a cardboard partition behind which he hid about 10 airmen whose Best Blues was not up to scratch. While being escorted round, HRH clearly curious about the partition, drew his ceremonial sword and slashed the screen with it, his actual words were 'Carry on Chaps!'

Later on, his visit to 11, HRH was invited to hit the button to send the Battle Flight airborne on a scramble. NCO crew Bob Kelly & I were no. 2, so No.1 were scrambled by HRH, they were on the take-off run when they aborted with air in the hydraulic lines to the flying controls. HRH asked the CO 'why this was happening'. The Wingco thought he'd found a good reason; as it was now snowing, he said the take-off was stopped due to inclement weather. Just then, after a 20 second wait, Bob & I took off & HRH said to the Boss, 'Well where the B***** ***L are they going to then?!' Exit Boss with a red face! Oh, great days, score was HRH 3 & the Wingco 0!

Roy Evans (navigator, 11 Sqn, Geilenkirchen)

Absorbing Local Culture

Our first RAFG tour was Gütersloh, 1967, young and raw. Among early purchase were beer glasses, Warsteiner, Becks, and several others. One evening after a few I focused on the glass. '0.3 L, Rastal,' with a horizontal line.

'Did you know,' said I, 'that the German for the 0.3 line is the Rastal?'

Forever afterwards the growing and expanding family insisted on beer 'up to the rastal'.

Only in very recent years we discovered that Rastal is a glass maker firm.

It will make not the slightest difference here: the line is forever a Rastal.

David Edward Langley

RAF Order of Battle in 2nd Tactical Air Force as of 1 April 1957

No 2 Group

Base	Sqn	Type	Role	UE
Alhorn	96	Meteor NF11	AWF/Attack	16
	213	Canberra B(I)6	Light Bomber	12
	256	Meteor NF11	AWF/Attack	16
Gütersloh	59	Canberra B2/(I)8	Light Bomber	12
	79	Swift FR5	Armed Recce	12
Jever	4	Hunter F6	Day Fighter	16
	93	Hunter F6	Day Fighter	16
	98	Hunter F4	Day Fighter	16
	118	Hunter F4	Day Fighter	16
Laarbruch	31	Canberra PR7	Tactical Recce	12
	69	Canberra PR3	Tactical Recce	12
	80	Canberra PR7	Tactical Recce	12
Oldenburg	14	Hunter F4/F6	Day Fighter	16
	20	Hunter F4	Day Fighter	16
	26	Hunter F4	Day Fighter	16
Wunstorf	5	Venom FB4	Ground Attack	16
	11	Venom FB4	Ground Attack	16
	266	Venom FB4	Ground Attack	16
	541	Meteor PR10	Tactical Recce	12

83 Group

Brüggen	67	Hunter F4	Day Fighter	16
	71	Hunter F4	Day Fighter	16
	112	Hunter F4	Day Fighter	16
	130	Hunter F4	Day Fighter	16
Celle	94	Venom FB1	Ground Attack	16
	145	Venom FB1	Ground Attack	16
Geilenkirchen	2	Swift FR5	Armed Recce	12
	3	Hunter F4	Day Fighter	16
	234	Hunter F4	Day Fighter	16
Wahn	17	Canberra PR7	Tactical Recce	12
	68	Meteor NF11	AWF/Tactical	12
	87	Meteor NF11	AWF/Tactical	12
Wildenrath	88	Canberra B(I)8	Light Bomber	12

RAFG Order of Battle as of 1 April 1963 Following Restructure

Brüggen	80	Canberra PR7	Tactical Recce		12
	213	Canberra B(I)6	Tactical Strike		12
Geilenkirchen	3	Canberra B(I)8	Tactical Strike		12
	5	Javelin FAW9	AWI		16
	11	Javelin FAW9	AWI		16
Gütersloh	2	Hunter FR10	Fighter Recce		8
	4	Hunter FR10	Fighter Recce		8
	230	Whirlwind HAC10	Troop Support	Approx.	10
Laarbruch	16	Canberra B(I)8	Light Bomber	Tactical Strike	12
	31	Canberra PR7	Tactical Recce		12
Wildenrath	14	Canberra B(I)8	Light Bomber	Tactical Strike	12
	17	Canberra PR7	Tactical Recce		12

RAFG Order of Battle as of November 1989 When the Berlin Wall Collapsed

BASE	SQN	TYPE	ROLE	UE
Brüggen	9	Tornado GR1	IDS	12
Brüggen	14	Tornado GR1	IDS	12
Brüggen	17	Tornado GR1	IDS	12
Brüggen	31	Tornado GR1	IDS	12
Gütersloh	3	Harrier GR3	CAS/BAI	18
Gütersloh	4	Harrier GR3	CAS/BAI	18
Gütersloh	18	Chinook HC1	Troop Support	10
Gütersloh	230	Puma HC1	Troop Support	13
Laarbruch	2	Tornado GR1	Recce	12
Laarbruch	15	Tornado GR1	IDS	12
Laarbruch	16	Tornado GR1	IDS	12
Laarbruch	20	Tornado GR1	IDS	12
Wildenrath	19	F-4M Phantom	AD	12
Wildenrath	92	F-4M Phantom	AD	12
Wildenrath	60	Various	VIP/Comms	10

The aircraft on 60 Squadron were a mix of types, including HS Andover CC2 and BAE 125.

RAF Regiment units

Brüggen	37	Rapier SAM	8 fire units (4 x missiles each) *
	51	15 x Spartan/6 x Scorpion	Light Armoured Support
Gütersloh	63	Rapier SAM	8 fire units (4 × missiles each) *
Laarbruch	26	Rapier SAM	8 fire units (4 × missiles each) *
	1	15 × Spartan/6 × Scorpion	Light Armoured Support
Wildenrath	16	Rapier SAM	8 fire units (4 × missiles each) *

*Each fire unit/launch station was armed with a maximum of four missiles; depending on stock levels, they would be re-loaded as required.

Rest of NATO Central Region Air Forces Order of Battle

Wing/Base	Sqn	Type	Role	UE

2 ATAF (USAF)

20 TFW

Wing/Base	Sqn	Type	Role	UE
Upper Heyford	55	F-111E	IDS	21
Upper Heyford	77	F-111E	IDS	21
Upper Heyford	79	F-111E	IDS	21
Upper Heyford	42	EF-111A	ECM	14

48 TFW

Wing/Base	Sqn	Type	Role	UE
Lakenheath	492	F-111F	IDS	24
Lakenheath	493	F-111F	IDS	24
Lakenheath	494	F-111F	IDS	24
Lakenheath	495	F-111F	IDS	24

10 TFW

Wing/Base	Sqn	Type	Role	UE
Alconbury	509	A-10A	CAS	18
Alconbury	511	A-10A	CAS	18

81 TFW

Wing/Base	Sqn	Type	Role	UE
Bentwaters	92	A-10A	CAS	18
Bentwaters	510	A-10A	CAS	18
Woodbridge	78	A-10A	CAS	18
Woodbridge	91	A-10A	CAS	18
Soesterberg	32	F-15C	AWI	18

WGAF

JG 72

Witmundhaven	721	F-4F	AWI	15
Witmundhaven	722	F-4F	AWI	15

JBG 36

Hopsten	361	F-4F	CAS	15
Hopsten	362	F-4F	CAS	15

JBG 31

Norvenich	311	Tornado IDS	IDS	15
Norvenich	312	Tornado IDS	IDS	15

JBG 34

Memminghem	341	Tornado IDS	IDS	15
Memminghem	342	Tornado IDS	IDS	15

JBG 43

Oldenburg	431	Alpha Jet	CAS	21
Oldenburg	432	Alpha Jet	CAS	21

Aufklärung Geschwader 52

Leck	521	RF-4E	Recce	15
Leck	522	RF-4E	Recce	15

RNLAF

Leeuwarden	322	F-16A	AD	18
Leeuwarden	323	F-16A	AD	18
Volkel	306	F-16A	Recce	18
Volkel	311	F-16A	IDS	18
Volkel	312	F-16A	IDS	18
Twenthe	313	F-16A	TF	18
Twenthe	315	F-16A	TF	18
Eindhoven	316	NF-5	CAS	18
Gilze-Rijen	314	NF-5	CAS	18

BAF

Beauvechain	349	F-16A	AD	18
Beauvechain	350	F-16A	AD	18
Klein Brogel	23	F-16A	IDS	18
Klein Brogel	31	F-16A	IDS	18
Florennes	8	Mirage V	CAS/BAI	18
Florennes	42	Mirage VR	Recce	18
Beirset	1	Mirage V	CAS/BAI	18
Beirset	2	Mirage V	CAS/BAI	18

4 ATAF (USAF)

86 TFW

Ramstein	512	F-16C	TF	24
Ramstein	526	F-16C	TF	24

36 TFW

Bitburg	523	F-15C	AWI	24
Bitburg	524	F-15C	AWI	24
Bitburg	525	F-15C	AWI	24

50 TFW

Hahn	10	F-16C	IDS	24
Hahn	313	F-16C	IDS	24
Hahn	496	F-16C	IDS	24

52 TFW

Spangdahlem	23	F-16C	SAM Sup	24
Spangdahlem	81	F-16C	SAM Sup	24
Spangdahlem	480	F-4G	SAM Sup	24

26 TRW

Zweibrucken	38	RF-4C	Recce	18

WGAF

JBG 35

Pferdsfeld	351	F-4F	CAS	15
Pferdsfeld	352	F-4F	CAS	15

JG 74

Neuburg	741	F-4F	AWI	15
Neuburg	742	F-4F	AWI	15

JBG 32

Lechfeld	321	Tornado IDS	IDS	15
Lechfeld	322	Tornado IDS	IDS	15

JBG 33

Buchel	331	Tornado IDS	IDS	15
Buchel	332	Tornado IDS	IDS	15

JBG 42

Fuerstenfeldbruck	421	Alpha Jet	CAS	21
Fuerstenfeldbruck	422	Alpha Jet	CAS	21

Aufklärung Geschwader 51

Bremgarten	511	RF-4E	Recce	15
Bremgarten	512	RF-4E	Recce	15

RCAF

1 CAG

Baden Sollingen	421	CF-18	TF	12
Baden Sollingen	431	CF-18	TF	12
Baden Sollingen	439	CF-18	TF	12